KV-371-606

Boots

Angela Hollest | Penelope Gaine

Party Party was originally published as two
separate books – *Children's Parties*, covering
dozens of party ideas for children up to eight years
old, and *Parties for Older Children*, which was
packed with original and exciting ideas for
entertaining 8–14 year olds.

Following the huge popularity of these two
volumes, they have been amalgamated into one
bumper, value-for-money edition specially for
Boots. Whether your child is a toddler or a
teenager, in **Party Party** you will find everything
you need to know to make your next party the most
successful one ever!

Children's Parties

Ideas, Planning, Cakes, Food, and Games.

Angela Hollest
and
Penelope Gaine

To David, Edward and Clare,
and Michael, David and Daniel.

Authors' acknowledgement
We would like to thank Christine Curzon, who typed the manuscript and
struggled with our handwriting; Cetra Long, who so cleverly visualized our
ideas; all our friends who generously shared their experiences with us —
both the triumphs and the disasters; and our families for their patience and
willingness to try and test everything.

Children's Parties © 1983 Angela Hollest &
    Penelope Gaine

First published in
Great Britain in 1983 by
Judy Piatkus (Publishers) Ltd

Reprinted 1984, 1985, 1986

Parties for Older Children © 1986 Angela Hollest &
    Penelope Gaine

First published in
Great Britain in 1986 by
Judy Piatkus (Publishers) Ltd

This joint paperback edition
first published in Great Britain in 1986
for Boots of Nottingham by
Judy Piatkus (Publishers) Ltd of
5 Windmill Street, London W1

British Library Cataloguing in Publication Data

Hollest, Angela
    Party, party.
    1. Children's parties   2. Cookery
    I. Title   II. Gaine, Penelope
    III. Hollest, Angela. Children's parties.
    IV. Hollest, Angela. Parties for older children.
    793.2′1   TX731

    ISBN 0-86188-593-7

Printed in Great Britain

Contents

Introduction

We are not qualified cooks or entertainers, but we are, like you, qualified mothers! This book evolved because we found there was neither a realistic nor complete guide to the nerve-racking experience of giving a children's party. We decided, in between feeding the puppy, digging the veg patch and coping with the measles, to produce this reference book for others who may similarly have searched in vain.

This book is designed to give you plenty of scope to plan your style of party. The chapter on cakes includes simple designs, as well as more complicated ones – although all of them can be achieved without any particular culinary skill! The section on ice cream cakes is deliberately simple – there is little cooking – and similarly, the party food chapter is designed to allow you plenty of choice, showing you how to cater for your children's party as diversely and economically as possible. We have tried to produce the party planning and games chapters in a realistic way, so that you can choose how to organize your event according to your budget and time. And although this is basically a book for parties, you can also make use of the ideas just for a special tea, following, for example, a holiday outing to the zoo.

Above all, we want you to be able to adapt it to your own lifestyle. It's great if you have time to make your own invitations, but don't be disheartened if not – maybe next year you won't be coping with night feeds, or you could start planning a little earlier. Don't despair if that doesn't work, though – there is no stigma in not producing home-made invitations, food and presents. You can't do everything! But we hope that we have provided you with plenty of possibilities, so that at the end of the day you will have that special hug and be thanked for the best party ever!

1. TEA PARTY PLANNING

In this part of the book, there are ideas for making invitations, for decorations, for presents, and for party themes. We also have a section on fancy dress, directed particularly at non-sewers like us, which relies basically on making do with what is at hand, with only a few simple instructions for making the odd garment or hat. Our aim is to achieve easy but effective outfits.

Although we give you plenty of suggestions for everything, don't panic if you feel you can't cope: a few balloons can be quite enough decoration. All these ideas are for you to put into practice only if you have the time and energy. And indeed, if you share your party with a friend, you could each take a section on which to concentrate your time and skills – for instance, one of you could make decorations, and the other some fudge or other presents to take home.

First things first

First fix the date, numbers and venue of your party. If you are using a church or village hall, then you will have to organize this well ahead. Do check your facilities if using a venue other than your home. A friend organized a Christmas party for fifty under-fives in a local hall, with Father Christmas and all the trimmings; horror-struck, she sat up in bed the night before the party, realizing the function was to raise money to provide loos for the hall. . . . She managed with a row of potties behind a screen, and very little orange to drink for tea!

Make a list of the names of the children you are inviting to the party. If you are planning a joint effort with another mother make sure that you both know how many you are inviting. If your party is being held at home, limit the number of children to the capacity of the house (half a dozen seven-year-olds can seem like a herd of elephants) and to your capacity for coping. Even in a hall and sharing a party, don't be tempted to go mad with your numbers unless you have sufficient helpers.

Send your invitations out about three weeks to a fortnight before the date of the party. You can of course just telephone the mothers, but children do love to receive their own post, and have a written invitation especially for them. You can deliver them by hand, particularly to children attending the same school as yours. If you cannot manage to ask the whole class give them to the teacher, so that she can distribute them discreetly. If your party is going to be held in the holidays, be sure you know all the children's names and addresses from school, so that you can contact them if your child develops mumps, and you need to cancel the party! Tick off the names of the children who have accepted, but be sufficiently flexible to allow enough room and food for the occasional child you thought wasn't coming, but turns up anyway.

When planning your party, above all else, have sufficient helpers to organize a trail of children needing to go to the loo after tea (don't let them lock the door), to hand out the coats, balloons and presents at the end, and generally to assist where necessary. You cannot run a party single-handed even when the children are older, so try to have two helpers, so that two of you can run the games while the third organizes tea.

A few simple rules will keep the party running smoothly and avoid confusion. We are great believers in lists – they make life so much easier.

1. Make a list of your guests (plus telephone numbers).

2. Have a list of the food you are planning and check that it is all on the table. We found some cheese straws sitting in a tin in solitary splendour several days after one party.

3. Make a detailed shopping list, including anything you are buying for the table – paper plates, napkins, etc – as well as balloons, prizes, going-home presents, and food.

4. Make a list of the games you intend the children to play, and check that all the equipment (eg, a parcel for Pass the Parcel) is organized. Make sure you have enough little prizes. If you are having musical games, check that you have a suitable record or tape, and that your helper knows how to work the machine. Don't be too proud to look at the games list halfway through the party if your mind goes blank.

5. If you are having an entertainer (see below) have ready a contingency plan of games in case he is late or fails to turn up. Be prepared for the worst and it will never happen.

6. Do not have any open fires, even with very satisfactory guards. Accidents do happen, particularly with flimsy party dresses, in the general excitement. Use electric blow heaters if you need extra heat quickly.

7. Have a simple first aid kit available in case of need (always keep Waspeze to hand for summer outdoor parties).

8. Have your camera, film and flash light ready and working.

9. Don't forget a box of matches for the cake candles.

Escape routes

We do not suggest that you have entertainers for very young children. The children have to be at an age when they can concentrate sufficiently to enjoy and appreciate the treat, and not get restless and fidget. Older chil-

dren, from five upwards, love having entertainment of some sort at their parties, but this does not mean they do not want games as well. So time your party to have warm-up games before tea, tea itself, the entertainment and

more games at the end of the party. We feel that three-quarters of an hour is sufficient time for the entertainer for five- to seven-year-olds, but after that the shows can last for an hour or more.

It is best to have entertainers recommended by friends and acquaintances, but if you look in your local newspaper advertisements and in the Yellow Pages, you can find several alternatives for entertainment: a film show, a magician, a balloon man, or a Punch and Judy (our man once swallowed Punch's voice whistle!). Some entertainers take over the entire party, and all you do is provide tea, which they even help to serve – what a doddle!

Whoever you use, you will need to book them early. Some need four to five months' advance booking, especially if you are planning a party at a weekend, a bank holiday or Christmas. It is also very important to check whether or not they have done any shows in your area, and with a similar age group to the one for which you are catering. They can alter their programme accordingly. Always check, if having a film show, exactly which films you will be getting. Don't forget to write and confirm the booking, and if there is any doubt, enclose a set of clear instructions of how to find your home. There is nothing worse than the feeling of panic that creeps over one while waiting for the 'pièce de résistance' of the party to make an entry, and trying to organize extra games to occupy restless and expectant children! We have both had this experience, and both times the excuse was that the entertainer had got lost. The other result of a later start to the show is that you will have parents arriving at the given time to collect children and you may have to entertain *them* for longer than anticipated, unless they can squeeze in and watch the show too. (At all times have this book to hand to whisk up some impromptu games for the children or liquid refreshments for the adults!)

When booking the entertainer, check how long his programme will last. You can then organize what time to serve tea, remembering to leave enough time to ferry everyone to the loo before they sit down for the treat. Despite this efficiency, you will find some children will need to get up in the middle of the show, so when arranging seating leave sufficient space for them to squeeze out comparatively easily and quietly. Also remember that your guests will fidget least if they are 'sitting comfortably'. Even if you haven't enough chairs, put cushions, rugs or pillows on the floor for them to sit on. If you are having a long film for older and less messy children, why not hand out a small packet of crisps or Monster Munch, etc, for each child, half way through – although think twice about this if they are sitting on your beautifully upholstered chairs.

Always remember, when planning to have an entertainer, to be practical. It is not easy to have to remove the remains of tea, tables, chairs, etc, to make way for the conjuror's equipment. You really need to have separate rooms for tea and the show, especially as nearly all entertainers want to set up their props beforehand.

If you are using your own video, and hiring a film to show, again remember to check the time the film will last. Also do not invite more guests to this sort of party than can comfortably sit and watch a small television screen.

Entertainers are not cheap. They are extremely popular, but don't worry if you cannot afford to employ one. So long as you have sufficient games organized, the children will be just as happy.

Party themes

If you like the idea of giving a party with a special theme linking all the different elements in the party, then here are lots of ideas for you – games, decorations, cake, take-home presents, and so on. You may decide to give a fancy dress party, inviting all the children to come as pirates or as nursery rhyme characters; or you could give a simpler kind of fancy dress party – a kings and queens party, for instance, where the children only need a cloak and a crown, and their usual clothes underneath – or a hat party which is self-explanatory. The fancy dress section at the end of this chapter is very simple and involves very little sewing. The most important thing is that the children must be happy in their outfits or they will be uncomfortable for the whole party.

Keep your party simple – use our ideas as a basis, but don't feel you have to do everything we suggest: adapt them to suit you, your child and your own lifestyle. A party is meant to be fun and not all hard work.

Teddy Bear's Picnic

If the weather is good enough have the party outside (if you are only having a few children then a picnic in the countryside or in a park would be more exciting.) Make teddy bear invitations, invite teddies too. Use Winnie the Pooh wrapping paper, tea towels, etc, to decorate the room or house if the party is indoors. Make a teddy bear cake or ice cream cake. Sit teddy bears on the table and label, 'Paddington's marmalade sandwiches' and

'Pooh's honey treats' for the children's sandwiches. Pin the nose on the Teddy and have a suitable mini Paddington or Pooh prize in the Pass the Parcel game.

Army Party

You could use this theme if you are giving your child an Action Man, a fort or a tank as his birthday present. The cake could be the castle or the tank, as well. Decorate the table with toy soldiers, and give one to each boy as a going-home present. The boys could come dressed as soldiers. Use the assault course in the summer (see the games section).

Space Age Party

This theme would be ideal if you are giving your child a space rocket or space Lego for a present. Make the space ship invitations and the space ship cake. Decorate the room with *Star Wars* or space ship posters, record sleeves, or whatever you have. Use silver foil to decorate the table.

Cowboy and Indian Party

Ask the children to come as cowboys and Indians. Divide the guests into two teams – one cowboys and one Indians – for games, going into tea and so on. This theme would go well if you are giving your child a fort, a cowboy outfit or wigwam. Make the cowboy and Indian cake and use more plastic cowboys and

Indians to decorate the table. Use them as prizes and play Pinning the tail on the Bronco, and Shoeing the Horse etc.

Motor Party

Give your son a garage or a lorry as a present. Make a motor racing cake, a car cake or a garage cake. Have toy cars on the tea table. Put a toy car in the centre of the pass-the-parcel as the prize. (If you do put cars on the table, then be prepared for spills!)

Clock Party

This could be combined with giving your child a toy clock to help him learn the time, or a real child's clock or watch. Make clock invitations, and make the clock cake. Give toy watches as prizes or going-home presents. If it's a party for tiny children, start off with, What's the time, Mr Wolf?

Riding Party

Very popular with little girls! If you are lucky you might be able to borrow a pony (good tempered) for pony rides (in which case, remember to specify jeans or riding clothes on the invitations). Make sure you have efficient help. Give your child a present relevant to riding – a riding hat, jodphurs or a crop. Make a gymkhana cake. Decorate the room with horsy posters and rosettes, if you have any. You could play Pin the Tail on the Pony (*not* the real one) as one of the games.

Football Party

Make football invitations. Ask the boys to come dressed as footballers. Hang up a pair of boots on the front door instead of balloons. Cut up old football magazines and put up as decorations. Use the colours and rosettes of your son's favourite soccer team to decorate the table. Make the football match cake. Have a football game, out of doors, if you have room. In any case, divide the children into two teams for playing games, and give each child the name of a famous footballer – you could have the name and a photograph of him on a piece of card to pin to the child's jumper. Wrap the going-home presents in the colours of your son's favourite football team.

Pirate Party

Make the skull and crossbone invitations. You could decorate the room with cutlasses (cut out of card and covered in foil) or skulls and crossbones. Have one on the front door, instead of balloons. Make the galleon cake for tea. Play pirate games like Musical Islands (with cushions), Pin the treasure on the Island, with a big picture of an island (like Pinning the tail on the Donkey), and have a treasure hunt. Give chocolate money in gold foil as prizes. Also have a big box of treasure trove from which to dispense the presents at the end of the party.

Farm Party

If you are giving your child a model farm, or tractor as his main birthday present, then why not make this the theme of the party? Make a tractor cake, put little farm animals on the table and give these to the children, as their going-home presents. If your son has toy tractors have them down the centre of the table, as decoration (but don't be surprised if the children play around with them). Play farm games – The Farmer's in his Den, Old Macdonald had a Farm, and so on.

Noah's Ark Party

Ask the guests to come as animals. Use an animal template, or stencil, for the invitations. Pair the children off for games and for going in to tea two by two. Make a Noah's Ark cake for tea, and animal biscuits. Put plastic animals on the table, two by two if you wish. If you can find any suitable posters, or magazine pictures, you could Blu-tack them to the walls, or make concertina cut-outs of animals and attach them around the room, and on the doors. Stick little animals on their bags for presents. Play animal orientated games – the Tail on the donkey game, What's the time, Mr Wolf?, and so on. If you have anything that looks like a Noah's Ark, use it for the going-home presents if it's large enough. You could make animal felt finger puppets (see page 37) for going-home presents.

Zoo Party

This would be fun if you were taking children to the zoo for a treat first. Make a zoo cake for tea, and see Noah's Ark party, above, for other ideas.

Hallowe'en or Witches and Wizards Party

Ask the guests to come as witches or wizards – this only needs a hat and cloak. Make witch or wizard invitations. Decorate the room with hollowed-out pumpkins with holes for eyes and mouth. Put night lights in them, but keep them well out of harm's way. If you can't get hold of pumpkins, put nightlights in jam jars and sellotape coloured tissue paper around the *outside* of the jar. Again, keep them well out of reach. Hang up moons and stars cut out of foil, or fasten them to the walls. You could replace your ordinary light bulbs with blue or red ones, which is particularly effective at tea time. Play Apple Bobbing, and make a witch cake for tea, and toffee apples for the children to take home.

Firework Party

You can either let off your own fireworks, or go to a local firework display first, and bring the children back to tea. Send rocket cards for the invitations. If you are having your own firework party at home, then remember to keep the children well back from the fireworks. Very small children may be frightened so let them watch from indoors. Always have plenty of adult helpers. Make a rocket cake for tea and lots of sausages.

Easter Party

Send egg-shaped invitation cards. Have an Easter egg hunt as one of the games. Decorate the table with chocolate Easter eggs, or decorated hard-boiled eggs and with Easter chicks. You could give the eggs and the chicks and egg cosies (see page 38) to the guests to take home. Make a Humpty Dumpty cake, or an Easter nest cake for tea.

Hat Party

Make hat invitations, and ask all the children to come in a special hat, for instance: top hat, bowler, cap, riding hat, cowboy hat, Indian feathers, crown, saucepan hat, scarecrow hat, witch's hat, medieval lady's hat, straw hat, poke bonnet, chef's hat, hat with a salad on it, flower hat, etc, etc. Play Musical Hats with them all!

Kings and Queens Party

Send out invitations in the shape of crowns, using gold card if you can. Ask the guests to come as kings and queens (they only need a cloak and crown). Decorate the room and the tea table with crowns cut out of foil, and red crepe paper cut into strips. If you like, you could use red crepe paper to cover the table and staple crowns to it. Use red paper napkins. Games to play: Treasure Hunt, Oranges and Lemons, Musical Crowns. Make the castle cake for tea, and if you can find a model king and queen put them on their castle cake. Give red balloons and gold chocolate money as going-home presents.

Nursery Rhyme Party

Stencil a nursery rhyme figure for the invitations, and ask the guests to come as a nursery rhyme character. Decorate the room with nursery rhyme wrapping paper fastened to the walls. You can also cover the table with it if you like. For tea you could make either a Humpty Dumpty cake, a farm cake or a Little Bo Peep cake (make the doll cake on page 62 and add a shepherd's crook made out of a pipe cleaner, and some little lambs). Give the children little nursery rhyme books to take home.

Seasonal Party

If your child's birthday falls at an inconvenient time, or if you are working, consider giving a Christmas, Easter or Summer holiday party instead.

Wurzel Gummidge and Aunt Sally Party

Ask the children to dress up as Wurzels and Aunt Sallys. Make a farm cake for tea, and put a plastic scarecrow on it. Make a simple scarecrow with a broom handle securely fixed in sand or earth in a large pot, and a bamboo cane tied horizontally: dress him in old clothes, and hang the going-home presents from his arms. If the party is in the garden, tuck straw into his clothes; if indoors, stand him in the corner of the room, and forget the straw!

Party Invitations

Some very attractive invitations can be bought, but they are not at all difficult to make, and are great fun to do, although they take time. Try and involve the children in making their own invitations, but remember that until they are about seven years old their help will be more enthusiastic than practical. Make the wording of the invitation absolutely clear. It is very easy to forget a vital ingredient, such as the date of the party or address! Use your own wording but check that you include all the details given on the right:

> LAURA invites DANIEL to come to her
> BIRTHDAY PARTY
> On 2 April
> From 4 pm to 6 pm
>
> At   RSVP
> 12, Princes Drive,   *or*
> Blenheim   Please answer

If you are having the party in the garden or after school, put 'garden' or 'school' clothes. There is nothing worse than arriving in a long dress when everyone else is in wellington boots. If you have decided to give a fancy dress party or one with a particular theme – pirates, scarecrows, nursery rhymes, etc – then put this on the invitation as well.

When making your own invitations, in order to avoid a happy fun idea getting into a muddle and causing frayed tempers, decide on your design in advance. Assemble your materials on the kitchen table, or on any other large flat surface that won't get damaged by paint, scissors, and so on, and organize your children into helping sensibly as far as they are able, colouring the cards, for instance. Don't be disappointed if your child is not the constructive type, or if you find he/she simply cannot concentrate for long enough. Be prepared to do nearly all the work and let your child have all the credit!

For all the ideas below, you will need some fairly stiff coloured card, coloured felt pens, sharp scissors, ruler, and envelopes to fit the finished cards. The invitations here are designed to fit p.o.p. (Post Office preferred) envelopes $4\frac{1}{2} \times 6\frac{1}{2}''$ (11·5 × 16·5 cm). If you are coordinating the party to follow a specific theme this can be introduced at the invitation stage.

Cut-out Invitations

For the simplest invitation, cut the shapes from single card, and write the details on the back and front of the shape.

Trace the outline of one of the drawings we include here and on the next two pages, of a gingerbread man, a flower, balloons, cat, space rocket and clown. If these don't fit your theme, draw for yourself a clock (with hands pointing to party time or child's age), ship, crown, teddy bear, etc. Keep the outline bold and simple and make sure there is plenty of space for all the party details.

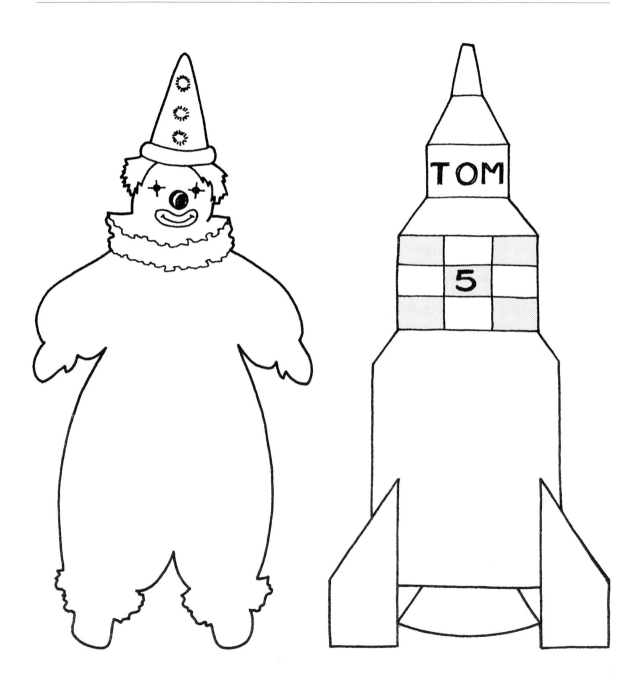

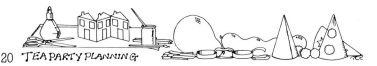

Folded Invitations

Another kind of card is one that is folded in half, and stands up on its own. Decide on the finished size of your invitations, making sure they fit your envelopes. Measure out the coloured card, fold the card in half, and cut it out very neatly. You could use pinking shears for an attractive zig-zag edge. Trace or draw your design, and decorate the front by colouring it or using a stick of glue (Pritt Stick) to make a pattern and then shaking glitter over it (allow time for the glue to dry before shaking off the glitter). Use the inside of the card to write all the details of the invitation.

Try one of these designs on the front of your folded card: skull and crossbones, Easter egg. Alternatively, you could draw for yourself a birthday cake, football, crown, wrapped present, cracker, and so on, or adapt a drawing from one of the other sections, adding more detail and colour or glitter.

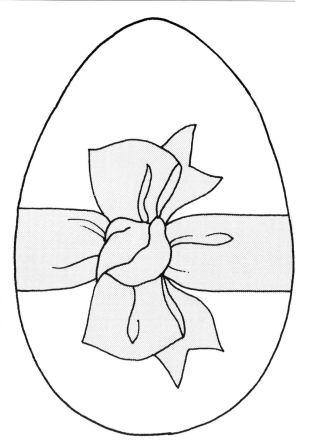

Concertina Cards

A more interesting and slightly more complicated invitation is a concertina card. Decide on the size of the finished invitations. Multiply the width by four, measure with a ruler and cut it out. Mark out four widths with little pencil marks top and bottom and fold them as shown. Draw a shape on the top layer and cut round it through all the layers, remembering to leave a join on each side. Colour all layers and write the invitation on the inside. The elephant, house and Christmas tree look very effective, or you could experiment with your own designs.

Mask Invitations

If you are having a fancy dress party, send mask invitations. Cut out a piece of coloured card to shape. Pierce two holes either side and put on a hole reinforcer on each one. Thread through two pieces of string or shirring elastic, and then decorate mask with stick-on shapes, and write the invitation on the back. Suggest your guests come in the mask to the fancy dress party. Have a few extra masks in reserve.

Fancy dress costumes

The majority of the costumes listed are simply made from old shirts, dresses, pieces of material etc. – and most of them require no sewing at all. Accessories are often found in the toy cupboard, or can be put together with a little imagination, occasionally with a little glue. There are ideas for boys and for girls.

Cowboy

A cowboy hat and plenty of guns. If your cowboy is still quite little let him ride a hobby horse. Spotted handkerchief to tie around his neck. A check or gingham shirt. A pair of jeans tucked into wellington boots to look more like cowboy boots. Sheriff's badge.

Coalman

Cap (black) with peak turned back to front. Old shirt. Long trousers with string tied round just below the knee. A pair of wellington boots. Plenty of black face paint and, if possible, a sack (not too dirty!).

Ghost

One small sheet (depending on the size of your child). Cover the child with the sheet and mark on the centre with a pencil, very carefully, where the eyes come, then remove the sheet and cut out the eye holes. Sew some elastic to fit your child's head by the side of each eye so that it goes around the back of the head, to hold the sheet in place. If you have any old black net, you could tack this over the top of the sheet to give an eerie cloud effect.

Soldier

You can purchase camouflage outfits. If you have one of these send your child with a rifle and his face blacked in non-toxic face paints. You can assemble your own camouflage or similar army kit if you have an army jersey (with elbow and shoulder patches), a pair of green or brown trousers and a green beret.

Wee Willie Winkie

If you do not have a suitable night gown, then one of Dad's old collarless shirts (or one of your own!) might be suitable. Some sort of a nightcap – perhaps you have a suitable bobble hat, which could be made to look like a nightcap – and a candle and candle holder.

Surgeon or Doctor

A man's white collarless shirt, worn back to front, or a painting overall. A white face mask. A pair of wellington boots. A doctor's kit. Make the face mask out of a piece of muslin or thin cotton. Sew two lengths of tape on either side so that the mask can be worn over the nose and mouth. If he has a doctor's kit then put the stethoscope around his neck.

Chef

White jeans, man's white collarless shirt as tunic over trousers. Catch waist with belt and tuck a white napkin into this. Chef's hat (see diagram). If you have a stripy butcher's apron, he could wear that. If you have a meat tenderizer, let him take this but *never* let your child carry a knife of any sort. Or he could carry a tray full of buns he has 'just baked'!

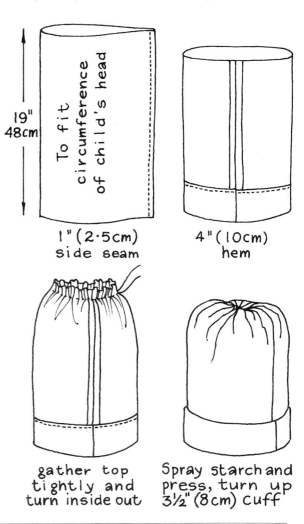

19"
48cm

To fit circumference of child's head

1" (2.5cm) side seam

4" (10cm) hem

gather top tightly and turn inside out

Spray starch and press, turn up 3½" (8cm) cuff

Straw hat tied with ribbon

Rosebud mouth, lashes drawn on lids, circles of blusher on cheeks

Pretty dress and lace petticoats

White tights

Black shoes

Old hat with straw

'carrot' nose

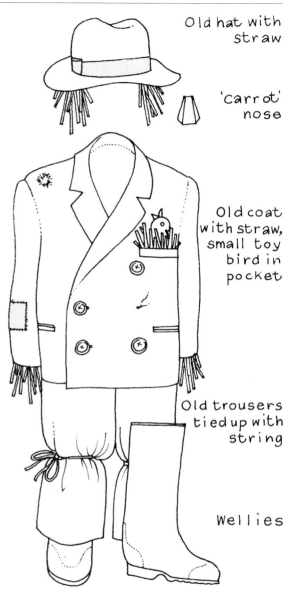

Old coat with straw, small toy bird in pocket

Old trousers tied up with string

Wellies

Aunt Sally

Follow the drawing to create this very easy but attractive costume. Finish off with round red cheeks, made-up eyes and heart-shaped lips.

Wurzel Gummidge

The drawing shows details of this costume. You will need to stitch the straw (or raffia) to the jacket and the hat. Cut the nose (right) out of carrot-coloured card, and glue flaps.

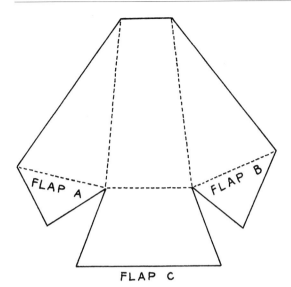

FLAP A

FLAP B

FLAP C

Fold along dotted lines and glue Flap A and Flap B to Flap C.

King or Queen

Measure your child's head and make a suitably-sized crown out of card. Cover the crown with silver foil by stapling it, or by gluing it to the inside of the crown. Decorate by spreading glue on the tips and edge of the crown and sprinkle glitter over it. Leave to dry and shake off extra glitter. Glue on cotton wool ermine and contrasting coloured-foil jewels.

Use a plain coloured dressing gown as the king's robe, and fasten an old gilt chain round his neck, and a gold belt round his middle. Or make this simple cloak (see right), in red or purple, with a tie fastening. You can dress up his shoes with a bobble of fur or some jewels, stick a sword in his belt, and make an orb or sceptre for him to carry.

You will need a long party dress or pretty night dress for your Queen, and give her a full-length cloak and glittering jewellery.

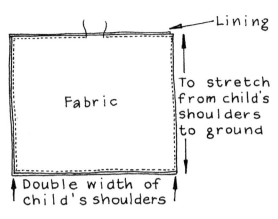

Lining

Fabric

To stretch from child's shoulders to ground

Double width of child's shoulders

Machine round edges leaving opening, turn inside out and press

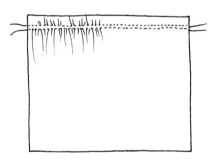

Sew 2 rows gathering Pull up to fit

Attach neck band and ties

Footballer

Football shorts, football shirt, football boots, football socks, and football, will probably be your son's favourite outfit, particularly if you can organize this in the colour of his favourite team.

Robin Hood

Green tunic (see page 30) with shirt. If your child does not object you could also put him into some green tights. Stick a feather in the side of a suitable hat. Make the hat out of green felt (see diagram). A bow and arrow to carry.

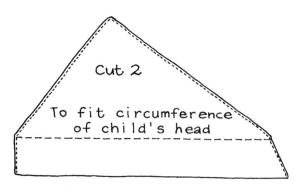

Cut 2

To fit circumference of child's head

Sew sides and crown
Turn inside out

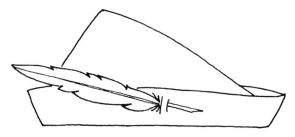

Fold up brim along dotted line, attach feather

Christopher Robin

Ideal for a shy boy as basically there is no dressing up! Summer: white sunhat, wellingtons, shorts and shirt, and a teddy to carry. Winter: sou'wester and matching mackintosh, wellingtons and a teddy.

Clown

There are endless possibilities here. Make a fat clown by putting a cushion inside large pyjamas with braces to keep them up. Use a stuffed pair of large shoes but let your child take ordinary shoes for wearing after the fancy dress parade as he might trip over. Hat with droopy paper flowers. Sew patches onto clothes. Use face paints to make either a sad or happy clown or make one side of his face smiling and one crying.

Paddington Bear

A suitable man's hat (it doesn't matter if it's rather large); a duffle coat (the longer the better), a pair of corduroy trousers, and wellington boots. A luggage label with the usual message 'Please look after this bear'. He will need a small suitcase to carry, and a marmalade sandwich if you can trust him! Put suitable labels on the suitcase too.

Highwayman

Make a mask (see page 22) and dress him in cowboy hat, black trousers, black cape (see cloak, page 25) or use an old curtain, black polo-neck jumper and black gumboots. Let him ride a hobby horse, if you have one. Give him some old jewellery in a jewel case or little sack for his booty, and a couple of pistols to carry.

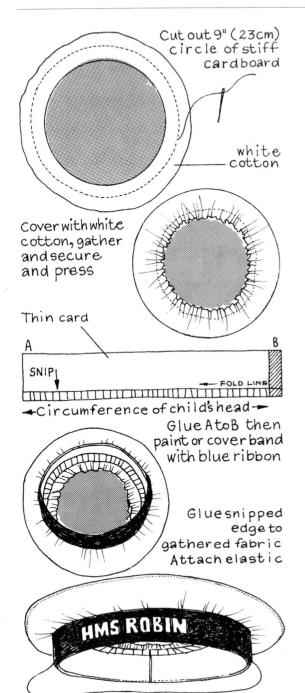

Cut out 9" (23cm) circle of stiff cardboard

white cotton

Cover with white cotton, gather and secure and press

Thin card

A   B

SNIP↓

←——— FOLD LINE

←Circumference of child's head→

Glue A to B then paint or cover band with blue ribbon

Glue snipped edge to gathered fabric
Attach elastic

HMS ROBIN

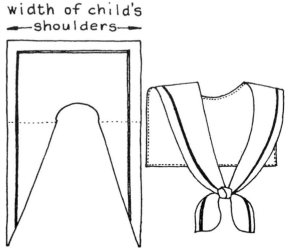

width of child's
←—shoulders—→

White cotton, hemmed, with blue trimming

Sailor

Blue and white striped T-shirt, and blue trousers. Make a collar and a hat (see diagrams). He should carry a toy telescope.

Dick Whittington

A toy cat. A man's shirt belted at the waist, tights, wellington boots, and large red and white spotted hanky tied into a bag round a stick – for his traditional bundle of possessions. Optional hat (see Robin Hood's hat, page 26).

Birds

One long-sleeved polo-neck jumper, or brown long-sleeved T-shirt. Brown woollen balaclava, if you have one, with a beak (see next page) stapled on to the front. Brown, yellow or black tights. Dancing shoes, plimsolls or brown sandals. Brown wings attached to the child's wrists and back (see Fairy's

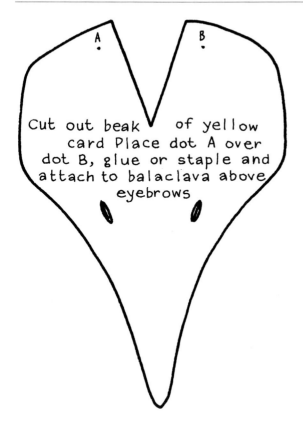

A   B

Cut out beak   of yellow
card Place dot A over
dot B, glue or staple and
attach to balaclava above
eyebrows

Animals

Use a similar basic outfit as for the birds. Make felt ears for a rabbit (see diagrams on how to make these). Use a puff of cotton wool for his tail. For a donkey (Eeyore) make the outfit in grey or brown with long ears and a donkey's tail with a red bow on it. Make the tail out of a brown stocking or half a pair of tights stuffed and sewn on to the child's tights. For a cat, black tights, polo neck and balaclava (see diagram for pussy cat ears). Stuff a black stocking as above for the tail. Use face paints to draw whiskers on face.

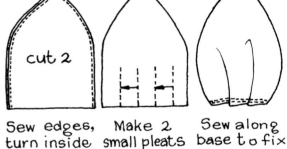

cut 2

Sew edges,   Make 2   Sew along
turn inside   small pleats base to fix
out, press   pleats

wings on page 30 for detailed instructions). You could staple pieces of overlapping feather-shaped paper to the material. For the tail, if you can get hold of some pheasant feathers (ask your butcher) make an arrangement of these, and carefully sew them on to the back of the tights, at waist height (remind the child to be careful when he sits down).

You could also have a completely black outfit, for a blackbird, or a completely white outfit, for a swan. For an owl use a cloak or curtain (see page 25) as a base and staple paper feather shapes to it. Attach two clusters of feathers to the balaclava for the owl's ears. Use brown face paints, and leave a large circle of white round each eye.

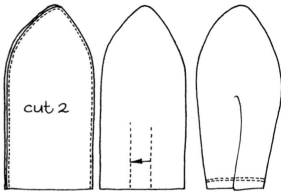

cut 2

Sew edges,   Make 1   Sew along
turn inside   small pleat   base to fix
out, press   pleats

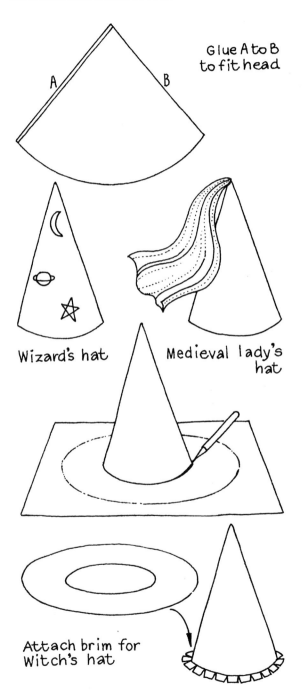

Glue A to B
to fit head

A   B

Wizard's hat

Medieval lady's hat

Attach brim for
Witch's hat

Sorcerer or Wizard

A long dressing gown or cloak (page 25). A witch's hat cut out from coloured paper, covered with stars and moons made out of foil (see diagram). Make some more to attach to the dressing gown or cloak. Give him a wand (see fairy's wand diagram), and a very fat book labelled spells.

Fine Lady from Banbury Cross

Cover a medieval style hat (see left) with foil. A light piece of net or nylon (part of an old lacy petticoat) could be attached to flow from the top of the cone. Secure the hat by a band of elastic stapled inside the cone to go under the chin. A long dress or pretty nightie will look most suitable, together with a cloak (see page 25). If you can manage it give her plenty of rings and jewellery and if you have any little bells attach these to the front of her shoes. You can buy lovely sounding bells which children use to play in a band, for her to hold. She could ride a hobby horse, if you have one.

Japanese Girl

You will need a suitable robe – a dressing gown, for instance. Make a cummerbund out of a wide piece of brightly coloured material. Wrap the cummerbund around the waist, and tie firmly at the back with a big bow. If your child has long hair, make the most of this by putting it into a bun, and use two coloured plastic knitting needles as long hair pins, sticking out of the bun. If your child has got short hair, you can make a bun from wool. Make up her face with white face paint, and give her slanting eyes, and red lips.

Tinkerbell or Fairy

Follow the drawings to make the separate items for this costume. If your daughter has a tutu let her wear this, instead of the tunic. Dancing shoes, if she has them. Make a flower hat in coloured tissue or crepe paper to match the dress.

To make the wings, you will need a piece of net or light material of the same colour as the dress. For the wand you need a piece of stick or a dowel rod 18″ (45 cm) long. Follow the diagram and then cover the corner staples with little pieces of tinsel sellotaped to the foil. Then take a long piece of tinsel and twist it around the rod, and secure firmly. If you want, you can add tinsel to her shoes and around the elastic bracelets. Cut out a little silver-foil bell, if you do not have one, for her to hold in her other hand as Tinkerbell.

Width of child's shoulders

Measure length from shoulder to below knee

Cut zig zag edge. Hem arms and neck

Add tie belt

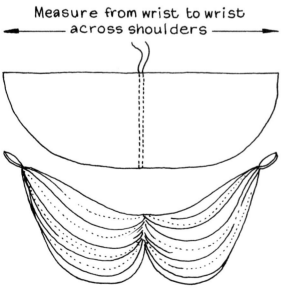

Measure from wrist to wrist across shoulders

Gather centre and sew to back of dress. Attach elastic loops to fit wrists

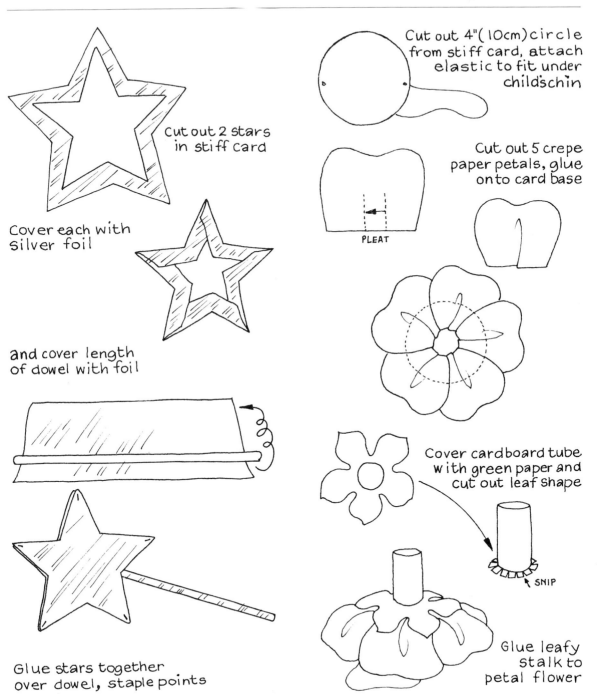

Cut out 2 stars in stiff card

Cover each with silver foil

and cover length of dowel with foil

Glue stars together over dowel, staple points

Cut out 4"(10cm) circle from stiff card, attach elastic to fit under child's chin

Cut out 5 crepe paper petals, glue onto card base

PLEAT

Cover cardboard tube with green paper and cut out leaf shape

SNIP

Glue leafy stalk to petal flower

Right: A pirates' tea party in full swing.

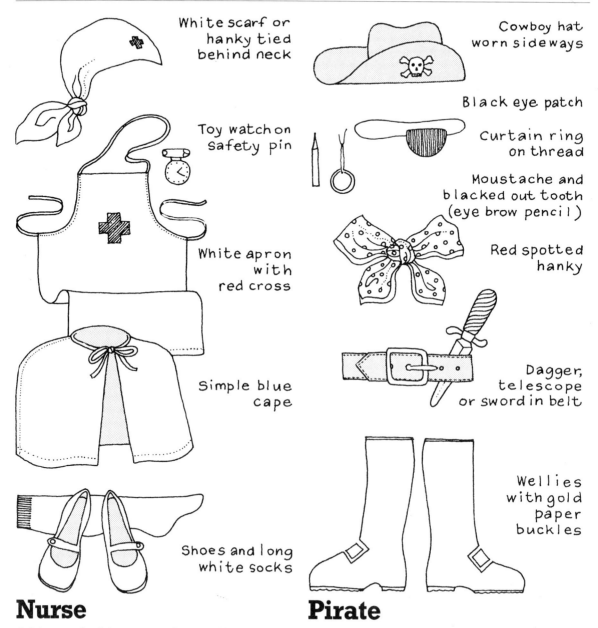

White scarf or hanky tied behind neck

Toy watch on safety pin

White apron with red cross

Simple blue cape

Shoes and long white socks

Cowboy hat worn sideways

Black eye patch

Curtain ring on thread

Moustache and blacked out tooth (eye brow pencil)

Red spotted hanky

Dagger, telescope or sword in belt

Wellies with gold paper buckles

Nurse

A blue and white cotton dress, either striped or checked, in other words a typical summer uniform dress, is the basis for this outfit which is shown in the drawing.

Pirate

The drawing shows everything you will need for this outfit. Start off by dressing him in a brightly coloured T-shirt and jeans and wellington boots.

Little Bo Peep

Dress your daughter in a pretty nightie. Give her a walking stick as a crook, wound with pink and white crepe paper, tied at the top with a bow. Secure the paper with sticky tape at the bottom and top, and fasten some small flowers and add lots of bows at the top. Make a mob cap (see diagram) or use a pretty bath hat. Give her a woolly lamb to carry.

Mary Mary Quite Contrary

A pretty nightie. A child's watering can, decorated with ribbons on the handle, tied in a bow. If you have any bells left over from Christmas, you could sew these if they are small enough, on to a hair band. Attach them also to the ribbon around the watering can, and make little wrist bands. Or make a mob cap, or use a pretty bath hat (see Little Bo Peep above).

Little Miss Muffet

Little Miss Muffet should really carry a toy spider, a bowl and spoon. Either make the spider out of pipe cleaners, dyed black with black ink or buy a horrid black plastic one. Attach a piece of cotton or thin elastic to the spider and tie this around your little girl's wrist. Put her in a nightie, with a mob cap (see above) and give her a bowl and spoon, for her curds and whey.

Waitress

Black tights, black skirt, white blouse, and little pinny and cap. Tray with plastic utensils on it.

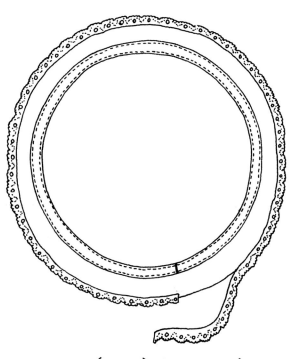

Cut out 28" (71 cm) diameter circle of fabric, trim with lace and attach a wide bias binding channel 4" (10 cm) from outside edge

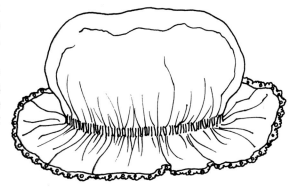

Insert elastic and pull up to fit child's head

Rider

This is a good outfit if your daughter already has riding gear. You could send her as a famous rider. You could put a number on a piece of card and tie it around her middle with a piece of string, as if she is competing in a show. If she has a riding crop she could carry that, or if she is young enough she could ride a hobby horse. If you have a rosette attach this to her horse!

Little Red Riding Hood

Make a red cloak and hood as in the drawing. Pretty little red or white dress to wear underneath, with an apron. A wicker basket with a gingham (red and white if possible) napkin over the top.

Cinderella

She could either be Cinderella going to the ball or Cinders. If Cinderella, she will need a pretty long dress or nightie, decorated with jewellery or tinsel and a little crown (see instructions for King's crown, page 25, but make it smaller to sit just on top of her head and staple elastic to either side to go under her chin). Decorate her shoes with tinsel and make her a foil clock face with the hands set at 12 o'clock to carry, or perhaps a small pumpkin.

If she is going as Cinders then blacken her face and give her really tatty clothes to wear. Cut or tear an old dress into spikes around the hem. Let her carry a besom broom (see opposite page).

For the Ugly Sisters, see page 36.

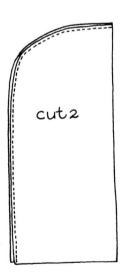

Wrong sides together, sew back seam

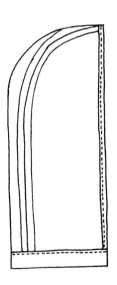

Hem all edges

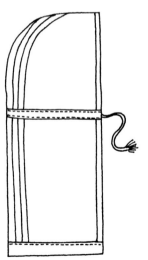

Attach wide bias binding, insert cord

Pull up cords and tie at neck

Alice in Wonderland

This is most suitable for a fair haired child. You will need a blue alice band, a blue and white striped dress (a similar school uniform dress would be fine), a white apron, a pair of white tights or long white socks. A plastic bottle with a label marked 'Drink me'.

Ballet Dancer

Use a tutu and ballet shoes, if you have them, and thin tights. If not, she could wear a leotard and leg warmers. If her hair is long, draw it back into a bun.

Witch

A black T-shirt, and long black skirt. Make the skirt by simply buying some very cheap black material and turning one end up to use as the waistline with elastic, and just join up the seams. If you have any black net, this is ideal for a cape to tack on to her shoulders, or make a simple black cloak (see page 25). A friend once even strung some old chop bones (scrubbed meticulously clean) to make a ghoulish necklace. Green nail varnish. A white powdered face, use child's talcum powder, or white face paints. Suitable eye make-up, and a couple of teeth blacked out. Strands of black wool sewn or stapled to the rim of a conical hat (see drawing on page 29) from underneath, and hanging down as hair.

If you have a suitably short broom handle, make it into a besom, by collecting some twigs, and firmly tying these with string to the broom handle. If you have a soft black toy cat she could take this under one arm, or attach it to the besom. An old book could be used as a book of spells.

Punk Rocker

Mini skirt or whatever 'with-it' gear you have! Washable coloured hair spray. Packet of glitter, packet of stars. (You can buy in chemists a special gel for sticking these on.) Coloured nail varnish. Bright face paint (non toxic) make-up. Sprinkle glitter in hair and on face, and decorate both with stars etc. Your child will enlighten you anyway as to the current trend!

Gipsy

Gold gipsy earrings, or brass curtain rings. Pretty frilly blouse, and pretty flower patterned skirt. Plenty of satin ribbons tied in bows, at the sleeves of the blouse and on either side of a hair band. An old lacy shawl. Black ballet shoes, or black canvas gym or tennis shoes. A tambourine if you have one, with satin ribbons as streamers.

Double Acts

If two of your children, or your child and a friend, are going to the same fancy dress party, then why not dress them up as a double act? Some of our suggestions are for boys and girls, but some could be either two boys or two girls.

Jack and Jill

Jack could be dressed in fairly traditional clothes, such as dungarees. Put brown paper as bandages around his head, and let him carry a large bottle labelled vinegar. Jill could wear a simple striped dress, or a long dress or nightie, with a pretty bow around her waist. Give her a bucket to carry. Decorate it with bows on the handle to make it look attractive.

Doctor and Patient

Doctor as on page 23. To make a patient, put him/her in pyjamas, dressing gown and slippers. Cut up an old sheet and bandage his head, one leg and arm and make a sling for his arm. If you have a walking stick let him use this.

Queen and Knave of Hearts

Dress the girl up as a queen (see page 25), and staple or tack lots of red paper hearts to the costume. Make some jam tarts and put them on an open tin or little tray (not to be eaten straight away). The Knave can wear either a man's shirt or one of yours, particularly if it has full sleeves, decorated with paper hearts. Belt it in at the waist. Or make a cardboard 'tabard' with shoulder and waist ties. Cover with foil and decorate with red paper hearts. Wear a red T-shirt underneath. Tights if he will wear them (if not, trousers).

Owl and Pussy Cat

See page 28. Let them carry between them a jar marked honey, lots of toy Monopoly money, with a £5 note on the outside, a toy guitar and a curtain ring for the wedding ring.

Ugly Sisters (for boys and girls!)

Anything goes for these outfits! Very brightly clashing colours for shirts and blouses. Let them wear bloomers (thermal underwear will do!) and stripy stockings if you have them. Large shoes. Tie hair up with lots of bows all in different colours and very exaggerated hideous make-up.

Indian and Squaw

In summer decorate a boy's chest, back and face with war paint, using suitable face paints. Stick some feathers on to a band to fit your child's head. Put him into suitable trousers or jeans and moccasin shoes or slippers, if possible. Give him a bow and arrow to carry.

A squaw can wear a tunic, fringed if possible, moccasins, a head band and feather, and could paint her face. Two black woollen plaits could be fixed to the head band.

Peter Pan and Wendy

For Wendy a nightdress. She could be hugging a teddy bear, and wearing slippers. Peter Pan in a green tunic (see page 30), or a green, belted shirt as for the Knave of Hearts. Give Peter Pan a large box labelled flying powder.

Other Pairings

Witch and Cat
See pages 35 and 28 for each outfit.

Alice and the White Rabbit
See pages 35 and 28 for each outfit.

Chef and Waitress
See pages 23 and 33 for outfits.

Dick Whittington and His Cat
See pages 27 and 28 for outfits.

Doctor and Nurse
See pages 23 and 32 for outfits.

Wurzel Gummidge and Aunt Sally
See page 24 for Wurzel and Aunt Sally outfits.

Presents

You could give little presents as prizes for winning games, and most people give small going-home presents at the end of the party, as well as a balloon, to each child. Instead of simply handing out presents at the end, it is more fun to wrap each little gift either in tissue paper, or used wrapping paper (iron it if creased). Have a present hunt at the end of the party, having hidden them either around the house, or if the weather is fine, around the garden. This is ideal for younger children whose mothers have stayed with them, and who can help them find the presents. For older children have a bran tub or box, and decorate it with crepe paper, tied around with a big ribbon. Cut out lots of strips of newspaper and put these in the box with the presents.

If you are inviting both sexes to the party, then remember that the presents should be suitable for both boys and girls, or else make separate boy/girl presents, and wrap the girls' presents in pink paper, and the boys' in blue. You can of course put your guests' names on their respective presents. If it is Christmas, then Santa Claus can appear suitably garbed, anonymous, and armed with a sack full of goodies. If you are privileged enough to have an inglenook fireplace, put a pair of kitchen steps inside the fireplace, and at the end of the party 'find' Father Christmas 'coming down the chimney', lightly sprinkled with soot! Younger children are totally captivated by this.

The presents need be only small, although depending on the number of your guests, it is amazing how fast the 10p's add up! Or if you have time, try and make some goodies yourself.

Bought Presents

Either from the local toy shop, in the pocket money section, or from W. H. Smith or Woolworth:

> *Pencil sharpeners*
> *Little books*
> *Little pencils and notebooks*
> *Sweets* – tiny packets of Smarties, fun-size Mars Bars, or perhaps a packet of sugar cigarettes.
> *Sweet lollipops* – if outside and fine weather, suspend them from the branches of a tree for a lollipop tree.
> *Toys* – a cheap farm animal, car etc, to carry through your party theme.

Home-made Presents

Felt Finger Puppets

You can buy felt at a local craft shop. It is probably worth asking if they have any off-cuts, if you do not need the felt for any other purpose. If not, buy a small amount of felt in different colours. We have given you several designs to choose from – rabbit, pirate, owl, little girl, cat – or you can design your own puppet, around your party theme perhaps. The finger puppets can either be sewn or glued. If you choose the latter method, then we suggest a clear adhesive like Bostik.

Cut out your finger shape, approximately $2\frac{1}{2}$ inches long (6 cm) long by $1\frac{1}{2}$ inches (3·5 cm) wide (this is to allow for your glued or sewn seam). Cut another matching piece and either glue or sew together. If you are making an

animal which requires ears, you could insert these between the two halves prior to the gluing or sewing, or you could sew them on afterwards. Cut out contrasting colour eyes, mouth, or animal nose, and glue these in the appropriate place. It always looks more realistic to add a little tiny pupil to the eye and the mouth can be simply made by cutting a triangle and with the long base side at the top, this gives a smile effect. To produce suitable ears, beak, etc, follow the diagrams. For animal whiskers, thread a needle and with the cotton doubled pass the needle at the nose point, just through the snout, and cut to a suitable length and repeat until you have sufficient whiskers, as in the diagram. If you wish to make hair for the little girl, use pieces of wool, or embroidery thread glued at a centre parting, and tie the wool or thread in bunches at ear level, with bits of either very narrow ribbon or contrasting threads. You could easily cut out hat shapes, buttons or collars to put on top if you wish.

Egg Cosies

For an Easter Party make little egg cosies. Make them in the same way, using the same design suggestions, as for felt finger puppets, but sew rather than glue the seams. The two pieces of felt should be 2 inches (5 cm) high and $3\frac{1}{2}$ inches (9 cm) wide. Include a small chocolate Easter egg.

Bean Bags

Use odd remnants of material (don't worry if these are all totally different, do one side one design and the other another). Cut the material into approximately 7 inch (17·5 cm) squares, and machine sew up very firmly, with a double seam to make approximately 6 inch (15 cm) square bags. Leave a small hole at one corner, and then turn the bag inside out, so that your seams are on the inside. Fill with dried peas, or whatever you choose, and sew up the hole very firmly. These should perhaps not be given to younger children, depending on the firmness of your stitching!

Masks

Make a mask-shaped template out of newspaper and cut your masks out of coloured firm paper or card. Then make your two eye holes, and decorate the mask with self-adhesive coloured shapes, which you can buy in packets. If you wish you could put clear adhesive on part of the mask and sprinkle with glitter. Make two small holes on either side, and using your child as a guide to the size, attach either shirring elastic or a single piece of wool or ribbon from each hole, to tie at the back of the head. It is a good idea to place hole reinforcers over the holes first, to strengthen them. (See the mask invitations on page 22).

Peg Dolls

You can still buy the old fashioned springless type of peg at ironmongers. It will depend on your ability as a seamstress as to how elaborate you make these peg dolls, but using a few remnants of material and felt you can make very satisfactory gifts without much expertise. In fact, you can use a clear adhesive glue like Bostik, instead of sewing, to keep the making of the doll very simple.

First of all make the doll's face. As these pegs are unvarnished you may find biro the easiest medium to work with, as it will not 'splodge'. If you have any model enthusiasts in the family 'borrow' a little enamel paint and paint the doll's face. If you have time and energy, perhaps paint the feet of the doll black, otherwise just leave them plain. Then twist a piece of pipe-cleaner around the doll's neck to form the two arms. Then make the dress, add sleeves if you can, then finish off with pink felt for her hands. If you are making a girl doll, then you could put a little petticoat underneath the main piece of material for the outer garment. Don't forget to trim her with the odd piece of lace, which gives a more

professional finish. To make your doll's hair, you could glue either embroidery thread or wool. You may need to catch it back in bunches, either with a couple of little stitches or a thin ribbon bow, to prevent the hair sticking out too much.

Home-made Sweets

These sweets are really quite easy to make and are popular presents. Wrap three or four sweets together in cellophane and tie with a pretty ribbon.

Peppermint Creams

See photograph on page 76.

10 oz (275 g) icing sugar, sieved
1 egg white, stiffly beaten
A few drops of peppermint essence
Green food colouring
Cellophane or cling film
Very narrow satin/nylon ribbon or wrapping
  ribbon

Add the sieved icing sugar to the whisked egg white, and mix with a wooden spoon (if not stiff enough add a little more icing sugar). Stir in the peppermint essence, and green food colouring. Roll out the peppermint mixture on to a board sprinkled with icing sugar, and cut out shapes (diamonds, stars etc) with a knife or the smallest sized pastry cutter, or suitably sized lid.

Leave the peppermints in a cool place until they are set hard (this may take several hours). Then cut pieces of cellophane or cling film into 6 inch (15 cm) squares, and wrap the peppermints up, gathering up the ends and securing them with pretty, narrow ribbon.

Fudge

1 lb (450 g) sugar
5 oz (150 g) butter
$\frac{1}{4}$ pint (150 ml) milk
Cellophane or cling film
Narrow ribbon (as for Peppermint Creams)

Grease a tin about 8 inches (20 cm) square. Put all the ingredients into a saucepan over a gentle heat and stir until the sugar is dissolved. Bring to the boil, stirring all the time, and boil until a small spoonful of the mixture dropped into a cup of cold water forms a small ball. Take off the heat and beat for a couple of moments until the mixture has cooled slightly. Pour into the tin and cut into squares when cold. Wrap as in Peppermint Cream recipe.

Chocolate Fudge

Make as above, adding 2 tablespoons cocoa, and make sure the cocoa is completely dissolved before the mixture comes to the boil.

Gingerbread Men

These are rather large for small children to eat as part of a tea, so they make interesting take-home gifts wrapped in cling film. Have some spare ones, in case of breakages, and if you have time pipe your guests' names on them. See page 86 for the recipe.

Toffee Apples

6–8 unblemished eating apples
1 lb (450 g) demerara sugar
2 oz (50 g) butter
¼ pint (150 ml) water
2 tablespoons golden syrup
One wooden stick per apple (or lolly stick)

First of all prepare your apples: wipe them clean, dry them and insert the sticks. In a large heavy bottomed pan, melt the remaining ingredients over a gentle heat (do not stir too much as this may cause the toffee to crystallize). When the sugar has dissolved, boil rapidly for about 5 minutes, until the temperature is about 290° F (143° C) or test the toffee by popping a little into cold water – it should divide into fairly hard threads. Remove the pan from the heat. Tipping it slightly, dip in your apples and coat each one completely. Stand the apples either on a buttered tray or on wax paper. When quite cold, wrap each one in a piece of cellophane or waxed paper, and hold with a ribbon, rubber band or freezer twist tie. You can prepare these toffee apples a couple of days before the party, but keep them somewhere dry.

Peanut and Chocolate Balls

3½ oz (100 g) plain chocolate
1 oz (25 g) butter
2 oz (50 g) peanuts
1 teaspoon vanilla essence

Break up the chocolate, put in a bowl and stand over a pan of hot water. Add the butter and leave until both are melted. Chop the peanuts coarsely and add to the chocolate with the vanilla essence. Form into balls, and leave to firm before wrapping.

Coconut Ice

Makes 64 pieces

1 lb (450 g) sugar
¼ pint (150 ml) milk
5 oz (150 g) desiccated coconut
pink colouring

Grease a tin, 8 × 8 inches (20 × 20 cm) square. Put the sugar and milk into a saucepan and heat gently until the sugar has dissolved. Bring to the boil, stirring continuously, and cook until a spoonful dropped into cold water forms a soft ball. Remove from the heat and stir in the coconut. Pour half the mixture into the tin, add pink colouring to the remaining half and then pour over the first portion. Divide into 1 inch (2.5 cm) squares while the coconut ice is cooling. Don't take out of tin until completely cold.

Party decorations

It is a good idea to show where the party is being held by putting a bunch of balloons on your gate post or front door. If you are intending to have a theme running throughout the party, start it off by drawing a suitable poster, or make a cut-out concertina of dolls or animals, such as elephants joined trunk to tail, to reflect the theme, and attach these to the gate or front door. See the invitation section for ideas.

Balloons

Lots of balloons around the house will give a festive atmosphere without much effort or inconvenience other than a lot of puff from someone! If you are desperate you can buy a balloon pump from stationers. Once you have blown the balloons up you can write each child's name on a balloon or draw faces on them with a felt-tipped pen. Always remember to have some extra balloons in case of accidental bursts! Tie a piece of string, wool or ribbon to each balloon, and, mixing the colours and shapes, group them into however many bunches you require to decorate the room. Tie a slip knot in the bunch of strings so that when the children go home you can easily take the balloon cluster down and free them by simply pulling the right end.

The Party Room

If you are having your party at home, clear the room that you have chosen for the games of all breakable objects to avoid any embarrassing accidents. If you are lucky enough to have a nursery or play room, then hold the party there, and, depending on your time and energy, decorate the room to the best of your ability. If you can carry the party theme through from the invitations into decorations then do so. Use posters or drawings of the chosen theme, sheets of wrapping paper of a suitable design, record sleeves, pictures from magazines, etc. Use sheets of silver foil for a spaceman's party. Blu-tack is ideal to use as an adhesive for these, but obviously it depends on the surface of your wall. If you wish to make your decorations, you could have more strings of concertina figures as you did for the outside of the house, strung on the walls indoors.

Streamers

One easy but effective form of decoration is crepe paper streamers. Keep the paper folded as in its original packet, cut it across into 2 inch (5 cm) strips, then frill the edges by running the back of the scissors down either side. Unwind the strips, join ends with sellotape (you can buy double sided sellotape which is expensive, but extremely strong and durable), twist the strips and fasten around the walls and across the ceiling with Blu-tack. Don't destroy these decorations as they will come in handy for other occasions.

If you are having your party in a hall, then go down there well before the party date, have a look around and see if there is any way in which you can quickly and easily decorate before the party. Often at these places one can only have the hall a little while before your party is due to start, and you may well find that you have no time at all to decorate. However, if you do have time, remember that in a room of large proportions small decorations get rather

lost, and plenty of streamers and balloons and the like are probably the most effective way of decorating.

Party Tea

If you have the space, we suggest that you set tea in another room, simply to avoid over-enthusiastic premature nibblings! If you are planning to use your dining-room table, or any wooden table for the tea party, then cover it first of all with a polythene sheet (cleaner's bags sellotaped together will suffice) and place your cloth on top. Use benches if you have any, as they take up less room than chairs, but try not to overcrowd your guests; each child takes up more room than one would imagine.

The Tea Table

You can buy very attractive matching paper sets, which include table cloths, napkins, mugs, plates in varying sizes, and jelly containers. These are expensive, but labour saving (wash up unstained items at leisure and keep them for picnics, and they will not be quite as extravagant as they might seem at first sight). However, you can make the table look very attractive using your own equipment, so long as you have enough. Instead of napkins, you could economize by using coloured kitchen roll, folded into individual squares for each child. A cheerful gingham tablecloth will not need further decoration, but a plain white cloth could be jollied up with foil strips, cut out and stapled in criss-crosses over the cloth, or cut-out shapes of animals, stars, moons, in foil or coloured card which might fit in to your party theme and again could be stapled to the cloth. If you are not using paper sets then try and make sure that your colours at least blend, even if you haven't sufficient matching equipment. But remember not to use glasses for small children to drink from. If you have time, cut out place names from coloured card – carrying on the theme or simply cut oblongs, fold them in half, write each child's name on one and stand them on their long sides. Use pinking shears to give a fancy edge, if you like.

If you have room on your table, and if you don't mind the prospect of games being played while eating progresses, then decorate your table further by putting plastic animals, if you have an animal theme, or small cars, etc, around the table. Suspend a bunch of balloons or Blu-tack some mobiles over the tea table. The sets of bought plates, etc, often come in packets which do not necessarily match up with the numbers of guests, so if you have any of these left over, it is very easy to thread a piece of cotton through the rim of one of these, knot the thread, and use this as a mobile above the table. You could make foil or coloured card shapes, and similarly suspend these. Remember that it is best to glue the foil to firmer card as it may curl up with the heat in the party room, and lose its effect.

2. PARTY CAKES

However daunting it may be for the mother, the focal point of any child's tea party is the cake! The climax lies in the candle blowing and singing ritual, not in eating the master-piece – so don't be disappointed or offended if most of the cake is left (you can always cut up slices to be taken home in paper napkins, if you've time). Nevertheless, the centrepiece must be on show, and the more interesting or amusing, the more likely it is to be devoured. If your party has a specific theme, try to keep the cake in line with it, or, if your child asks for a specific cake such as a train or a ship, then shape your ideas for the party around it. In our cake section we provide lots of ideas for different cakes which look effective and can be achieved quite simply.

Once you have decided on your cake, then is the time to think of the rest of the party food.

In this chapter we provide detailed recipes for the basic cakes and icings. These are followed by the recipe for each individual cake which tells you which basic cake is required, and we have numbered these basic cakes for extra clarity. Don't worry at all if your cake might look a little crooked, bumpy or otherwise not quite perfect – it all adds to the charm of a home-made cake and the children will love it.

We have both experienced the feeling of horrible inadequacy when our children have demanded what seems like an impossibly exotic cake – 'Make me a hedgehog/a car/a space ship/a house' – but our recipes are genuinely easy to follow and we promise that most effective results can be achieved even by the most unconfident or inexperienced cake-maker.

If you have never made a cake before, then start off with the all-in-one sponge. This is the never-fail cake with a light perfect texture. Use it to make one of the simpler cakes which do not require any shaping; the zoo cake, clock, or football match, for instance. As the texture tends to be rather brittle, we do not recommend it for any of the cakes which need cutting into shape. But it does keep very well so you can make it two or three days in advance.

If you are making a Victoria sponge, you can make it two days before the party and ice it the day before. This gives time for the icing to harden and avoids last-minute panics on the party day itself. Alternatively any cake made with butter icing can be made in advance, iced, and put into the freezer on a cake board. Take it out on the morning of the party. Don't freeze a cake decorated with glacé icing – the colour goes blotchy and the icing tends to melt on defrosting. Smarties do not freeze well and should be added as decoration on the day of the party.

We have also included a section on ice cream cakes, which are extremely easy to make, and very popular with children. We have found by experience that it is not a good idea to mix ice cream and sponge in the same cake – the sponge gets soggy and the children don't eat it – so, other than the snow princess which requires a sponge base, our ice cream cakes can be assembled from start to finish in a few minutes. For the sake of hygiene, we have made sure that instructions do not involve a lot of refreezing of the ice cream – in most cases the cake can be assembled in one operation and put straight back in the freezer until required.

Cake boards come in many shapes and sizes. However, a large table mat or bread board, covered with foil with the shiny side up, can be a cheap but effective alternative.

We know that time is the vital factor. Due to unforeseen circumstances (the typical experience of any mum!) one of us had ten minutes to assemble the crinoline lady doll cake one day – but it worked and looked lovely.

Metric conversions are approximate, so stick to either metric or imperial in any one recipe. Finally, don't forget the matches – and, why not try the candles that relight themselves.

Basic cakes and cake ideas

Basic Swiss Roll

Oven Temperature: 425°F, 220°C, Gas Mark 7

3 large eggs
3 oz (75 g) caster sugar
3 oz (75 g) self-raising flour, sieved
4 level tablespoons warmed jam, or softened
   butter icing (see page 49)

Preheat the oven and grease and line a swiss roll tin of 8 × 12 inches (20 ×30 cm). Whisk the eggs (at room temperature) with the sugar, until the mixture is light and fluffy. (There should be a trail when the whisk is taken out of the mixture.) Using a metal spoon, fold in the flour.

Turn this mixture into the tin, and level with a palette knife. Bake in the hot oven for 7–10 minutes, until the sponge begins to shrink from the edge of the tin, and is firm to the touch.

Turn the cake out on to a sheet of greaseproof paper which has been dredged with caster sugar. Trim off the edges of the cake, and roll up tightly with the paper inside. When it is cool, unroll the cake gently, remove the paper, and spread the cake with either jam or the softened butter icing, and then reroll it. If you are using jam, warm it to make it easier to spread, but do not make it too hot, or it will soak into the cake.

Basic Victoria Sponge Cake

Oven Temperature: 350°F, 180°C, Gas Mark 4

6 oz (175 g) soft butter or margarine
3 large eggs
6 oz (175 g) caster sugar
Pinch of salt
6 oz (175 g) self-raising flour, sieved
1 tablespoon milk or water, if necessary

Preheat the oven to the required temperature. Grease your chosen tin or bowl and line the base with greased greaseproof paper, with silicone paper or butter paper cut to fit. It is very important to have your fat and eggs at room temperature, and to warm your mixing bowl.

Cream the fat, sugar and salt until the ingredients are thoroughly combined and the texture is like whipped cream. Beat the eggs in a separate bowl and add them to the creamed mixture a little at a time, beating well after each addition, until the mixture returns to its fluffy state. Sift the flour into the bowl from a height, thereby allowing the flour to take in air. Carefully fold in the flour with a metal spoon. Add the milk or water if the mixture does not fall easily from the spoon.

Turn the mixture into the prepared tin or bowl and bake for the appropriate time (see below). To test if the cake is cooked, press it and if it springs back into shape, it is ready. (Another sign of the cake being thoroughly cooked is when it starts to shrink away from the sides of the cake tin or bowl.) Take out of the oven and after a minute run a palette knife around the edge of the container and turn the cake on to a wire tray. Peel off the greaseproof paper and allow to cool.

Flavour and Colouring Suggestions

Vanilla: $\frac{1}{2}$ teaspoon vanilla essence – add to the fat and sugar
Chocolate: 1 tablespoon cocoa powder – add to the flour, sieved
Orange: 1 teaspoon grated rind and juice from $\frac{1}{2}$ orange – add to fat and sugar
Lemon: 1 teaspoon grated rind and juice from $\frac{1}{2}$ lemon – add to fat and sugar
Marble: A few drops of pink colouring, and 1 dessertspoon chocolate powder. This makes a very pretty three colour cake. Divide the prepared sponge mixture equally between three bowls, then colour one pink, one chocolate, and leave the last one plain. Take 1 tablespoon from each bowl, and drop it into the prepared baking tin or bowl. Continue until the mixture is used up. Slightly hollow the centre of the cake and give *one* swirl with a metal spoon. Place in the centre of the oven, and bake according to the specific instructions for the shape of the tin or bowl used.

Basic Cakes 1–8

1. Two round sandwich cakes, baked in 8 inch (20 cm) sandwich tins. 20–25 minutes.
2. One square cake, baked in 8 inch (20 cm) square cake tin. 45 minutes.
3. One round cake, baked in 8 inch (20 cm) sandwich tin. 30–35 minutes.
4. One loaf shaped cake, baked in loaf tin, top approximately 9 × 5 × 3 inches (22·5 × 12·5 × 7·5 cm). 50–55 minutes.
5. Two basin shaped cakes, baked in $\frac{1}{2}$ pint (300 ml) and $1\frac{1}{2}$ pint (900 ml) pudding

basins, each two-thirds full. (Use white china pudding basins, as pyrex are too flat bottomed.) Cooking time for large basin, 1 hour; for small basin, 30–35 minutes.

6. One large 2 pint (1·1 litre) pudding basin. (Again use white china basin rather than pyrex.) 1 hour 15 minutes.

7. Rectangular cake, baked in swiss roll tin 8 × 12 inches (20 × 30 cm). 30–35 minutes.

8. One ring mould cake, baked in 9 inch (22·5 cm) ring mould tin. 40 minutes.

Basic All-in-one Sponge Cake

Oven Temperature: 325°F, 170°C, Gas Mark 3

8 oz (225 g) self-raising flour
1¾ level teaspoons baking powder
8 oz (225 g) soft margarine
8 oz (225 g) caster sugar
4 large eggs

Preheat the oven, grease the baking tin(s), and line with silicone or greaseproof paper.

Sift the flour and baking powder into a bowl, shaking the sieve from quite high above the bowl, so that the flour takes in air. Add all the other ingredients, and whisk well (with an electric hand beater if you have one) for about a minute until well mixed. The mixture should be firm but not stiff – add 1 or 2 tablespoons of warm water if necessary until it is the right dropping consistency. Spoon it into the prepared tin(s), smooth the surface and cook in the centre of the oven for the required time (see below), until well risen and golden.

Gently press the cake with a finger and if it springs back into shape, it is cooked. Remove from the oven, allow to cool in the tin for a couple of minutes, run a palette knife around the sides of the tin then turn out on to a cake rack. Remove the paper very carefully, and leave until cool.

Flavour and Colouring Suggestions

Vanilla: ½ teaspoon vanilla essence – add to the margarine and sugar

Chocolate: 1 tablespoon cocoa powder – add to the flour, sieved

Orange: 1 teaspoon grated rind and juice from ½ orange – add to margarine and sugar

Lemon: 1 teaspoon grated rind and juice from ½ lemon – add to margarine and sugar

Basic Cakes 9–10

9. Two round sandwich cakes, baked in 8 inch (20 cm) sandwich tins. 20–25 minutes.

10. One rectangular cake, baked in a swiss roll tin 8 × 12 inches (20 × 30 cm). 45–50 minutes.

Butter Icing

4 oz (110 g) butter, at room temperature
10 oz (275 g) icing sugar, sieved
1 tablespoon liquid (fruit juice, water or
   milk)

Cream the butter with the appropriate flavouring and gradually beat in the icing sugar, and liquid if required. Beat the mixture until the consistency is smooth and creamy.

Flavourings

Vanilla: ½ teaspoon vanilla essence
Chocolate: 2 level tablespoons sieved cocoa, made into a paste with a little water
Lemon: 1 teaspoon lemon juice, with finely grated rind
Orange: 1 dessertspoon orange juice, with a little finely grated rind
Peppermint: A few drops of oil of peppermint, or peppermint essence with a couple of drops of green food colouring.

Colourings

You can buy food colourings – mix a few drops of whichever colour you wish with the basic icing. For blue icing you may prefer to use glacé or the 'white' butter icing recipe as the yellow of basic butter icing makes the colour rather green.

Apricot Glaze

3 tablespoons apricot jam, sieved
1 tablespoon lemon juice

If you are using glacé icing, you will need to cover the cake with a layer of apricot glaze first to prevent crumbs getting into the icing. Heat the jam with the lemon juice, and push through a plastic sieve into a basin with a wooden spoon. Use this mixture while still warm, but not too hot.

Pure White Butter Icing

4 oz (110 g) softened butter (unsalted, as
   this is the palest in colour)
10 oz (275 g) icing sugar, sieved
2 tablespoons cold milk

Beat the butter until very soft. Continue to beat while gradually adding the sifted icing sugar, alternately with the milk, until all the icing sugar and milk is used up. Continue beating until soft and white. This will make sufficient icing to fill the centre and cover the outside of an 8 inch (20 cm) sandwich cake.

Glacé Icing

8 oz (225 g) icing sugar, sieved
2–3 tablespoons hot water
Flavouring of choice (as in the butter icing
   recipe)
Colouring of choice – use a few drops

Gradually mix the sieved icing sugar with the hot water, beating well until a smooth coating consistency is achieved. Add the hot water very cautiously as it is easy to make the icing too runny. When ready to use it should still seem to be a little stiff – this is the correct consistency. Add the flavouring and colouring as required.

Dougal Cake

1 bought or home-made chocolate swiss roll
(page 46)
Chocolate butter icing (page 49)
1 Wagon Wheel
A few Smarties, to form eyes and nose
Candles and holders

If you can pipe the icing, use the number 8 vegetable nozzle (a large zig-zag nozzle) to pipe from Dougal's centre back downwards on either side to form his shaggy hair. Use the Wagon Wheel and Smarties (stick with a dab of icing) to make his face.

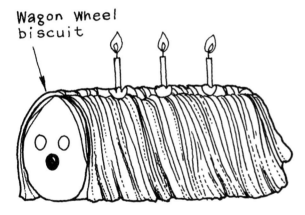

Wagon Wheel
biscuit

If you can't pipe then don't panic, but cover the cake with the butter icing, and smooth it with a palette knife. Then draw a line down the centre back, and from that use a fork to draw 'hair' lines down the sides of Dougal. Position candles along his back.

Teddy Bear Cake

2 basin shaped cakes (basic cake 5)
Chocolate butter icing (page 49: save an
egg-cupful)
2 Yoyos
2 Smarties for his eyes
1 Malteser for his nose
4 miniature chocolate covered swiss rolls
Cocktail sticks
2 Munchmallows
Candles and holders

Trim the base of the smaller cake to make the head a better shape. Put the large cake round side up on to a board, fasten the smaller one to it (also round side up) with a little butter icing, and cover both cakes with the rest of the icing. Add one extra

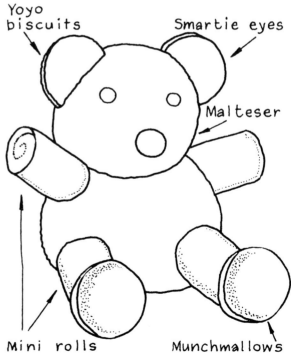

Yoyo
biscuits

Smartie eyes

Malteser

Mini rolls

Munchmallows

dollop of icing on one side of the bear's head, where his nose is going to be. Roughen the surface of the cake with a fork. For the bear's ears, cut two slits at the top of the bear's head with a sharp knife, and remove two very small slivers of cake. Put the Yoyos in the spaces provided and place the Smarties and Malteser in position. To make his arms and legs stick a cocktail stick halfway into the four swiss rolls and push the other half of the stick into the cake so that the arms stick out on either side of the bear, and the legs stick out in front, along the board. Use a dab of icing and fasten the two Munchmallows as the bear's feet to the end of his legs. Position candles on top of his head.

Hedgehog Cake

2 ×8 inch (20 cm) round chocolate
*   sandwich cakes (basic cake 1)*
Chocolate butter icing, made with 6 oz
*   (175 g) butter, 12 oz (350 g) icing sugar*
*   and 3 level tablespoons cocoa (page 49)*
1 packet of Matchmakers
2 large packets of chocolate buttons
1 Malteser
2 silver balls
Candles and holders

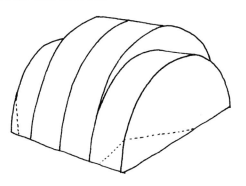

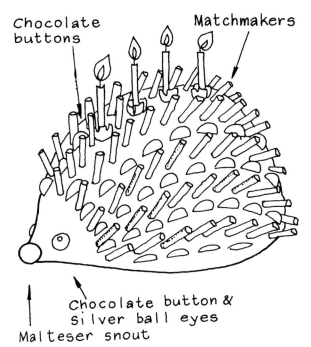

Put the two cakes on top of each other and cut straight across them, making slightly unequal portions. Then sandwich the four portions together with some of the butter icing, as shown in the diagram. Shape his face by cutting off a sliver of cake at one end on either side. Form the pointed nose with icing and fill in the gaps between the cakes with extra icing. Cover the cake with the remaining icing, and roughen it a little with a fork. Break the Matchmakers in half and stick these and the chocolate buttons into the icing as his prickles. Stick the two silver balls with a little icing on to his chocolate button eyes. The Malteser becomes his snout. Put candles on his back as extra spines.

Mouse Cake

2 × 8 inch (20 cm) round orange or chocolate flavoured sandwich cakes (basic cake 1)

Orange or chocolate butter icing, made with 6 oz (175 g) butter, 12 oz (350 g) icing sugar and 2 dessertspoons orange juice and rind, or 3 tablespoons cocoa (page 49)

2 Smarties or chocolate buttons (for eyes)

2 silver balls (for pupils)

1 Malteser (for nose)

Orange flavoured Matchmakers (about 6 for whiskers)

Thin liquorice (for tail)

2 more chocolate buttons (for ears)

Candles and holders

Assemble the Mouse cake as for the Hedgehog cake (page 51).

Wise Owl Cake

2 chocolate basin shaped cakes (basic cake 5)

Chocolate butter icing (page 49: reserve an egg-cupful)

5 chocolate flakes

2 yellow Smarties and 2 silver balls

1 skinned almond or shelled brazil nut for a beak

Candles and holders

Trim the edges of the smaller cake to make a rounder shape for the owl's head. Place the larger cake on a board with the round end at the top. Sandwich the flat wide end of the smaller cake to this, using a little of the icing. Cover the owl with the remaining icing. Break three of the flakes into slivers and sprinkle them on to the butter icing, leaving two circles side by side without flakes for his eyes. Cut two 1-inch (2·5 cm) pieces from a flake and press the two pieces on either side of his head for his ear feathers. Use a tiny dab of icing to stick the silver balls to his Smartie eyes, and position his beak. Cut the rest of the flake in half and position the pieces as the owl's feet. Cut the remaining flake in half and press the pieces into his sides as wings. Put the candles in their holders around the owl's ear feathers.

Brazil nut or almond beak→

Cat Cake

*2 × 8 inch (20 cm) round chocolate
sandwich cakes (basic cake 1)*
Chocolate butter icing (page 49)
*3 Smarties (2 green for eyes, and 1 orange
for the nose)*
*6 thin strips of liquorice or a liquorice
wheel (or Matchmakers)*
1 satin bow
Candles and holders

Sandwich the cakes together with butter
icing and assemble the cat's ears as in the
drawing.

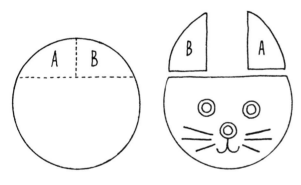

   Cover the cat's head and ears all over
with the chocolate butter icing, and
roughen it up with a palette knife to
simulate fur. 'Round' the cat's head between
his ears with extra icing. Place the two eyes
and nose on the cake. Cut the liquorice
wheel into thin strips and surround the eyes
and nose with an outline of liquorice Use six
thin strips of liquorice to make the cat's
whiskers. Shape the nose and mouth as in
the drawing. Sit a satin bow at his chin and
put the candles in his ears. •

Butterfly Cake

*8 inch (20 cm) round orange flavoured cake
(basic cake 3)*
Orange butter icing (page 49)
*2 packets orange and lemon crystallized
slices or 1 Terry's crystallized orange and
1 Terry's crystallized lemon*
2 Matchmakers
Candles and holders

Split the cake in half horizontally and
sandwich together with some of the butter
icing. Then cut it in half vertically, straight
down the middle. Place the two halves of
the cake on the board to form the butterfly
shape, as you can see in the drawing.
Cover with the remaining butter icing.
Make the head of the butterfly with a
rounded blob of icing, and stick the
Matchmakers in as antennae. Arrange the
orange and lemon slices alternately over
the top of the cake, to create the design of
the butterfly's wings. If you are using
Terry's crystallized orange and lemon, cut
the slices in half lengthways before
arranging them, otherwise they are too
thick.

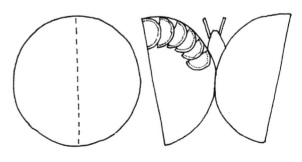

Humpty Dumpty Cake

See photograph facing page 97.

1 chocolate loaf shaped cake (basic cake 4)
Butter icing (page 49)
Few drops pink colouring
1 chocolate Easter egg about 5 inches (12·5 cm) high
1 skewer 6–8 inches (15–20 cm) long
Smarties (if not using piping bag)
2 silver balls
3 chocolate finger biscuits
Piece of ribbon 12 inches (30 cm) long
White paper to make Humpty Dumpty's collar and thin ribbon
Candles and holders

Although this is primarily an Easter cake or for birthdays around Easter time, you could make it later in the year, as a bought chocolate Easter egg will keep very well for several months in a cool dry place. It is extremely easy to make, very effective and younger children absolutely love it.

Level off the top of the cake if necessary. Cut in half and sandwich the two halves together with butter icing, as in the drawing. Put two tablespoons of the butter icing into a piping bag (if using one), and leave this in the fridge to harden. Colour the rest of the icing with the pink colouring (quite a deep pink, to represent the bricks). Cover the cake with the icing, and with the point of a knife, mark out the lines of the bricks all over the cake. If you do not wish to do any piping, then the bricks look quite effective as they are, but piping is very simple to do, and does look more striking. It does not matter if it is not quite accurate, in fact, this makes it look more like an old brick wall! Pipe along the lines made by

the knife point through a small nozzle. Do not use all the white icing, save the last little bit for Humpty Dumpty's face.

Make Humpty Dumpty's collar by following the diagram. To prepare Humpty Dumpty take a sharp knife and very gently scrape away some of the chocolate at the blunt end of one half of the egg. Remove just enough to make a hole for the head of the skewer to go through. Fill the egg with Smarties (the weight also helps him to balance). Tie the two halves of the egg together with the collar and the ribbon, making a nice bow in the centre of the collar. Push the skewer into the cake, making sure it tilts backwards and lower the egg gently on to the skewer, sitting it firmly on the cake. Then pipe in eyes, eyebrows, nose and mouth. If you are using Smarties for his face, then place these in

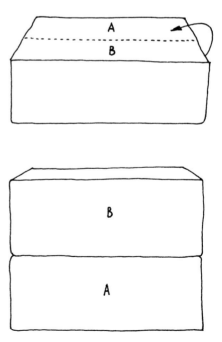

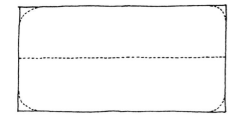

Cut out collar from white paper
Trim corners and fold

Fol · Insert ribbon tie

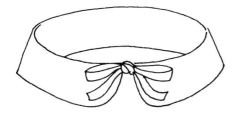

position with a little butter icing. Place the 2 silver balls in the centre of his eyes.

Finally make his legs by cutting two chocolate fingers in half, and place the pieces on the cake so that his knees stick outwards. Then cut about ½ inch (1·25 cm) from either end of the remaining chocolate finger, and place these two pieces for his feet, sticking them out from the ends of his legs. When positioning your candles along the cake, remember not to place them too near to Humpty in case he melts!

Cuckoo Clock Cake

8 × 12 inch (20 × 30 cm) rectangular chocolate cake (basic cake 7)
Chocolate butter icing (page 49)
1 packet of chocolate fingers or Matchmakers
1 packet of chocolate buttons
2 Matchmakers or a chocolate finger cut in half
1 packet of Smarties
1 bird (the robin off the Christmas cake!)
1 After Eight mint as the cuckoo's door (cut in 2 halves)
Candles and holders

Cut two corners from one end of the cake to form the inverted V shape of the roof. Cover the cake with the butter icing. Decorate with the chocolate fingers or Matchmakers and the chocolate buttons (pipe with numbers if you wish). Place the Smarties around the edge of the cake and straight across below doorway. Position mint halves and bird as in drawing. Position the candles around the cake.

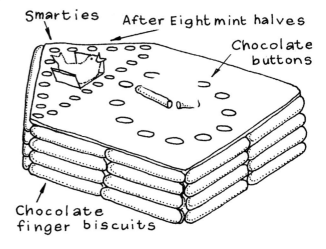

Smarties
After Eight mint halves
Chocolate buttons
Chocolate finger biscuits

Clock Cake

2 × 8 inch (20 cm) round chocolate
   sandwich cakes (basic cake 1 or 9)
Either (a)
White butter icing (page 49)
12 chocolate buttons
2 chocolate fingers
Small amount of glacé icing to pipe the
   numerals on to the clock face on the
   chocolate buttons
Candles and holders
Or (b)
Chocolate butter icing (page 49)
12 varying coloured Smarties
2 chocolate fingers
Candles and holders

Sandwich the cakes together with a third of
the butter icing and cover with the
remainder.

If using ingredients (a), place the
chocolate buttons to represent the hours of
the clock, and the chocolate fingers as the
hands of the clock. Use the glacé icing to
pipe the numerals on to the chocolate
buttons and place the candles around the
edge of the cake.

If you are using ingredients (b), place the
Smarties at the points of the clock, and the
chocolate fingers as the hands. Don't worry
about piping the numerals.

This is a very quick and easy cake.

House Cake

See photograph facing page 65.

8 inch (20 cm) square vanilla cake (basic
   cake 2)
Chocolate butter icing (page 49)
1 small bought chocolate covered swiss roll
1 packet chocolate fingers
White glacé icing and piping bag with
   small nozzle or 1 packet cigarette sweets
   to make the windows and doors
1 packet of Smarties for the garden and
   bought sugar icing flowers
Green butter icing
Candles and holders

Cut the cake into three sections, as in the
first diagram. Sandwich it together with
butter icing, and assemble it as in the
second diagram.

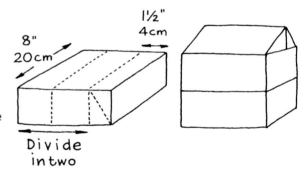

Cover the whole cake with the remaining
butter icing. Roughen the surface of the roof
with a fork in a downwards direction, to
simulate thatch. Smooth the rest of the
house with a palette knife. Cut the swiss roll
in half and place the halves at either side of
the roof as chimneys. Press the chocolate
fingers into the icing along the top and
around the edge of the roof to form the

ridge, the eaves, and the gables, as in the photograph. If you are using white glacé icing for the windows and doors, make sure it is very stiff, spoon it into the piping bag and pipe two windows and a door on either side of the house, and a window at each end. If you are using cigarette sweets, cut off the pink end and split them in half lengthways with a sharp knife, then put these in position as window and door frames. Use two of the Smarties for door handles. Stick a candle into each chimney and the rest along the top of the roof (on either side of the chocolate fingers).

Make the garden by spooning the green icing on to the board to make a lawn on either side of the door. Continue the icing round the sides of the house and press the Smarties upright around the edge of the lawn to represent flower beds. If you are using sugar flowers then arrange these in little groups around the edge of the lawn or have them growing up the cottage walls.

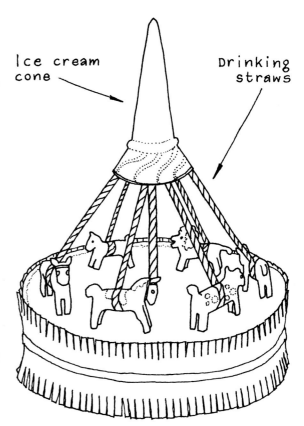

Merry-go-round Cake

8 inch (20 cm) round orange flavoured cake (basic cake 3)
Orange flavoured butter icing (page 49: save an egg-cupful)
7 stripy paper (not plastic) drinking straws
1 ice cream cone
6 small plastic riderless horses (anything suitable to represent the equipment on a real merry-go-round)
Paper frill (striped)
Candles and holders

Cover the top of the cake with the butter icing. Hold the cone wide side up and fill it with butter icing. Push one upright straw into this. Smooth some icing into every other division inside the lip of the cone and press the remaining straws into it. Turn the cone upside down, and push the centre straw into the centre of the cake. Bend the edges of the outside straws and secure them round the middle of the horses with sticky tape.

Fasten frill. Place the candles around the cake.

Farm Cake

See photograph facing page 65.

*8 × 12 inch (20 × 30 cm) rectangular cake
(basic cake 10)*
*Half green, half chocolate butter icing
(page 49)*
Plastic farm animals, tractor, plough, etc
Pottery or plastic farm house, trees, etc
Plastic farm fencing or Matchmakers
Candles and holders

Decide how much of the farm you wish to
be ploughed field, and how much pasture.
Cover the 'ploughed' area with chocolate
icing (mark lines with a fork to simulate
furrows) and place a tractor and plough on
this. Cover the pasture with green icing and
put the sheep or cows on it, together with
the farmhouse, if you have one. Extend the
farmyard round your cake with animals or
farm vehicles surrounding it on the board. If
you wish you could give each child one of
the animals to keep. Position candles.

Sea Cake

Cake as Farm cake
*Blue (sea) butter icing (page 49),
roughened up as waves (or use blue
glacé icing and apricot glaze, page 49)*
*Small plastic or wooden sailing ships (tip up
and down in 'waves')*
*Home-made chocolate fudge for rocks
(make it uneven)*
Candles and holders (lighthouse by rocks)

Zoo Cake

Cake as Farm cake
Green butter icing or glacé icing (page 49)
Apricot glaze if using glacé icing (page 49)
*Plastic farm fencing or Matchmakers (to
make enclosures to put animals into)*
*1 packet of Cadbury's chocolate animals,
wooden or plastic zoo animals (place in
enclosures, and any extra on board round
cake)*
*Plastic or wooden trees, etc (to dot around
as scenery)*
*A few pieces of home-made chocolate
fudge for rocks (page 40)*
*Small child's mirror or a piece of foil to
represent a water hole for the sea lion*
Candles and holders
*Place any extra animals on the board
around the cake*

Village Cake

Cake as Farm cake
Green butter icing for gardens, and
    chocolate butter icing for road winding
    across cake (page 49)
Little wooden or plastic houses
Little wooden or plastic church
Plastic dog, pony, people, etc
Candles and holders

Gymkhana Cake

Cake as Farm cake
Green butter icing (page 49)
Matchmakers or plastic farm fencing
Plastic jumps (for main ring)
Plastic ponies and riders strategically
    positioned
If you have plastic trailers, landrover, etc,
    put these on the board
Candles and holders

Match Cake

2 × 8 inch (20 cm) square orange or lemon
    flavoured cakes (basic cake 2) placed
    together on a board to form an oblong,
    16 × 8 inch (40 × 20 cm)
Green butter icing, or apricot glaze and
    green glacé icing (page 49)
Small quantity of white glacé icing

To make the goals, or goal posts:
Drinking straws or construct-a-straws, cut
    into correct lengths, sellotaped together,
    or bent to shape
Malteser or tiny plastic ball

To make a tennis net:
2 cocktail sticks, or 2 chocolate fingers for
    the posts. Netting from a plastic mesh
    bag used for nuts or oranges, cut to
    shape
Candles and holders

Players:
Subbuteo figures and ball if you have them

Place the cakes on the board. Coat the
sides of the cakes, and the top with green
icing, and smooth with a palette knife.
Using a fine nozzle, pipe white lines in the
appropriate positions for the game you have
chosen, and place the net or goal in
position. Place your players on the cake.
Place the candles around the edge of the
cake.

Crinoline Lady Cake

See photograph facing page 97.

1 × 2 pint (1·1 litre) basin shaped marble cake (basic cake 6)
Butter icing (page 49)
Pink colouring
Small plastic doll, approximately 9 inches (22·5 cm) high
A few inches of lace or other material (to make a little bodice for the doll)
Silver balls
Bought sugar-icing flowers if you cannot pipe
Pink and/or white candles and holders

This is an exceptionally pretty cake for a little girl's tea party, and should look elegant and delicate. It is a simple cake to produce, and looks very professional.

Prepare the doll before you start decorating the cake. Remove the legs, and make a bodice with the material – simple and strapless. Pin the back or put in a few stitches to hold it in place.

When the cake is completely cool, make sure that the bottom is level (if necessary trim it). Spread three-quarters of the white icing over the cake, smoothing it with a palette knife. To create the crinoline effect of the skirt, mark out the shape of the paniers (the draped effect of a Victorian dress) with the rim of a tablespoon (you should be able to make seven). Make sure that the markings are even, and at the same height. Run the handle end of a teaspoon gently up the lower part of the skirt to represent the gathers in the material. Take the doll and press her firmly into the cake. Mix the remaining icing with a very few

drops of pink colouring so that the colour is not too bright. If the icing is too soft it will not pipe well, so put it in the fridge for half an hour to make it easier to handle. Spoon this into a piping bag, and practise piping a few rosettes on to a board. Decorate the skirt with little rosettes. If you wish you can put silver balls on these. If you are using bought decorations place these carefully around the cake. Place candles on top of paniers.

Fairy Cake

As for the Crinoline Lady Cake, but add wings, a wand and a tinsel hair band.

To make the wings use a lace paper doily, rice paper or silver foil. Cut into two triangles. Fasten into the cake at the doll's waist, with a cocktail stick. (Be careful not to position the candles too near the wings or the Fairy may go up in smoke). To make the wand use a cocktail stick, covered with a little foil, and glue or sellotape a little tinsel to the top. To make the hair band, twist a little tinsel around the doll's hair. She makes a very effective Christmas Fairy cake.

Witch Cake

*2 chocolate or marble basin shaped cakes
    (basic cake 5)
Chocolate butter icing (page 49: save an
    egg-cupful)
1 large chocolate digestive biscuit
1 ice cream cone
A few Smarties
2 silver balls
Several Matchmakers
1 piece of black satin ribbon
2 chocolate fingers for arms
Candles and holders*

This cake is ideal for a November 5th or Hallowe'en party.

Place the large cake on your board, flat wide side down. Sandwich the narrow end of the smaller cake to this, using a little of the icing, and trimming the cake, if necessary, to make a good round shape. Cover the witch with the remaining icing. Make the hat from the chocolate biscuit and the ice cream cone, sticking them together with icing. Stick the silver balls on to the Smarties with a tiny dab of icing for her eyes. Place half a Matchmaker to make her

mouth and decorate as in the drawing with the Matchmakers, chocolate fingers, ribbon and Smarties. Position candles on board.

Scarecrow Cake

Adapt the witch. Give him the Snowman's hat (page 62) and a glacé cherry nose. Raise his arms and put a robin on his shoulder.

Space Ship Cake

1 swiss roll, either bought or home made
  (page 46)
Chocolate butter icing (page 49: save some
  for glueing)
1 Wagon Wheel biscuit
1 cone shaped ice cream cornet
1 packet Smarties
A few silver cake balls
4 After Eight mints
3 small bought chocolate swiss rolls
Plastic spacemen (Lego spacemen are
  particularly effective)
Candles and holders

For this cake, first organize the cake board.
A foil-covered board would be best for this
moon-landing cake. If you wish, use some
white glacé or butter icing to simulate the
uneven surface of the moon on the board,
and sprinkle this with some crushed silver
balls. Place the board to one side. If you
are using a home-made roll, it may topple
over if too long, so cut some off.

Stand the swiss roll on end on the Wagon
Wheel using some of the chocolate butter
icing. Cover the entire rocket with
chocolate butter icing and smooth with a
palette knife. Take the ice cream cone and
cut a small hole in its tip, using a very
sharp or fine serrated knife. Fix the wide
end of the cone to the top of the swiss roll
with a little butter icing. Cut a corner of
each mint off diagonally, to make a fin
shape (see diagram), and place the cut side
to the cake securely into the butter icing.
Decorate your rocket. Then put some butter
icing on either end of the three bought
chocolate swiss rolls and stand firmly on
end on the board. Place the assembled
rocket on top of these as in the drawing.

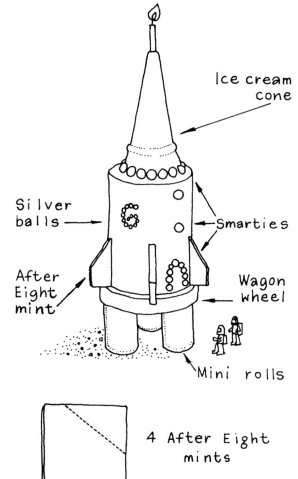

Ice cream cone

Silver balls

Smarties

After Eight mint

Wagon wheel

Mini rolls

4 After Eight mints

Place one of your candles in its holder
carefully in the hole that you have made in
the ice cream cone (again, you may need
to use a little butter icing in the hole to
secure it). Put the remaining candles at an
angle at the bottom of your swiss roll
rocket, to simulate lift off. Crash land to cut!

This Space Ship cake could be made for
a November 5th party.

Car Cake

1 chocolate loaf shaped cake (basic cake 4)
Chocolate butter icing (page 49: reserve an
egg-cupful)
4 Chocolate Munchmallows
Packet of Smarties
Silver balls
Matchmakers (optional)
Candles and holders

Turn the cake upside down, and cut segments from either end of the cake as in the diagram, so that the cake looks like a car. Cover the car with the chocolate butter icing and smooth with a palette knife. Cut two axles about 1 inch (2·5 cm) wide from the cut-off segments, and put these on the cake board. Place the cake on top of the axles. Then 'glue' with icing the four Munchmallow wheels into position on the axles and a Smartie as a hubcap on each.

Decorate the car with the Smarties, silver balls and Matchmakers, if you are using them. Place the candles on top of the cake, and position two as exhaust pipes.

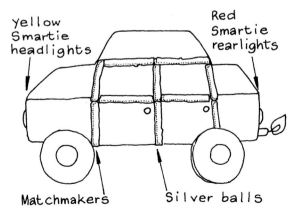

Yellow Smartie headlights — Red Smartie rearlights — Matchmakers — Silver balls

Tank Cake

8 inch (20 cm) square chocolate cake (basic
cake 2)
Chocolate butter icing (page 49)
1 Munchmallow
2 long strips of liquorice
Packet of Rolos
Packet of Smarties
1 Twix
Candles and holders

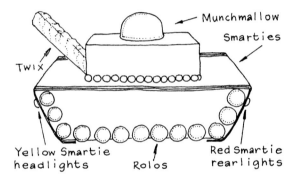

Munchmallow — Smarties — Twix — Yellow Smartie headlights — Rolos — Red Smartie rearlights

Take a 2 inch (5 cm) strip from the side of your cake. If it has risen up and this would make the cake lopsided then cut 1 inch (2·5 cm) from either side. Cut the front and the back of the tank to get the shape. Cover with the butter icing. Place a piece of the offcut 2 × 5 inches (5 × 12·5 cm) in the centre on top of tank and cover with icing.

Place the Munchmallow as the tank's hatch, your liquorice strips to simulate caterpillar tracks, and the Rolos to represent the wheels and have the ones at either end slightly higher than the rest – cut your cake here to get the shape. Place the Smarties as lights, and the Twix as the gun with the candle secured to 'fire' at the end of it. Decorate cab with more Smarties.

64 PARTY CAKES

Right: Train Cake.
Overleaf: *All the fun of the Sack Race.*

Train Cake

See photograph opposite.

---

2 large bought or home-made chocolate
   swiss rolls (page 46)
Chocolate butter icing made with 6 oz
   (175 g) butter, 12 oz (350 g) icing sugar
   and 3 level tablespoons cocoa (page 49)
   (save some for glueing Smarties etc)
3 long strips of liquorice, or Matchmakers
5 small bought chocolate covered swiss
   rolls
1 Munchmallow
1 packet of Smarties
1 packet of Maltesers
8 Rolos
Candles and holders

Lay two flat strips of liquorice or the
Matchmakers on the cake board to
represent the rails. Glue them down with a
dab of butter icing. Cut the other strip in
pieces to lay across the rails as sleepers.
Reserve a small amount for the 'coupling'
between the engine and the coal truck.

   Cover one large chocolate swiss roll with
icing, and smooth it with a palette knife.
Place two of the small bought swiss rolls
across the track to represent wheels. Place
the large swiss roll on top of these. The
wheels should be a little in from either end.
Place the third small bought chocolate roll
on the front of the engine as a funnel and
the Munchmallow as the engine's dome.

   Cut off about a quarter of your second
swiss roll. Position this, cut side down, to
form the cab and cover with some of the
remaining chocolate butter icing. Place the
Smarties in a circle around the front of the
engine. Using a little icing, place one
Smartie to each side of the swiss roll

wheels (in the centre) to make a hub. Put
bands of Smarties around the engine as
decoration and 4 of the Rolos for buffers. If
you like, decorate with piped chocolate
icing.

   Place the last two small bought chocolate
covered rolls on the track behind the
engine. Take the remaining large piece of
swiss roll and cut a hollow out in the centre
to form a container. Cover this with the
remaining chocolate butter icing and place
it on its wheels. Fill the hollow with
Maltesers (to represent coal). Attach the
piece of 'coupling' liquorice from the back
of the engine to the coal container.
Remember to put another Smartie hub on
the wheels of this section and your buffers
in position. Place one or more candles into
the funnel and place the rest along the top
of the engine.

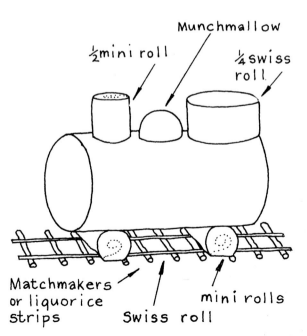

Munchmallow
½ mini roll
¼ swiss roll
Matchmakers or liquorice strips
Swiss roll
mini rolls

Tractor Cake

*1 large bought or home-made swiss roll
   (page 46)*
Chocolate butter icing (page 49)
*2 small bought chocolate covered swiss
   rolls*
2 Wagon Wheel biscuits
1 packet Smarties
*A little green butter or glacé icing
   (optional)*
Candles and holders

This cake is very easy to assemble if you
follow the diagram carefully. Use green
icing on the board for the grass and rough
it up with a palette knife. Place two small
swiss rolls on your board. Cut one-third off
the large swiss roll and set the larger piece
on the smaller swiss rolls. (If necessary, cut
the front mini roll in two so that you can see
the 'wheels' on each side.) Cover the large
roll with the butter icing. Position the
Wagon Wheels to form large tractor
wheels.

Cut a small section out of the back end of
the tractor on to which you position the
remaining one-third of swiss roll, cut side
down, to represent the cab. Cover with the
butter icing, and smooth with a palette
knife. Decorate with the smarties. Use a
candle as the exhaust for the tractor.

Tractor Trailer

*1 large bought or home-made chocolate
   swiss roll (page 46)*
Chocolate butter icing (page 49)
*2 small bought chocolate covered swiss
   rolls*
Maltesers or Smarties
1 chocolate finger for the coupling

If you are having a particularly large party,
make another swiss roll to use as a trailer
behind the tractor. Cut out the centre top
(see diagram), place the roll on two
chocolate swiss roll wheels, cover with the
butter icing and couple it to the tractor with
the chocolate finger. Pile the Maltesers or
Smarties into the trailer.

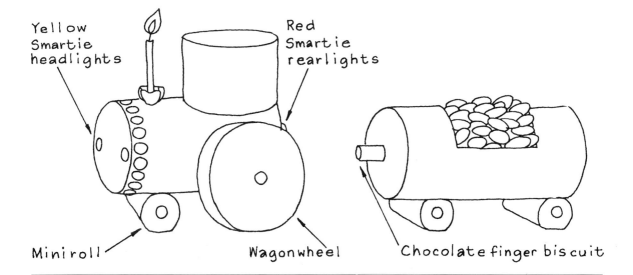

Yellow Smartie headlights

Red Smartie rearlights

Miniroll

Wagonwheel

Chocolate finger biscuit

Castle Cake

8 inch (20 cm) square chocolate cake (basic cake 2)
Chocolate butter icing (page 49: reserve 1 teaspoonful)
4 small bought chocolate swiss rolls (or 8 and put the extra four in the centre of the castle as the keep with arrow slits)
Matchmakers
2 packets of chocolate buttons
1 Penguin biscuit and 2 chocolate fingers
2 strands of liquorice
A little blue icing for a moat (optional)
Plastic knights in armour or plastic guardsmen
1 straw and label with Castle — (your child's name) written on it
Candles and holders

Cut the cake in half horizontally and sandwich the two halves together with butter icing. Trim the corners to allow room

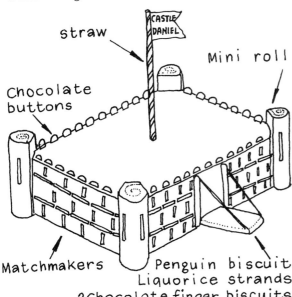

straw

Mini roll

Chocolate buttons

Matchmakers   Penguin biscuit
Liquorice strands
2 Chocolate finger biscuits

for the turrets, and cover with the rest of the icing, smoothing with a palette knife. Place the swiss roll turrets at the cut corners. Arrange the Matchmakers to simulate a stone wall. Using some icing fix matchmaker arrow slits. Place the buttons as battlements and the chocolate fingers as gateposts, the Penguin biscuit and liquorice strands, fixed with icing, as the drawbridge.

If you are using the moat icing, surround the cake with this. Place your plastic knights around the castle, the candles in the turrets and the flag pole in the centre of the cake.

Noah's Ark Cake

See photograph facing page 65.

8 inch (20 cm) round chocolate cake (basic cake 3)
Chocolate butter icing (page 49), reserve an egg-cupful)
1 packet chocolate finger biscuits
1 packet Matchmakers
1 packet Smarties
4 Penguins or similar biscuits
1 packet of Cadbury's Chocolate animals (or plastic animals) and a small plastic man to represent Noah
Candles and holders
Small amount of blue glacé or butter icing for sea (optional)

Cut the cake in half (into half-moon shapes) and sandwich the two halves together with some of the butter icing. Then slice off a *very narrow* sliver from the bottom of the semi-circular slice so that the ark rests on a firm base. Cover the cake with the rest of the butter icing. Run a palette knife along the sides to create a plank effect, or edge the sides with chocolate fingers. Make

portholes with Smarties, and place more Smarties upright at intervals along the edge of the deck and stick chocolate fingers or Matchmakers (using a little butter icing) along the top to make a deck rail.

Press in four chocolate fingers upright on the deck and stick (again with the butter icing) one of the large biscuits on top to form the roof. Make a ramp with the Penguin biscuits at the end of the Ark. Position the animals going up the ramp and around the deck etc. Place your candles as lights at intervals along the deck rail. Spread the blue icing on the board to represent the sea, and make waves with a fork.

Galleon or Pirate Ship

See photograph on page 44.

8 inch (20 cm) round chocolate cake (basic cake 3)
Chocolate butter icing (page 49)
1 packet of Matchmakers
1 packet Smarties
Rice paper
3 knitting needles
Very fine liquorice strands for rigging
Candles and holders
Optional Extras:
Small quantity of blue icing for the sea
Small pennant with skull and crossbones
Small box with Smarties or gold chocolate coins to represent treasure chest
Maltesers, as cannon balls

Make and assemble as for the Noah's Ark cake to the end of the first paragraph.

To form the sails, cut 3 rectangles of rice paper 8 × 4 inches (20 × 10 cm) and one smaller rectangle 5 × 3 inches (2·5 × 7·5

Matchmaker and Smartie railings

cm), then follow the diagram to assemble the sails and masts. If you have time cut out some small pennants to tape or glue to the tops of the masts. If you are making a pirate ship make a skull and crossbones pennant. Sellotape the liquorice carefully across the needles to give the effect of rigging.

Place the treasure chest (if you are using one) on the deck or arrange the Maltesers in neat piles on the deck. If you are making a pirate ship firmly press the end of one chocolate finger flat side upwards on to the deck, so that it makes a plank, and if you have a suitable plastic sailor let him be 'walking' it! Use the candles as cannons.

Cross Road Cake

*2 × 8 inch (20 cm) round chocolate
  sandwich cakes (basic cake 1)*
*Chocolate butter icing (page 49: reserve an
  egg-cupful)*
*2 packets of Smarties (reserve 4 red, 4
  green and 4 orange)*
4 chocolate fingers
White peppermint Tic-Tacs
Model cars, lorries, motor cycles, etc
Candles and holders

Cut the centre out of each of the cakes with
a 3½ inch (8·5 cm) cutter – or cut around the
rim of a similar sized cup with a sharp knife
(use the small cake circles for a tiny extra
birthday cake). Place the cake on a
largeish board. Cut a sliver off both cakes
about 2 inches (5 cm) long on the outer
edge. Join the two circles at this point so
that you have a figure-of-eight. Cover the
cake with the icing and smooth with a
palette knife. Use the Smarties, Tic-Tacs
and the model cars to decorate the cake as
shown in the drawing. Make the traffic
lights using the icing to fix on the Smarties
to the flat side of the chocolate fingers.
Place your candles around the cake as
street lights, or on a 'traffic island'.

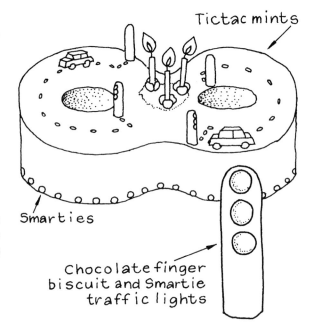

Tictac mints

Smarties

Chocolate finger
biscuit and Smartie
traffic lights

Race Track Cake

The Cross Road cake could be adapted to
make either a motorbike or car race track.
Have the start at one side of the centre of
the figure-of-eight and the end opposite so
that there is a continuous track. You could
have a green Smartie on a chocolate finger
to start the race and a red one to end it, or
you could use Scalectrix flags or similar.

Railway Cake

The Cross Road cake can be made into a
railway track, using Matchmakers as rails
and sleepers with a signal at either end.
Place a plastic train and carriages on the
track.

Wild West Cake

*8 inch (20 cm) square chocolate cake (basic
   cake 2)*
Chocolate butter icing (page 49)
*4 small bought chocolate covered swiss
   rolls*
2 packets chocolate fingers
2 Penguin biscuits
*1 drinking straw and label, with Fort —
   (your child's name) written on it*
Plastic cowboys or soldiers and Indians
Candles and holders

Cut the cake in half horizontally. Sandwich
the two halves together with butter icing,
and cover with the rest of the icing.

Place the swiss rolls and chocolate
fingers as shown in the drawing. On the
fourth side leave a gap in the centre and
put the Penguin biscuits as two open gates.
Put the drinking straw and label in the
centre of the fort as the flag pole, position
the cowboys on top of the cake and the
Indians around the board attacking.

Position candles on the swiss rolls.

UFO Cake *(for failures!)*

*2 round chocolate cakes (basic cake 3) or
   whichever cake you have made*
Chocolate butter icing (page 49)
4 chocolate flakes, cut in half
8 Smarties
Candles and holders

If you find that your cake is a complete
failure, then just turn it into this unidentified
flying object! Sandwich the two cakes
together with some chocolate icing and
cover with the rest. Roughen it into peaks.
Place the chocolate flakes at any old angle,
and, using a little of the butter icing, stick a
Smartie at the end of each flake to
represent lights. Position the candles at
random.

Easter Nest Cake

1 chocolate or orange ring mould cake
   (basic cake 8)
Chocolate butter icing (page 49)
4 chocolate flakes
A large quantity of small Easter eggs to fill
   the centre of the ring mould
1 or more Easter chicks (optional)

Cover the nest with the butter icing. Cut
the milk flakes in half widthways with a
sharp knife, and then cut the pieces in half
lengthways to simulate twigs. It doesn't
matter if some of the bits crumble. Arrange
the best bits around the top of the nest, to
make an overlapping circle and then
sprinkle all the remaining bits over the top
– the effect should not be too tidy. Arrange
the eggs and the Easter chicks in the nest.

Snowman Cake

2 marble or vanilla flavoured basin shaped
   cakes (basic cake 5)
White butter icing (page 49: reserve an
   egg-cupful)
1 large chocolate digestive biscuit
1 Munchmallow
5 chocolate buttons for 2 eyes, 3 buttons
1 red Smartie as a red nose
1 Matchmaker or cut-down liquorice pipe
1 piece of satin ribbon as a neck tie or
   scarf (to camouflage the join between the
   head and body of the snowman)
2 chocolate fingers as arms (optional)

Place the large cake, wide flat side down
on the board. Sandwich the narrow end of
the smaller cake to it with a little of the
icing. Trim the smaller cake, if necessary,

Munchmallow

Chocolate
buttons

Chocolate
digestive
biscuit

Red
Smartie
nose

Chocolate finger biscuits

to make it a good round shape. Cover the
snowman with the remaining icing. Using a
dab of icing make the chocolate digestive
biscuit and the Munchmallow into his hat.
Place the Smartie, chocolate buttons, the
Matchmaker cigar or the cut-down
liquorice pipe, the scarf, and the fingers
into position.

Snow Scene Cake

8 inch (20 cm) round chocolate or orange
  cake (basic cake 3)
White butter icing (page 49)
Crushed silver balls
Seasonal decorations, such as Father
  Christmas, angels, etc

Children often do not like the traditional
Christmas fruit cake, so this simple sponge
cake is specifically for them. Cut the cake
in half horizontally, and sandwich the two
halves together with some of the butter
icing. Place the cake on the board, cover
with the rest of the icing and roughen up
the surface into peaks with a fork. Cover
with crushed silver balls and decorations.

Alternatively, sandwich the cake with a
small quantity of butter icing (chocolate or
orange, to match the cake), and cover with
white glacé icing (see page 49).

Christmas Log

1 bought or home-made chocolate swiss roll
  (page 46)
Chocolate butter icing (page 49)
2 chocolate flakes
Seasonal decorations (holly, robin, etc)

Place the cake on your board. Cut a
diagonal piece off one end of the cake, and
stick the cut edge with a little icing to the
side of the log to represent a side branch.
Cover the cake with the chocolate icing.
Cut the milk flakes lengthways with a sharp
knife (it doesn't matter if they crumble), and
arrange the bits along the cake to simulate
bark. Arrange the robins and the holly on
top of the cake.

Igloo Cake

1 marble basin shaped cake (basic cake 6)
White butter icing (page 49)
1 packet Matchmakers (optional)
1 small bought chocolate covered swiss roll
Candles and holders

This is the only cake that we recommend
you make in a Pyrex bowl, to get the right
shape.

Cover the cake with white butter icing,
reserving a little, and smooth with a palette
knife. Mark out the lines of the snow blocks
with the point of a knife, or use
Matchmakers. Use half the swiss roll as a
chimney, half as the tunnel doorway. Cover
them both with the remaining icing. Put one
candle on the chimney and the others
around the top of the igloo.

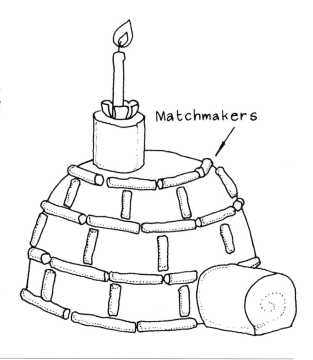

Matchmakers

Numeral Cakes

Special tins can be purchased. Numbers 1 to 9 can be bought at Harrods, Knightsbridge, London SW1, at William Page & Co., 87 Shaftesbury Avenue, London W1, or Divertimenti, Marylebone Lane, London. Many tins can be hired from specialist shops. However, some numbers are easily formed using conventional cake tins. Numbers 1, 3, 7, 8 and 10 can be undertaken as follows.

Number 1

Use a loaf shaped cake (basic cake 4) and if you wish, cut a triangular wedge from the top part of the cake, approximately 2 inches (5 cm) long, to make an angle at the top of your number 1. Cover with butter icing (page 49).

Numbers 3 and 8

Use two ring mould cakes (basic cake 8) and simply place them together on a board to form a figure 8. Cut off a small portion from both to make a good shaped 3. Cover both with double quantity butter icing (page 49). If you do not have a ring mould, use two round cakes (basic cake 1) and cut out the centres with a circular pastry cutter to make your shape.

If you are not having very many people to your party, you could make only one ring mould cake or circular cake, cutting it in half (take out the centre if you are using the circular cake) and then 'glue' the 2 halves together to make the number 3. However, the shape does not look as effective as when you allow more than a semi-circle for each half of the number. If you have made the circular cake, make a little butter icing and sandwich the two leftover circles together to make a little extra cake, either for another day, or to pop in the freezer.

Number 7

Make a rectangular shaped cake (basic cake 7) and cut it as one piece, into your number 7. There will be quite a bit of wastage. Cover with butter icing.

Number 10

Make two cakes – a loaf shaped cake (basic cake 4) and a ring mould cake (basic cake 8). Place them to form the number 10, and cover with a double quantity of butter icing. If you have not got a ring mould, then refer to the instructions for making a number 3.

Initial Cakes

Instead of going through all the letters of the alphabet, here are a few guidelines which, if you refer back to the number cakes, you can adapt to the initial you require.

If you are making a letter which involves straight lines – A, T. Z, H, etc – we suggest that you make it from the rectangular cake (basic cake 7). Place the entire rectangle on the board and cut your cake to shape, keeping it in one piece. Always use a very sharp knife.

For rounded letters, use your ring mould cake (basic cake 8) or cut the centre from a basic cake, numbers 1 or 3, with a pastry cutter. If you haven't the appropriate sized ring moulds, etc, to fit our recipes, adapt what you have, but remember to measure your tins together so that, when assembling your letters, the proportion of one cake balances with that of the other. If you have this problem, cut your cakes to fit – icing hides a multitude of sins!

Ice cream cakes

The ideas we give here are deliberately simple and effortless. You can use all bought ingredients and the time involved in assembling is minimal. We have found that a 'proper' ice cream cake – sponge enclosing a layer of ice cream – is not very popular with children, as they just eat the middle and leave the cake. The most important thing is to have sufficient space either in your fridge or freezer to put your assembled cake in prior to the party. Once removed from the cold atmosphere, don't expect this cake to last for hours! Add candles and holders if appropriate.

There is no reason why you could not simply jolly up a Sunday lunch pudding by using one of these ideas.

Lorry

2 small bought chocolate swiss rolls
1¾ pint (1 litre) family block of Neapolitan
  ice cream
A punnet of strawberries, if in season
4 Jaffa cakes (optional)
Candles and holders

Place the swiss rolls on the board, and cut the ice cream in its carton, into a one-quarter and a three-quarters division. Use the quarter piece to form the cab of a flat fronted lorry, and place the block on the suitably positioned swiss rolls. Put your strawberries on top of the ice cream, as the lorry's load. When you are ready to serve, position your candles along the roof, or at either of the corners of your lorry. If you wish to have larger wheels than the chocolate swiss rolls, then use the Jaffa cakes, and put them in position just prior to serving.

Yellow Teddy Bear's Face

2½ pints (1·5 litres) vanilla ice cream
3 chocolate buttons
1 bow for bow tie (optional)
Matchmakers for whiskers
Candles and holders
(You need an ice cream scoop for this
  cake.)

Pack ice cream into a chilled 8 inch (20 cm) round spring release or loose based tin, and refreeze. Leave some ice cream in the carton, to use with an ice cream scoop later. Before your party, take formed ice cream round out of the freezer, and place on a suitable board. Decorate with ears, made from two scoops of the remaining ice cream. If necessary, replace in the freezer until required. Just before serving decorate the teddy with the chocolate buttons as eyes and nose, and if you wish stick in a few Matchmakers for whiskers, and place his bow tie at his chin, and add candles.

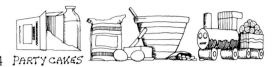

Tractor

2 small bought small chocolate swiss rolls
1¾ pint (1 litre) family block Neapolitan ice
*   cream*
2 thick slices of Arctic Log
1 chocolate finger
Candles and holders

Place the two chocolate swiss rolls on the board. Cut your ice cream in its carton, into a two-thirds and a one-third division. Cut the one-third in half again. Place the large piece of ice cream on top of the two swiss rolls, and at one end place the two remaining pieces on top of each other to represent the cab. Use the two slices of Arctic Log on either side at the cab end, as large rear tractor wheels. (You need the chocolate roll underneath to have the tractor raised at the back, even though it doesn't show.) Just prior to serving stick the chocolate finger into the engine part of the tractor as the exhaust. Place the candles on the roof of your tractor.

Trailer Cake

If you are having a large party, then add a trailer to the tractor.

3 small bought chocolate covered swiss
*   rolls*
1¾ pint (1 litre) block of ice cream
*   (whichever flavour you wish)*
Large punnet of strawberries
1 chocolate finger

Put the swiss rolls on a board. Position the ice cream on top, and pile the strawberries on to the ice cream. Join the trailer to the tractor by sticking the chocolate finger into the back of the tractor and the front of the trailer.

Train

5 small bought chocolate swiss rolls
1 Arctic Log
Bird's Ice Magic
1 choc ice
1 Munchmallow
1¾ pint (1 litre) family block of ice cream
1 Matchmaker, or chocolate finger
Strawberries, if in season
Small amount of chocolate butter icing
*   (page 49) and Smarties for decoration*
*   (optional)*
Candles and holders

Place two of the swiss rolls on to a board, and place the Arctic Log on top. Cover the engine with Ice Magic and smooth with a palette knife. Unwrap the choc ice and position it on its side across the top of the log as the engine cab. Then place the dome of the train (the Munchmallow) on the log, and finally the third mini roll, upright, as the funnel of the train. Place the remaining two swiss rolls behind the train and put the family block of ice cream on top as a trailer. Use a chocolate finger or matchmaker as coupling, and put a load of strawberries (if you have them) on the trailer. If you wish, use the chocolate butter icing to fix the Smartie hubs on the swiss rolls and use remaining Smarties to make a face on the front of the engine.

Snow Princess

Oven temperature: 450°F, 230°C, Gas Mark 8

7 inch (17·5 cm) diameter single layer round sponge cake (see below)
5 egg whites
10 oz (275 g) caster sugar
1¾ pint (1 litre) Italiano ice cream (round)
Cheap plastic doll of suitable size, and foil for her bodice (remove her legs)
Sugar flowers
Candles and holders

Follow the Victoria sponge recipe (page 47) but only use *half* quantities. When the cake is completely cold, whisk the egg whites until stiff. Add half the caster sugar, and whisk this mixture again until stiff. Fold in the remaining sugar with a metal spoon. Place the round shaped ice cream on top of your sponge cake, and either spoon the meringue mixture to cover the ice cream, or pipe the meringue, using a large star vegetable nozzle, around the ice cream. Decorate around the top with meringue rosettes, if you wish. It is vital to enclose completely the ice cream within the meringue mixture.

Put the Princess's skirt in the preheated oven and leave for approximately 4 minutes. The meringue should be soft on the inside but a little crisp on the outside. (If you wish you can freeze her at this point. When you wish to serve her you will need to remove her half an hour beforehand, and keep her in the refrigerator.) Then just before serving the Princess, position the top half of your doll (use a piece of foil as her bodice, see page 60) on top of the meringue. Camouflage the join with sugar flowers. If the doll you use has a hollow body with a 'waist' the size of the top of a skewer, you could secure her by putting the skewer in her body and placing the pointed end into the meringue and ice cream.

Clock

1¾ pint (1 litre) ice cream
Chocolate buttons to make a 'frame' for the clock
12 chocolate buttons
2 chocolate fingers
Candles and holders

Pack the ice cream in a chilled 8 inch (20 cm) round spring release or loose based tin, and refreeze. When well set, place the ice cream circle on a board. Just before serving, decorate the very edge of the clock face with chocolate buttons. Place the twelve buttons at each hour, and the chocolate fingers as hands. Place candles around the edge.

3. TEA PARTY FOOD

It is important that the food on the table (apart from the cake of course) should be very small, practically bite size, especially for small children. They will be so excited by the spread of goodies, and so eager to have a taste of everything, that a bite is all they will have in any case, and you don't want to end up with a lot of half-eaten leftovers. For this reason, we have suggested that where a recipe needs paper cases, you use the tiny *petit fours* cases, rather than the ordinary cake sized ones.

There are bound to be leftovers. It is far less nerve-racking for you to know that you have provided too much rather than to risk possible screams of rage because you have run out of a popular item. Leftovers need not be wasted – they can brighten up tea time for the next few days, as all the cakes and biscuit recipes keep well. Leftover sandwiches are excellent toasted or fried, or they can be frozen. One economy tip: don't open all the packets of crisps at once, but keep some back until the first lot are eaten; opened packets don't keep and soggy crisps are sad.

Children love crisps, twiglets, and other savoury nibbles and it is a good idea to buy some ready-made food for the party. You can of course also buy chocolate fingers, iced gems, playbox biscuits, Penguins, etc, but it is very expensive to have nothing but bought food and less satisfying for you, so a mixture of bought and home-made is the best answer. It is not worth providing vast amounts of sandwiches as you will find that with so many other goodies on the table they will only be ignored, but children love savoury food so we have given lots of suggestions for more interesting sandwiches and other savouries.

The first thing is to sit down and plan the menu. Go through the recipe section and make a list of the ones you want to do. At the same time, make a separate list of the ingredients you will need that you don't have in the store cupboard. This will only take five minutes, and saves a lot of time later. All the recipes are extremely easy to make, and require the minimum of cooking and preparation time. Children at parties are not interested in elaborate food, but do want it to look and taste delicious – and it goes without saying that all the following recipes do just that!

Start with one of the jelly recipes for the one to four year olds, and an ice cream recipe for older children, then savouries, followed by sweet things, and finally of course the cake.

Quantities

By now you will know roughly how many guests are coming to the party, and you know how old they are, so you should be able to work out the quantities of food that you will need. Children up to the age of four are usually accompanied by their mothers, and it is surprising how much the mothers can eat!

For this reason we have allowed the same quantities of food for small children's parties as for the older ones.

A rough guide to quantities might be as follows.

For each child:

1 helping of jelly or ice cream (1 packet of jelly makes 8 servings)
¼ packet of family size crisps, potato hoops or other
2 sausages for 2–4 year olds
4 sausages for 5–9 year olds
4 pinwheel sandwiches (the mothers will eat these)
1 bridge roll boat
4 cheese straws
1 Munchmallow
3 shortbread faces
3 coloured meringue drops (some children eat nothing but)
2 little gems
2 chocolate crispies

This is quite a varied menu, but if you want to do less cooking and have a smaller number of different items, you might like to try the following quantities.

For each child:

1 helping of jelly or ice cream
¼ family size packet crisps, etc
3 sausages for 2–4 year olds
4 sausages for 5–9 year olds
4 triple decker sandwiches
1 Penguin, Club, etc
1 Munchmallow
1 peppermint square
1 uncooked chocolate cake

Pre-party Schedule

Having decided on what to eat and how much, the next step is to work out your cooking schedule. We indicate in the recipes whether they can be frozen, or made in advance, and if so how far in advance. Try to make one or two of the recipes each day for a week before the party, rather than leaving everything to the day before and getting in a panic. For instance, make the sandwiches a week early and freeze them (all the recipes freeze well, except those containing egg, which goes leathery). Next make the meringues, flap-jacks, cheese straws, chocolate crispies, etc, and store in a *really airtight tin*. If you don't quite trust your tins, put a layer of greaseproof paper or plastic between the lid and the tin to get a good tight fit. This is vital if you do plan to cook in advance.

Two days before the party make the uncooked chocolate cake, or chocolate truffles, and keep in the fridge. Make the shortbread faces or other shapes, but don't ice them. On this day, you will also have made the cake, but not yet iced it. The day before the party make the jelly or jellies, and keep in fridge. Make, for instance, the cheese scones, ice the shortbread faces (we put them in the airing cupboard overnight to keep them crisp, as you can't stack them into a tin until the icing is really hard). You will also have iced the cake the day before the party.

On the day of the party, take the sandwiches out of the freezer, and slice them while still half frozen. If you haven't frozen your sandwiches, make them now, also make the bridge roll boats, etc. Keep in fridge until required, covered with cling film. In the afternoon, lay the table, arrange your food on plates, cover with cling film and put on table. Check your list to make sure that none of the food is lurking forgotten in your cupboards! Don't forget to put the cake on the table. Arrange the drinks on a side table. Lay cups for mothers (if present) also on a side table, plus milk and sugar. Check that the camera flashlight and film are at the ready for when the candles on the cake are lit and of course, check that the matches are to hand. Check too, that you have several damp cloths for mopping faces and spillages. Finally, just before tea, decorate the jellies or ice creams and put them on the table. Meanwhile, organize the helpers:

1. To take the children to the loo, if required, and wash hands, then to sit them down at table;

2. To pour drinks;

3. To make tea for mothers.

Up to your child's third or fourth birthday you will probably find that the party will go better if the mothers stay and help. Make a nice big pot of tea for them, and include the numbers of mothers in your estimate of the required size of birthday cake, as they will probably all like to have a slice. Once the children reach the age of four or five, parents will merely act as chauffeurs, ferrying their children to and from parties. But try, if you can, to organize a cup of tea or a drink for them when they collect their children, to make them feel welcome too. In the summer make a big jug of iced coffee or tea, which you can make in advance. Keep in the fridge during the party, and bring it out as required. (See the section on drinks for recipes.) Another good idea is to buy a big 5 litre bottle of wine (put it in the fridge before the party if it is white wine). Have the glasses arranged ready in a corner and offer one to each parent as they arrive to collect their offspring. Have one yourself too!

Metric conversions are approximate, so stick to either metric or imperial measures in any one recipe.

Starters

Start the tea with an individual bowl of jelly or ice cream for each child. For very small children, it is a good idea to make an egg custard to go with jelly. In this way the children get some sensible nourishment before the rest of the party food. All the jelly recipes can be made the day before the party.

We give lots of ice cream cake recipes (pages 73–75), but if you are not making an ice cream cake, then you can start the party with a serving of ice cream. Preparing the bowls of ice cream should be a last-minute job, but if you've room in your freezer, you can do it in advance, putting the bowls of ice cream on a tray and the tray in the freezer until required.

If you are having a summer party, where the children can run around the garden, you can finish tea by giving each child an ice cream cornet with a chocolate flake (obtainable in bulk from Bejams) to be eaten out of doors. (NB, this is *not* recommended for indoor parties!)

Egg Custard and Jelly

Serves 8–10

1 tablespoon cornflour
1 tablespoon sugar
1 pint (570 ml) milk
3 eggs
1 packet jelly
Hundreds and thousands

Mix the cornflour and sugar in a bowl with 2 tablespoons of cold milk. Add the eggs, and beat until the mixture is smooth. Heat the rest of the milk in a saucepan until almost boiling, then pour gently over the mixture in the bowl, stirring all the time. Pour back into the saucepan, and cook very gently, stirring all the time, so that the mixture thickens, but does not go lumpy. When it is thick enough to coat the back of a spoon, take it off the heat and continue to stir until fairly cool. Pour about 2 tablespoons of the custard into the bottom of each dish and leave to set.

Make up the jelly according to the instructions on the packet and leave it to cool. Just before it begins to set, pour it gently over the custard in each dish, and leave to set. Before serving sprinkle coloured hundreds and thousands over the top (not before or they melt into the jelly).

Fruit Salad Jelly

Make up the jelly according to the instructions on the packet, but minus ½ pint (300 ml) cold water. Add a can of fruit salad, including the juice, to the jelly and mix well. Pour gently into individual dishes and leave to set.

Multicoloured Jelly

A good way to serve jelly is to make two jellies of different colours in separate bowls – for instance, red and green, or yellow and purple. When they are set, chop them up roughly with a knife, and spoon them into the dishes with the darker colour at the bottom. This makes a pretty sparkly effect. If you are adding decorations, such as hundreds and thousands, do it at the last minute, just before you serve up, otherwise they will melt and the colours will run, and look very sad.

Jelly Froth

Serves 8–10

1 packet jelly
Small can evaporated milk
Hundreds and thousands

Dissolve the jelly in a bowl, in ½ pint (300 ml) boiling water, stirring all the time. Put in the fridge until the jelly begins to set. Whisk the evaporated milk, until the mixture is thick and frothy. Add to the jelly and whisk again. Pour into individual jelly cases, and put back in the fridge to set.

Decorate with hundreds and thousands or other decorations just before serving.

Simple Sundae

Put two scoops of different coloured ice cream into each dish, sprinkle with hundreds and thousands, or stick a glacé cherry, Smartie or chocolate button on to the top of each scoop, and serve immediately.

Chocolate Lemon Cups

Makes 12

A slightly more complicated recipe, but older children will find it very sophisticated. The chocolate cases can be made in advance and kept in the fridge, but keep the paper cases around them until required.

For the cases
8 oz (225 g) plain chocolate or chocolate cake covering
Knob of butter
12 paper cases

For the jelly
1 packet lemon jelly
1 small can evaporated milk

Melt the chocolate with the butter over a very gentle heat, stirring all the time. Pour some gently into each paper case, spooning it up the sides, so that the chocolate makes quite a thick layer. Put in the fridge to set.

Make up the jelly in a bowl with ½ pint (300 ml) boiling water, and stir until dissolved. Put the bowl in the fridge until it has almost set, then add the evaporated milk and whisk until the mixture is frothy.

Carefully remove the paper cases from the chocolate cups, and spoon the jelly into each cup. Return to the fridge to set. Decorate with chocolate vermicelli or a chocolate button just before serving.

Cat's Whiskers' Ice Cream

Put a layer of chocolate ice cream into each dish and make domes for the cats' heads by using a scoop of vanilla ice cream. Stick two chocolate buttons on top of the head for ears, use sultanas to make the eyes, nose and mouth, then break Matchmakers in half and stick in three on either side of the mouth to form whiskers. Serve immediately.

Sailing Ships Ice Cream and Peaches

Place a canned peach half flat side up in the bottom of each bowl. Put a scoop of chocolate ice cream on top, and stick in a triangular sail, made by cutting wafer biscuits in half, diagonally.

Knickerbocker Glory

Serves 12

1 packet red jelly
1 packet yellow jelly
1 can mandarin oranges, drained
1 can pineapple, drained and chopped
1¾ pint (1 litre) block ice cream

Make up the two jellies following the instructions on the packet, using the juice from the canned fruit in the pint of liquid. Mix the fruit and spoon it into ten tall sundae glasses. Chop the jelly when set, and add in layers. Top with a scoop of ice cream. Decorate with hundreds and thousands, and serve at once.

Savouries

There is no point in making large amounts of ordinary sandwiches, but children do seem to love savouries nowadays, and it is a good idea to make some extra special party sandwiches that look as appetizing as they taste. You can make these in advance and freeze them. Take out of the freezer 2 hours before the party. If the sandwiches have not been frozen before, you can also freeze the leftovers. Never freeze sandwiches containing hard-boiled egg.

Single Deckers

These freeze well, are simplicity itself to make, and small children love them.

Small brown or white loaf
Softened butter
Hundreds and thousands
Chocolate vermicelli

Slice the bread into $\frac{1}{2}$ inch (1·25 cm) thick slices. Cut off the crusts. Butter the slices and cut into neat squares, or use pastry cutters to cut into shapes (which means a lot of wasted bread). Stand the squares on a wire rack over a sheet of greaseproof paper, and sprinkle with hundreds and thousands. Pick up the paper under the rack and re-use the hundreds and thousands that have fallen through. Repeat the procedure using the chocolate vermicelli, and arrange them alternately in the serving dish.

Pinwheels

See photograph on page 76.

This makes about 25 sandwiches, which can be made in advance and frozen.

1 small loaf of brown bread
Softened butter
5 slices cooked ham, thinly sliced
3 oz (75 g) packet of Philadelphia cream cheese or Dairylea cheese (for very young children)

Put the loaf in the freezer for 2 hours, as this makes it much easier to cut thinly. Take it out of the freezer, cut away the rounded crust from the top, and trim away the side crusts and the ends. Cut five thin slices lengthways from the loaf, and butter them. If there is any of the loaf left, use it for making Single Decker Sandwiches. Put a slice of ham on top of the butter, and then spread cream cheese thinly over the ham. Roll up lengthways, and wrap tightly in foil, or cling film, and chill for 2 hours in the fridge. Take out of the fridge, and cut each roll into $\frac{1}{2}$ inch (1·25 cm) slices – you should be able to cut at least five from each roll.

If you don't have any ham, use Marmite or Bovril. Spread it over the butter, and then spread the cheese on top. This way the colour does not run into the bread.

Triple Decker Sandwiches

This makes 20 sandwiches, which can be made in advance, and frozen (all except for those filled with egg).

Small loaf of brown bread
Softened butter

Suggested fillings
Thinly sliced ham
Sliced cheese
Cream cheese with a little salt and pepper
Hard boiled eggs, chopped up with salad cream, or softened butter, with salt and pepper (do not freeze)
Cream cheese and chopped dates, mixed
Cream cheese and chopped apple or pineapple, mixed
Cream cheese coloured with a little tomato ketchup
Sandwich spread
Marmite or Bovril
Peanut butter

Put the loaf in the freezer for 2 hours, as this makes it easier to cut. Take out of the freezer, cut away the rounded crust from the top, the side crusts, and the ends, and slice lengthways. Take three of the slices, butter them and spread two of them with two of the suggested fillings. Place one slice on the other and press the third slice firmly down on top. Wrap in foil or cling film, and chill for 2 hours. Repeat with the remaining slices of bread, either using the same fillings, or varying them. Take out of the fridge, and cut downwards into half-inch slices. You should be able to cut ten sandwiches from each section.

Bridge Roll Boats

See photograph on page 76.

Miniature bridge rolls
Some thinly sliced ham
Lettuce
Cocktail sticks

Fillings
Slice of cheese, slice of tomato
Hard boiled eggs chopped up with salad cream or softened butter
Cream cheese and chopped dates mixed
Cream cheese, chopped apple or pineapple mixed
Sandwich spread

Allow one or two boats per child. This will be plenty as they are quite filling. Bridge rolls are much easier to cut and butter if they are frozen. Cut each bridge roll in half, butter the halves and put a layer of ham over the butter, followed by the chosen filling. To make the sail, cut or tear out a triangular piece of lettuce, push the cocktail stick through the lettuce in two places to hold it upright, and then push the end of a stick into the centre of each bridge roll.

Cheese Straws

You can make these in the traditional straw shape, or use cutters in the shape of animals, ducks, gingerbread men, and so on to make amusing shapes for the children. Make them up to a week in advance, but store in an airtight tin.

Oven Temperature: 350°F, 180°C, Gas Mark 5

4 oz (110 g) plain flour
1 teaspoon salt
2 oz (50 g) butter
2 oz (50 g) Cheddar cheese, grated
1 egg yolk
1 tablespoon cold water

Sift flour and salt together, and rub in the butter to give a texture of fine breadcrumbs. Stir in the cheese and egg yolk, and add enough cold water to give a stiff dough, but be careful not to add too much. Roll the pastry thinly, and if you are making straws trim into 8 inch (20 cm) squares. Put on a greased baking tray, and cut into straws, 2 inches (5 cm) long and ¼ inch (6 mm) wide, separating them gently with the knife. If you are using cutters, cut out the shapes before you put them on the tray. You can use up the leftovers by re-rolling them, but this will produce a slightly tougher result. Bake in the centre of the oven for 10–15 minutes, until golden.

Sausages

Children love sausages, and you should allow three or four per child. Cook them the day before the party, and put in the fridge when cool. If you can buy small cocktail sausages, then do so, but if not you can make your own.

To make your own, buy chipolata sausages, and before you cook them, untwist the skin and squeeze each sausage gently in half, and re-twist. Do not cut them apart until cooked. Put them on a tray in the oven with a little cooking fat at 350°F, 180°C, or Gas Mark 5, for about 20 minutes. Drain off the fat, leave to drain on kitchen roll, and then separate with a sharp knife or scissors. Pierce each with a cocktail stick and arrange on two suitable dishes, so that you have one at either end of the table (or see next recipe).

Sausage and Cheese Party Piece

See photograph on page 76.

Cooked sausages (see above)
½ inch (1·25 cm) cubes of Cheddar cheese
2 oranges
Coloured cocktail sticks

Cut a small slice off one end of each orange to make a firm base, and place the oranges, cut ends down, on small saucers. Stick the sausages and the cubes of cheese onto the cocktail sticks, and then push the sticks into the oranges, spreading them evenly around. These make very pretty table decorations, as well as being extremely popular to eat.

Baby Sausage Rolls

Makes 20
Oven Temperature: 350°F, 180°C,
Gas Mark 5

The pastry

2 oz (50 g) butter (but do not *cut it off the
block)*
3 oz (75 g) self-raising flour
1 dessertspoon water
or
8 oz (225 g) packet Jusrol Flaky Pastry

Filling

4 oz (110 g) sausage meat
A little milk

Make these the day before the party. Use a
block of very cold butter, or better still put
it in the freezer for 2 hours. Unwrap one
end of the block and mark off a 2 oz (50 g)
section. Sift a little of the flour into a bowl,
and with a coarse grater grate the butter on
top of the flour. Then add more flour, and
continue until both are used up. Mix
together very gently, with a metal spoon,
until the mixture resembles fine
breadcrumbs, then add water to mix. The
finished mixture should feel light and
require no kneading. Roll out into a
rectangle on a floured board, again very
gently, and cut into two strips lengthways.
Divide the sausage meat in two halves, and
roll with your hands into two sausages, the
same length as the pastry. Brush the long
edges of the pastry with milk, and lay the
roll of sausage meat down the length of the
pastry and bring the edges up to the centre
to cover the sausage meat. Press the edges
firmly together, making an indented edge
with your finger tips, and brush the pastry
with milk. Place on a greased baking tray

and cut into rolls, 1 inch (2·5 cm) long, with
the knife, and cook for 15 minutes. Reduce
the oven temperature to 300°F, 170°C, Gas
Mark 4, and cook for a further 10 minutes,
but don't let them get too brown. They
should rise well and be deep gold to light
brown in colour.

Miniature Cheese Scones

Makes 28

These can be made a day or two before the
party and kept in an airtight tin.

Oven Temperature: 350°F, 180°C,
Gas Mark 5

4 oz (110 g) self-raising flour
1 teaspoon salt
1 oz (25 g) butter
2 oz (50 g) Cheddar cheese, grated
A little milk

Stir the flour and salt together and rub in
the fat, until the mixture resembles fine
breadcrumbs. Add the cheese and enough
milk to make a soft dough, but be careful
not to make it too slack. Roll it out to a
thickness of about $\frac{1}{2}$ inch (1·25 cm), or pat it
out with your hands, and cut it into rounds
with a 1 inch (2·5 cm) diameter pastry
cutter. If you do not have a small enough
cutter, use the well-washed plastic top of an
aerosol spray or any bottle top with a sharp
edge (a Stergene bottle top is ideal). Place
on a greased baking tray, brush the tops
with milk, and cook for about 10 minutes.
You can cut them in half and spread the
halves with butter before serving.

Small cakes and biscuits

Gingerbread Biscuits

Makes 20

These can be made several days in advance if kept in an airtight tin.

Oven Temperature: 350°F, 180°C, Gas Mark 4

2 oz (50 g) butter
2 oz (50 g) sugar
4½ oz (125 g) plain flour
½ teaspoon bicarbonate of soda
1 teaspoon ground ginger
Warmed syrup

Cream the butter with the sugar until soft. Add the dry ingredients, mixed with a little warmed syrup to make a dough mixture. Having lightly kneaded this, flour a board and roll it out. If you wish, you could make gingerbread men (see following recipe), but these tend to be very large for smaller children to eat, so we suggest that you use instead your duck or dog cutters. Place your shapes on to a greased tray, and decorate with currants for eyes, etc. Bake for 10–15 minutes and allow to cool before placing on a wire rack.

Gingerbread Men

See photograph on page 76.

On page 40 we suggest that these make lovely presents for the children to take home, even if they are a little too large for younger children to eat at the tea table. Follow the previous recipe, and cut out the men with your man-shaped cutter. Cook and leave to cool as above. Decorate in one of several ways:
1. Use chocolate polka dots for the eyes, nose, mouth and buttons, and stick them on with a touch of slightly whisked egg white.
2. Make up a small quantity of icing and pipe on eyes, nose, mouth and buttons.
3. Use a very thin nozzle with a piping bag, or a strong paper or plastic bag with a tiny snip off one corner. Pipe (if you are very clever) each child's name across the front of each gingerbread man. Have a few un-named ones for spares in case of break-ages. If the whole name is a bit difficult, and it does require practice, then why not just try a big initial for each child? If you do break any of them, don't despair. Use egg white as glue – it works a treat.

Coloured Meringue Drops

See photograph on page 76.

Makes 30

There is a certain mystique about making meringues, and some cooks feel reluctant to try them, but meringues are actually very easy and if you follow the instructions carefully you should have no trouble at all. Meringue making has been enormously simplified since the introduction of silicone paper: simply lift the meringues off the paper – they will never stick – and the paper can be brushed down and re-used a number of times.

You can make your meringues up to two weeks in advance, but they must be stored in an airtight tin.

Oven Temperature: 180°F, 90°C, Gas Mark ¾

2 egg whites
4 oz (110 g) caster sugar
Few drops green and pink colouring

These coloured meringues must be cooked very slowly indeed, so that they do not change colour, but remain a fresh pink, green or white. Whisk the egg whites with an electric beater until *very* stiff. Add 2 oz (50 g) of the sugar and continue to whisk until mixture holds a peak. Gently fold in the remaining sugar. Put a tiny blob of meringue under each corner of the paper on the baking trays to hold the paper down. Take a very small teaspoonful of meringue and, with another teaspoon, slide the mixture on to the tray, making a small round meringue. Do this until you have made 10 meringues and have used about one-third of the mixture. Put half the remaining mixture into a separate bowl, add a few drops of the pink colouring and mix gently until the colour is even. Make another 10 meringues using the two spoons. Colour the last part of the mixture with a few drops of green colouring, and spoon on to the remaining tray. Cook near the bottom of the oven for 40 minutes. When they are firm to the touch, turn off the oven and leave them until they are completely cold.

Chocolate Meringues

Makes 30

If you are worried about making coloured meringues because you feel that yours go brown however slowly you cook them, then why not try chocolate meringues. They can also be made well in advance.

Oven Temperature: 180°F, 90°C, Gas Mark ¾

2 egg whites
4 oz (110 g) caster sugar
1 tablespoon cocoa

Whisk the egg whites with an electric beater until they are stiff. Add 2 oz (50 g) of the sugar and continue to whisk until the mixture holds a peak. Gently fold in the cocoa and the remaining sugar. Spoon the meringue mixture on to the trays and cook as in the previous recipe.

2 3 4 Shortbread

Makes 30

This recipe never fails, and gets its name from the proportions of the ingredients. It keeps well in an airtight tin.

Oven Temperature: 300°F, 150°C, Gas Mark 2

2 oz (50 g) butter
3 oz (75 g) caster sugar
4 oz (110 g) plain flour

Grease a baking tin, approximately 8 inches (20 cm) square. Put the butter into a mixing bowl. Rub in the sifted sugar and flour until the mixture resembles fine breadcrumbs. Then gently knead it together with your hands, and pat out into the greased tin. Cook for 10 minutes. The mixture should not change colour. Take out of the oven and cut into thin fingers. Leave in tin until cool.

Shortbread Shapes

These are nice to make if you have cutters to make ducks, fish and other nice shapes. The man-shaped cutter makes biscuits that are a little too large for small children, so save it until your children are older. Follow the recipe for Shortbread Faces, but use your different shapes. Draw the duck's eye and wings and the fishes' eyes and fins with icing as before, and add chocolate polka dots for the eyes.

Shortbread Faces

See photograph on page 76.

Makes 35

You can make these a few days in advance, but ice them the day before the party.

Oven Temperature: 300°F, 150°C, Gas Mark 2

4 oz (110 g) softened butter or margarine
2 oz (50 g) caster sugar
6 oz (175 g) plain flour
Icing
3 oz (75 g) icing sugar
1 or 2 tablespoons boiling water
Pink colouring
Chocolate polka dots (optional)

Put the butter into a mixing bowl. Add the sugar and beat well, then add the flour. Gently knead with your hands into a soft ball. Pat on to a floured board and roll it out lightly and thinly to about ⅛ inch (3 mm) thick. Use a small round cutter, about 1½ inch (3·75 cm) in diameter. Cut out as many biscuits as you can, re-roll the leftovers, and cut these out also. Place the biscuits on a greased baking sheet and bake towards the top of the oven for 10–15 minutes, until pale gold. Cool.

To make the icing, add the water and colouring to the icing sugar, and mix well. The mixture should be a little more stiff than you think is right as it will soften when you hold it. Put the icing into a paper bag, cut a very small hole in one corner and pipe a face on to each biscuit (when they are quite cold) with small blobs of icing for eyes and nose, and a nice smiley line for a mouth. Place a polka dot on each of the eye blobs – children cannot resist them.

Little Gems

See photograph on page 76.

Makes 24

If you like you can use this recipe to make up half of the quantity Little Gems and make the rest into Butterflies (see following recipe). Both make very pretty little cakes, but young children may need a little help in taking off the paper cases. You could make these two days before the party, and ice them the day before.

Oven Temperature: 350°F, 180°C, Gas Mark 4

4 oz (110 g) butter or soft margarine
4 oz (110 g) caster sugar
2 eggs
4 oz (110 g) self-raising flour
24 petit fours cases

Icing

4 oz (110 g) icing sugar
1 or 2 tablespoons boiling water
Few drops pink colouring
Mixed decorations, including halved glacé cherries, chocolate buttons, Smarties, hundreds and thousands, Jelly Tots, etc.

Preheat the oven, and place the paper cases on a baking sheet. Beat the butter and sugar together until pale and smooth. Beat the eggs in a separate bowl and add to the mixture, a little at a time, beating well between each addition. Sieve the flour into the bowl from quite a height to help lighten it, and fold in with a metal spoon. (Add a few drops of milk if the mixture is a little stiff.) Spoon the mixture into the paper cases, filling each case about two-thirds full. Cook in the centre of the oven for about 15 minutes, until the cakes are golden brown. Remove from oven and leave to cool.

Make up the icing so that it is quite stiff, adding the boiling water very gradually. With a teaspoon spoon the icing on to half of the cakes, putting the decorations in place immediately. Colour the remaining icing pink and spoon on to the rest of the cakes, again adding your decorations at once.

Butterflies

Makes 24

Again small children may need a little help in taking off the paper cases. You can make them two days before the party, and ice them the day before – perhaps at the same time as the cake.

Oven Temperature: 350°F, 180°C, Gas Mark 4

4 oz (110 g) butter or soft margarine
4 oz (110 g) caster sugar
2 eggs
4 oz (110 g) self-raising flour
24 petit fours cases

Icing

1 oz (25 g) softened butter
2 oz (50 g) icing sugar
2 or 3 drops vanilla essence

Make the Butterflies in exactly the same way as Little Gems.

To make the butter icing, cream the butter with the icing sugar and beat until smooth. Cut off the tops of the cakes, and cut each top in half. Put a teaspoonful of butter icing on the top of each cake and stick the two pieces on as wings into the butter icing.

Chocolate Crispies

See photograph on page 76.

Makes 20

These will keep fresh for several days in an airtight tin.

Oven Temperature: 200°F, 100°C, Gas Mark 2

2 oz (50 g) cornflakes or rice krispies
6 oz (175 g) plain chocolate
1 oz (25 g) butter or margarine

Spread the cornflakes over a shallow baking tray, and put into the bottom of the oven for 10 minutes. Remove from the oven and leave to cool. When they are cool crumble them up until fairly small. They should be very crisp. Melt the chocolate and butter over a gentle heat (do *not* add water as this will make the cornflakes go soggy). Stir in the cornflakes and shape the mixture into small conical heaps on a greased baking tray, and leave to set.

Coconut Pyramids

Makes 30

You can make these two or three days before the party.

Oven Temperature: 250°F, 120°C, Gas Mark 1

2 egg whites
8 oz (225 g) caster sugar
4 oz (110 g) desiccated coconut
Few drops of pink colouring

Whisk the egg whites until very stiff. Whisk in half the caster sugar, again until very stiff. Gently fold in the remaining sugar and the coconut. Shape half the mixture into small pyramids, on a greased baking sheet. Add a few drops of pink colouring to the remaining mixture, and shape into small pink pyramids. Cook for 30 minutes at the bottom of the oven.

Scrumptious Coconut Bars

Makes 16

Make two or three days in advance.

Oven Temperature: 350°F, 180°C, Gas Mark 4

4 oz (110 g) self-raising flour
4 oz (110 g) caster sugar
4 oz (110 g) desiccated coconut
2 oz (50 g) cornflakes
5 oz (150 g) butter
Icing
2 tablespoons boiling water
2 teaspoons instant coffee
6 oz (175 g) icing sugar

Mix the dry ingredients in a bowl. Melt the butter, pour over dry ingredients and mix well. Press into a greased baking tin. Cook for 15 minutes until golden brown.

Meanwhile, to make the icing, pour the boiling water over the coffee and stir into the icing sugar. Add a little more water if necessary. Pour the icing over the biscuits as soon as you take them out of the oven. Leave to cool and cut into small bars.

Chocolate Peppermint Creams

Makes 30

Make these up to a week before the party.

4 oz (110 g) plain chocolate
4 oz (110 g) margarine
4 tablespoons golden syrup
Few drops peppermint essence
Petit fours *paper cases*
Coloured hundreds and thousands

Melt the chocolate over a gentle heat. Cream the margarine with the syrup and beat in the melted chocolate. Add the drops of peppermint essence and mix well. Pour into *petit fours* cases, decorate the tops with hundreds and thousands, and leave to set. For very small children, peel off the cases before you serve the cakes.

Coconut Drops

Makes 20

Make these the day before the party.

Oven Temperature: 250°F, 120°C, Gas Mark 1

1 small can condensed milk
8 oz (225 g) desiccated coconut
Few drops pink and green colouring

Mix the condensed milk and coconut. Divide into three equal parts; leave one white and colour the others pink and green. Shape with a teaspoon into small moulds on a greased baking tray, and cook for about 30 minutes at the bottom of the oven. It is important that they do not go brown as they cook or the colouring will be spoiled.

Chocolate Crunch Cakes

Makes 30

Make two or three days in advance, and keep in the fridge.

8 oz (225 g) plain chocolate
1 egg yolk
2 oz (50 g) unsalted peanuts, chopped
2 oz (50 g) rice krispies
30 paper cases

Melt the chocolate over a very gentle heat, and stir in the egg yolk. Then stir in the dry ingredients, until they are well mixed. Put teaspoonfuls of the mixture into paper cases and leave to set.

Date Fingers

Makes 28

These are best when freshly made so try to make them no sooner than the day before the party.

Oven Temperature: 350°F, 180°C, Gas Mark 4

1 oz (25 g) butter
8 oz (225 g) chopped dates
1 tablespoon sugar
1 tablespoon self-raising flour
1 egg

Melt the butter and stir in all the other ingredients. Press the mixture into a greased baking tin. Don't worry if it looks like a sticky mess at this stage. Cook for 30 minutes and cut into fingers when cool.

Peppermint Squares

See photograph on page 76.

Makes 30

These are delicious, but rather rich, so keep them small. You can make them a day or two before the party.

Oven Temperature: 350°F, 180°C, Gas Mark 4

2 oz (50 g) cornflakes
3 oz (75 g) butter or margarine
2 oz (50 g) plain flour
2 oz (50 g) desiccated coconut
2 oz (50 g) sugar
½ teaspoon peppermint essence

Icing

4 oz (110 g) butter or margarine
8 oz (225 g) icing sugar
½ teaspoon peppermint essence
Chocolate buttons to decorate

Lightly crush the cornflakes. Melt the butter in a saucepan over a gentle heat and stir in the cornflakes, flour, coconut, sugar and peppermint essence. Press into a well-greased baking tin – use a fork – so that the mixture is evenly and thinly spread (not more than ¼ inch or 6 mm thick). Cook for 20 minutes until light gold in colour.

Make up the icing and when the biscuit mixture is cold, spread on top and roughen the surface with a fork. Cut into 1 inch (2·5 cm) squares, and press a chocolate button on to the centre of each square.

Chocolate Truffles

See photograph on page 76.

Makes 40

You can make these two or three days in advance, but keep them in the fridge.

4 oz (110 g) plain sweet biscuits
2 oz (50 g) digestive biscuits
3½ oz (85 g) butter or margarine
1 oz (25 g) caster sugar
3 tablespoons golden syrup
2 oz (50 g) cocoa
Chocolate vermicelli
Coloured hundreds and thousands
Petit fours cases

Crush the biscuits roughly with a rolling pin. Cream together the butter, sugar and golden syrup. Beat in the sifted cocoa and work in the crushed biscuits, mixing well. If the mixture is too soft, leave in the fridge for 30 minutes. When sufficiently firm, wash your hands well, and take teaspoonful size pieces of the dough, and roll between your hands to make neat round balls. Pour some coloured hundreds and thousands into a small bowl, and taking half the truffles roll each in the bowl until well covered. Place in *petit fours* cases to set. Roll the remaining half in chocolate vermicelli in the same way, put into cases, and arrange the truffles alternately on the serving dish. Put in the fridge to harden.

Chocolate Shortbread Treat

Makes 32

These are at their best when freshly made, but will keep well if necessary.

Oven Temperature: 350°F, 180°C, or Gas Mark 4

Shortbread base
6 oz (175 g) flour
1 oz (25 g) caster sugar
4 oz (110 g) butter
Filling
4 oz (110 g) butter
4 oz (110 g) soft brown sugar
2 level tablespoons golden syrup
1 small can condensed milk
Icing
8 oz (225 g) plain dessert chocolate
1 oz (25 g) butter

Grease the baking tin. Sift the flour into a bowl, add the sugar and rub in the butter until the mixture looks like breadcrumbs. Knead it into a ball and press it well into the tin. Cook for 15 minutes. Leave to cool in the tin.

To make the filling, put all the ingredients into a saucepan and stir over a gentle heat until the sugar has dissolved. Bring to the boil and, stirring continuously, boil gently for 7 minutes. Take off the heat and beat well, and pour on to the shortbread base. Allow to cool before adding the icing.

To make the icing, cut the chocolate up roughly and melt over a very gentle heat with the butter. Spread it evenly over the filling. When the chocolate is quite cold, cut the mixture into 32 squares.

Julianna's Uncooked Cookies

Makes 36

Make a day or two in advance, and keep in the fridge.

8 oz (225 g) sweet tea biscuits
2 tablespoons golden syrup
4 oz (110 g) butter
4 oz (110 g) sugar

Put the biscuits into a plastic bag, fasten the top and crush with a rolling pin. Dissolve the golden syrup and butter, mix in the crushed biscuits and the sugar, and press with a fork into a greased baking tray to set. When firm cut into fingers.

Cherry Crisps

Makes 30

Don't make this recipe too far in advance – a day or two if possible, and keep in an airtight tin.

2 oz (50 g) butter
2 oz (50 g) sugar
4 oz (110 g) dates, chopped
2 oz (50 g) cherries, chopped
2 oz (50 g) rice krispies

Melt the butter and sugar in a saucepan over a low heat. Add the chopped dates and cherries. Stir in the (very crisp) rice krispies and form into small pyramids on a greased baking tray. Leave to set.

5 6 7 Flapjacks

So called because of the quantities used! The easiest never-fail recipe there is. Flapjacks keep very well, for weeks if necessary, but are at their best when fresh. Keep in an airtight tin.

Oven Temperature: 350°F, 180°C, Gas Mark 4

5 oz (150 g) butter or margarine
6 oz (175 g) granulated sugar
7 oz (200 g) porridge oats

Melt the butter over a low heat, with the sugar (you will find that the sugar will not really dissolve, but don't worry, it's not meant to!). Stir in the porridge oats and pour into a shallow well-greased tray. Cook in the centre of the oven for 20 minutes, until golden brown. Remove from oven and mark into narrow fingers. Leave to cool in the tin.

Uncooked Chocolate Cake

Make two or three days in advance, and keep in the fridge.

4 oz (110 g) butter
4 oz (110 g) dark chocolate
2 tablespoons golden syrup
8 oz (225 g) digestive biscuits

Melt the butter, chocolate and syrup – do not allow to boil – then take off the heat. Put the biscuits into a plastic bag, fasten at the top, and crush with a rolling pin, until the biscuits are in small even crumbs. Mix with the other ingredients, and press into a greased baking tray. Smooth the surface and leave to set, then cut into squares, as many as you like.

Drinks

Very small children (one to four year olds) are perfectly happy with a big jug of orangeade, but the older children would appreciate a little variety. They love, needless to say, Coca-Cola, fizzy lemonade etc, but they also love the fresh taste of home-made drinks, with their ice cubes, little bits of fruit, pretty colours and so on. If you are having a big party, why not compromise: buy some ready-made drinks and make a fizzy orange or apple punch as well. If you are having a small party, or special teatime treat for about six children, then try some of the more adventurous milk or ice cream shakes. They are delicious as well as nourishing.

The first eight children's recipes in this section will serve about ten, depending on the weather and spillages, but keep some orange squash or fizzy lemonade in reserve. The milk shakes will serve about six.

Iced Coffee *For the mothers.*

Serves 8

3 tablespoons instant coffee
Sugar to taste (about 2 tablespoons)
¼ pint (150 ml) boiling water
2 pints (1 litre) cold milk
Ice cubes
Scoops of ice cream (optional)

Put the coffee and sugar in a large jug, add the boiling water and stir well. Then add the cold milk and ice cubes. Keep in the fridge until needed. Put a scoop of ice cream into each glass and pour the coffee over it.

Iced Tea *For the mothers.*

Serves 8

4 large teaspoons tea (half China tea if you have it)
1 pint (570 ml) boiling water
1 pint (570 ml) cold water
Ice cubes
8 slices of lemon
Sugar (optional)

Make a strong pot of tea with the boiling water. Allow to brew for 5 minutes, then strain into a large jug and add the cold water and lemon slices. When tea is cold add ice cubes and keep in fridge. Offer sugar individually.

Home-made Lemonade

4 lemons
4 tablespoons sugar
3 pints (1·5 litres) boiling water
10 ice cubes

Cut the lemons into quarters. Put them with the sugar into a heat-resistant jug. Pour on the boiling water and leave to stand for 30 minutes. Strain, cool, add the ice cubes, and serve.

Home-made Orangeade

Follow the recipe for lemonade as above. When it is cool, squeeze the juice of four oranges into the lemonade, add the ice cubes and serve.

Home-made Blender Lemonade

4 thin skinned lemons
4 tablespoons sugar
10 ice cubes
3 pints (1·5 litres) cold water

Cut the lemons into quarters. Put all the ingredients, reserving 2 pints (1 litre) of water and 5 ice cubes, into the blender and blend for 10 seconds. Strain, add remaining water and ice cubes and serve.

Fizzy Apple Punch

½ pint (300 ml) bottle concentrated apple
  juice
2 pints (1 litre) soda water
2 pints (1 litre) ginger ale
2 eating apples (red if possible)

Chill all the ingredients (except the apples)
for 2 hours. Quarter and core the apples,
but do not peel them, and cut the quarters
into small chunks. Put into a large jug. Pour
over the other ingredients and serve.

Fizzy Apricot Punch

1 × 10 oz (275 g) can apricots (stoned)
2 lemons
3 pints (1·5 litres) fizzy lemonade

Chill all the ingredients for at least 2 hours.
Cut the lemons into quarters, and put into a
blender with the apricots. Blend for 20
seconds. Strain into a serving jug, and mix
well with ½ pint (300 ml) lemonade.
Add the rest of the lemonade, and serve.

Fizzy Orange Punch I

1 large carton frozen orange juice
  concentrate
3 pints (1·5 litres) fizzy lemonade
10 ice cubes
A few slices of orange

Dilute the frozen orange juice with ½ pint
(300 ml) lemonade. When it is well mixed
pour into serving jug, add the rest of the
lemonade, the ice cubes and the slices of
orange, and serve.

Fizzy Orange Punch II

1 pint (570 ml) pure orange juice (tinned or
  bottled)
2 pints (1 litre) tonic water
10 ice cubes
A few orange slices

Chill the ingredients in the fridge for at
least 2 hours. Pour the orange juice into a
jug. Mix well with ½ pint (300 ml) of the
tonic water. Add the rest of the tonic water,
the ice cubes, the slices of orange, and
serve.

Banana Whiz

2 bananas
1 egg
2 pints (1 litre) cold milk
1 tablespoon sugar

Peel the bananas, chop, and put in the
blender. Break the egg into the blender,
and add the other ingredients, reserving 1
pint (570 ml) of milk. Blend for 20 seconds
until foaming. Add the remaining milk. Pour
into tall glasses and serve with straws.

Cola Surprise

3 pints (1·5 litres) Coca-Cola or Pepsi-Cola
Small carton of ice cream

Spoon or scoop the ice cream into each
serving glass. Pour the Cola over and
serve.

Chocolate Banana Shake

*2 bananas
2 pints (1 litre) cold milk
2 heaped tablespoons drinking chocolate
    or 1 tablespoon each cocoa and sugar*

Peel the bananas, chop, and put into the blender. Add the other ingredients, reserving 1 pint (570 ml) of milk, and blend for 20 seconds until foamy. Add remaining milk. Pour into tall glasses and serve with straws.

Pineapple Dream

*1 × 10 oz (275 g) can pineapple chunks
2 pints (1 litre) cold milk
Vanilla ice cream*

Put the pineapple, the juice and 1 pint (570 ml) milk into the liquidizer, and blend for 20 seconds. Add remaining milk. Pour into serving glasses and top with a scoopful of vanilla ice cream. Serve with straws.

Blackcurrant Delight

*5 tablespoons Ribena
2 pints (1 litre) cold milk
Vanilla ice cream*

Mix the Ribena and milk together. Pour into tall glasses. Top with a scoop of vanilla ice cream and serve with straws.

Peppermint Delight

*Few drops peppermint essence
Few drops green colouring
1 tablespoon sugar
2 pints (1 litre) cold milk
Soft ice cream*

Add the peppermint essence, the green colouring and the sugar to the cold milk, and stir well. Pour into tall glasses and top with a scoop of ice cream.

Apricot Delight

*1 × 10 oz (275 g) can apricots (stoned)
1 tablespoon sugar
2 pints (1 litre) milk
6 ice cubes*

Put all the ingredients into a blender, reserving 1 pint (570 ml) milk, and blend for 20 seconds. Add remaining milk. Pour into tall glasses and serve with straws.

Raspberry Soda

*8 oz (225 g) fresh or frozen raspberries
2 pints (1 litre) milk
Small bottle tonic water
Small block of Raspberry Ripple ice cream*

Partially defrost the frozen raspberries. Put the raspberries and 1 pint (570 ml) milk into a blender and blend for 20 seconds. Strain. Add remaining milk and tonic water. Pour into serving glasses. Top with a scoop of ice cream.

4. PARTY GAMES

The most important consideration, when planning what amusements to provide to stop the children being either shy, bored, or running riot through your house, is to base your choice of games on (a) the ages of your guests, and (b) the size of your house (or garden if you are planning a summer party). Make a list of the games which you think would be suitable and plan a rough timetable – it is amazing how quickly the children, especially the older ones, can get through the games. Keep the games coming thick and fast and don't allow gaps to develop between them.

For babies' parties just have lots of toys around – with the exception of your child's pride and joy, as tinies can be very possessive. Play nursery records and tapes to clap and jump to. Really these parties are a super excuse for a special tea with your friends and their children – and why not!

This chapter is divided into two parts. The first contains games suitable for the very young, but there are inevitably some games which overlap and continue to be popular with older children. The second part concentrates on the older group. We have tried to organize the sections chronologically, starting with the games aimed at involving everybody at the beginning of the party, while guests are arriving, continuing with something energetic before tea, followed by quieter games suitable for immediately afterwards, and finally suggesting a medley of ideas to draw the party to a conclusion on a high note. There are ideas for outdoor games for fine weather parties. You will find that little girls are happy to play party games longer than the boys – even at ten, girls are content to 'pass the parcel' although with forfeits, whereas boys would consider it 'sissy'!

It is a super treat for your guests to be given little prizes for winning games. The smallest token is quite sufficient – a pencil, sweet or marble (but not marbles for the under fives). Always have a few extra 'spare' prizes, in case of a draw or other problem!

It is a good idea to provide little bags for your guests to put their prizes into, especially if you are trying to cope with a lot of children – a lost prize is a major drama! You can either simply write each child's name on an ordinary paper bag or you could carry on your party theme by decorating a piece of card with, for instance, a pair of animals for a Noah's Ark party, printing the child's name on this, and stapling the card to your bag. An industrious and talented friend even made individual tiny carrier bags for each of her guests – needless to say the children were delighted.

It is a real bonus to have a children's party outside – thus avoiding any disturbance in your house – but it is always worth being prepared for rain. Plan sufficient games that can be played both indoors and outdoors, and have a room indoors cleared of furniture in case of need.

Indoor games for younger children

Grandmother's Footsteps

A suitable game to play when the children are arriving, with an adult as grandmother. This is the sort of game that children can join in at any stage of the proceedings. Ask the mothers to join in with their children to help break the ice. The 'grandmother' turns her back, and the children try to creep up on her from behind. Grandmother will, every now and again, suddenly turn around and if she sees anyone move they have to go back to the starting point.
Props: None.

'What's the time, Mr Wolf?'

'Mr Wolf' stands well in front of a line of children – with his back to them – as in Grandmother's Footsteps. The children creep up saying 'What's the time, Mr Wolf?'. He turns around to reply – '12 o'clock' – and if he sees anyone moving they have to go back to 'the House', ie, where they started from. At some point he replies 'Dinner time' and then tries to catch a child who is then Mr Wolf, and the game starts again. This is a good game to get the children shouting and joining in together.
Props: None.

Oranges and Lemons

The mothers form an arch and the children run in a line under the arch singing 'Oranges and lemons'. When they get to the 'chopping stage', whoever is chopped is out, until the last one is the winner. Here are the words:

> Oranges and lemons,
> say the bells of St Clements.
> You owe me five farthings,
> say the bells of St Martins.
> When will you pay me?
> say the bells of Old Bailey.
> When I grow rich,
> say the bells of Shoreditch.
> When will that be?
> say the bells of Stepney.
> I do not know,
> says the great bell of Bow.
>
> Here comes a candle
> to light you to bed.
> Here comes a chopper
> to chop off your head.
>
> Chop chop chop chop.

Why not end off with a 'tug of war' between the oranges and lemons? As each child is out they become an orange or lemon. At the end of the game the two teams have a good 'tug'! Any excuse for everyone to land on the floor!
Props: None.

'Simon Says'

One person stands in front of the rest as Simon. He faces them and calls out 'Simon says' (for example), 'put your hand on your head', and the children obey. But if he simply states 'Put your hand on your head' without the words 'Simon says...', then anyone who does it is out.
Props: None.

Musical Bumps

This is another excellent game to have before tea, to allow children to get rid of some excess energy. Have a practice run-through first. The children jump up and down to the music. When the music stops, they have to sit on the floor. Whoever sits down last is out, until eventually the winner is the last one left in.
Props: Music.

The Farmer's in his Den

The children stand in a circle with the mothers. Choose a farmer to be in his den. Then walk in a circle around the farmer singing 'The farmer's in his den', as the farmer chooses his wife, the wife a child and so on. When it comes to patting the 'bone', the last child to be chosen, make sure this is a gentle patting, and not an all-out-attack! For forgetful oldies the rhyme is as follows:

> The farmer's in his den
> The farmer's in his den
> Ee i diddily i
> The farmer's in his den.
>
> The farmer wants a wife
> The farmer wants a wife
> Ee i diddily i
> The farmer wants a wife.
>
> The wife wants a child
> The wife wants a child
> Ee i diddily i
> The wife wants a child.

Thereafter 'The child wants a nurse', 'The nurse wants a dog', 'The dog wants a bone', finishing off with 'We all pat the bone'.
Props: None.

Ring a Ring of Roses

The children hold hands and dance in a ring singing the words, then at 'we all fall down', they all fall down, usually roaring with laughter. Young children love this. Play this before sitting down to tea. Here are the words:

> Ring a ring of roses
> A pocket full of posies
> A-tishoo, A-tishoo
> We all fall down.

Props: None.

Pig, Sheep, Cow and Horse

Have a large picture of each of these animals and place them in each of the four corners of a room. Have the music playing and when it stops the children rush to whichever corner they choose. Some helper with their back turned calls out the name of one of the animals, and those in that particular corner are out. Continue until you find the winner.
Props: Four, if possible large, pictures of each of the animals; music.

Old Macdonald had a Farm

If you have a record for this, play it, and encourage the children to join in with all the animal noises. Or, if you are brave enough to sing it yourself, the words are as follows:

> Old Macdonald had a farm
> Ee i Ee i o
> Old Macdonald had a farm
> Ee i Ee i o
>
> And on that farm he had some hens
> Ee i Ee i o
> with a cluck cluck here
> and a cluck cluck there
> Here a cluck there a cluck
> everywhere a cluck cluck
> Old Macdonald had a farm
> Ee i Ee i o

Continue each verse with a different animal, but all the animal noises should be repeated in turn, in each verse, so that the verse gets longer and longer (perhaps give a prize to the child who can remember all the noises best?).
Props: None

Pass the Parcel

This is the best game to have after tea. Remember to prepare the parcel before the party. Choose a prize and then wrap it up – newspaper is fine – and then wrap this parcel in another layer of paper with a small present (for instance, a small wrapped sweet, not a large toffee) inside each layer, and continue wrapping layers with small presents, until you have allowed a layer for each child to unwrap Make sure that your maths is right! The children sit in a circle and pass the parcel from child to child, while the music is playing. Stop the music at intervals, and whoever is holding the parcel at that time, unwraps a layer. Each child should have a sweet, or whatever, by the end. Finally the last one is the main prize winner. Make sure that the host does not win the main prize.
Props: One small prize for last turn of game. Sufficient sheets of old wrapping or newspaper, and little sweet in between each layer to give each child a go; music.

Hunt the Thimble, Easter Eggs, or Sweets, etc

Another good game to play after tea. You can either play this so that there is only one prize, and whoever finds the thimble or the Easter egg, etc, wins, or you could have a little Easter egg or sweet for each child to find. Be careful that whichever way you play this game, the things are not hidden too near a fire, too high up, or near precious ornaments. For small children make the hiding places very easy. Once again, allow mums to help.
Props: Thimble, Easter eggs or sweets, whichever you decide to use.

Musical Cushions

Having had a less energetic game, Musical Cushions (or Bumps again) can let off a bit of energy. Have one less cushion than the number of children. The guests walk, dance, jump or whatever you want around the cushions to music. When the music stops, everyone has to find a cushion to sit on, and whoever does not is out. Remove one cushion and start the music again. Repeat this until one cushion is left, with two children contesting for it. When the children are tiny they may want their mothers to do this with them.

Props: One cushion per guest; music.

Musical Hats

Substitute hats for the cushions, though they're obviously not to sit on! Have one less hat than the number of children. The guests walk, dance or jump around the hats to music, and when the music stops, everyone has to find a hat to put on, and whoever does not is out. Continue as above, removing a hat each time the music starts again, until only one hat is left with two children contesting for it.

Props: One hat per guest, music.

Musical Newspapers

A good substitute for Musical Cushions as you may not have many cushions – a husband who shall be nameless tried to organize this game and forgot the need for twenty props! Cut about 1 foot (30 cm) square of newspaper per child, and the children have to jump on them.

Props: One newspaper per guest; music.

Here we go round the Mulberry Bush

The children join hands and dance in a circle miming the actions of each verse in turn. Here are some verses to show the structure of the song:

Here we go round the mulberry bush
The mulberry bush the mulberry bush
Here we go round the mulberry bush
On a cold and frosty morning.

This is the way we wash our hands
Wash our hands wash our hands
This is the way we wash our hands
On a cold and frosty morning.

Other verses are – 'This is the way we clean our teeth', 'This is the way we brush our hair', 'This is the way we eat our tea' and 'This is the way we jump for joy'. And so on.

Props: None.

'Hokey Kokey'

Mothers will have to help. Everyone stands in a circle and you all sing:

You put your left arm in, left arm out,
Left arm in and you shake it all about.
You do the Hokey Kokey and you turn around,
That's what it's all about!

Ooh the Hokey Kokey (all hold hands and go in to the centre of the circle and out again, throughout the chorus),
Ooh the Hokey Kokey, Ooh the Hokey Kokey,
Knees bend, arms stretch, ra, ra, ra.

Remember that you put your arms, legs, feet, etc, in!

Props: None.

Pinning the Tail on the Donkey

The donkey can be the conventional animal, on to which you pin your tail, but if your party is a pirate party for instance, then use a treasure map on which the treasure trove is to be found. Draw the outline on to a stiff card, or a piece of paper pinned to a board. You might be able to find a suitable picture on a poster or a piece of wrapping paper. (Or you can buy the donkey and the tails from some large stationers.) Then make a separate tail either using paper, raffia, string or wool. Place the picture against the wall and mark on it the position where the tail should be. Blindfold one child at a time, give them the tail through which there is a drawing pin, and whoever places the tail on the paper nearest to the correct position is the winner. Initial each attempt. Some little children do not like the thought of a blindfold, so don't force the shy ones – they have just as much fun watching. Let them say with you who they think is the winner.

Props: Card or paper pinned to board as donkey, or whatever symbol you plan to use. A pin with the tail, cross, etc. A blindfold. Pencil for initialling.

Shopping

This is a good game to end your party with, but it does need preparation beforehand. Wrap up little parcels of Smarties, chocolate buttons, Refreshers, Dolly Mixtures, etc, in cling film. If you have the time and inclination tie with a little ribbon. Any small objects can be used – rubbers, little pencils, whatever you wish. Have a bag with lots of either pennies or toy or real money (you can get bags of pennies from banks, but if using real money, be careful that

the children are not too young and try to eat it). 'Hide' the money around your house, wherever you want, and let the children go and find the money and come to 'buy' either the little packets of sweets, or toys. These can be considered their going-home presents. Allow enough time for the children to have a proper game before their parents arrive.

Props: A bag of pennies, or toy money, little presents; some sort of stall from which you can 'sell' these to the children.

In-Between Games

Here are a few ideas to keep the children who are 'out' occupied until the next game. Sometimes when children are very little you won't need to do anything, as they will be quite happy just watching their friends. If you have sufficient room, have lots of toys out for them to play with, but if space is a problem, and if you can have an extra pair of hands to help, then why not use another room, and have some other activity going on in there. For example, have a jar or bowl of Smarties, or pennies, and get the guests to guess how many there are in the jar. Whoever wins can have a little prize. Your helper will need a pencil and paper to write down the names and number the child guessed.

Alternatively, have a box of straws and some Smarties in a bowl or plate. The children have to suck the Smarties with a straw on to another plate and they can eat the proceeds! If you have enough space, little children love playing Musical Bumps. While you have a musical game going on, have an 'out' section, who can jump around and do the bumps just for fun when the music stops, but it is important to keep those playing the proper game and those that are just having fun separate. You will need space.

Outdoor games for younger children

Don't forget that conventional indoor games can perfectly well be played outside – Musical Bumps, Hats, etc, Pass the Parcel, Pig, Sheep, Cow and Horse, etc. Also don't try to keep the younger children running all the time: they are only tiny, so have a Pass the Parcel for a rest. Have plenty of orange squash outside, as they'll be thirsty. If you are short of unbreakable beakers, collect up well ahead of the party, either small yogurt or cream pots, or washing powder measure mugs. Wash these thoroughly and they will be fine.

Running Races

Little ones have fun just running races and mums can join in! If you have a small garden have people running to the end and back.
Props: Washing line, if possible, for start and finish lines.

Egg and Spoon Race

Give each child a dessertspoon with a small potato in it. Whoever crosses the line first with the potato still in the spoon is the winner. If you are being firm, or if the children are old enough to understand, they ought perhaps to either go back to the beginning and start again when they drop the potato, or turn a circle.
Props: A dessertspoon and small potato per child.

Dressing-up Race

Have the children run to individual heaps of dressing-up clothes. They get dressed and run back.
Props: Lots of old scarves, hats, etc. One per guest. If you haven't many such clothes, run heats of four children, say, and then have a 'final'.

Relay Race

Divide the children into two teams. The first one in each team runs to a marker and round back to their team. The second child takes the baton, and this is repeated until the first team to finish wins. NB, when dividing the teams, try and make them evenly balanced.
Props: 2 batons (a piece of smooth wood); 2 markers (tall bamboo sticks, for instance).

Pitch and Chuck

Divide your guests into two teams. Have the children run to a ping pong ball and throw the ball into a bowl or paddling pool full of water. When they are tiny they may need some help with their aim, and also have the bowls or pools quite close to the balls. They run back and the next child then goes. Meanwhile a helper has retrieved the ball from the water. First team to finish wins.
Props: 2 washing-up bowls filled with water, or 1 paddling pool; 2 ping pong balls.

Buckets and Balloons

Divide your guests into teams. The first child runs to the bucket and picks up a balloon from inside. They run back to the next child and hand over the balloon. The next child runs to the bucket and puts the balloon back into it. Continue this until everyone has had a go. The first team to finish wins. Have a helper at the bucket end.

Props: 2 balloons, 2 spares and don't make the balloons too big or it will be hard to get them out of the bucket; 2 buckets.

Prince Charles, Princess Diana and their carriage

If you have twelve guests divide into three groups of four. From each group choose a Prince Charles, a Princess Diana and two horses. Have 'Prince Charles' at one end of the garden with a pile of his clothes, and put 'Princess Diana' at the other end with her clothes. Have the two horses with their skipping rope 'reins' in the middle. When the off is given, Prince Charles and Princess Diana get dressed. Prince Charles, when ready, runs to pick up his horses, puts the skipping rope around them and drives them to Princess Diana. She and Prince Charles then both drive the horses back to the start.

Props: Clothes for Charles and Diana and skipping ropes.

Sandpit, etc

If you are having an outdoor party a sandpit will enable the children to amuse themselves for quite a while. Have plenty of other outside toys – a tricycle, playhouse made out of travelling rugs on clothes airer, truck, rope ladder, swing, slide, play tunnel, etc. If the weather is really fine and there are plenty of mothers to help, have lots of towels and the paddling pool out. Have old washing-up liquid containers, plastic cups, etc, for them to play with in the water.

Prizes and Presents

Why not make a lollipop tree, by hanging lollies (or any little toys) on to a little bush or tree and the children could either collect prizes for games from it, or their presents at going-home time. All you need to do is tie pieces of cotton in loops from the presents, and suspend them from the tree.

Indoor games for older children

Some of the earlier games are obviously just as suitable for older children, so don't neglect the old favourites of Pass the Parcel, etc.

Pairing

Once mothers no longer stay during the party you may wish to encourage shy children to gain confidence by having a pairing game at the beginning of the party. If the children are too young to read, make cut-out recognizable shapes. If you are having a zoo or Noah's Ark party, for example, make animal shapes (if you are not good enough at drawing trace from a book), and remember to cut out two of each. When a child arrives, pin one to his or her chest, and the other on to another child's chest. Then they can all go around and find their partner. Later they can go into tea two by two, especially if it is a Noah's Ark party. Older children can have photographs of famous pairs of personalities, for instance Starsky to pair with Hutch, or Tom with Jerry. Or you can draw on a piece of paper or cut out of magazines, matching objects and pin one to each child – for instance, a tennis racquet and a tennis ball, a bird and a nest, and so on. If it is a *Star Wars* party, use space scenes in your pairing. Having divided the children up like this, you can also use the same pairing to create teams, with half of each pair in opposing teams, or you can let them play games in pairs, as in the next game and the tray game.

Props: Some badge or marker per child (sticky labels for instance), designed as you want.

Hunt the Pennies

Buy £1 or £2 worth of pennies from the bank, and hide these around the house. When the children come, they can rush around finding the pennies, come back to you and be given Smarties as a prize. This is a very good game to start the party with, while everyone is arriving.

Props: Sufficient pennies and Smarties for your guests.

Guess what or who they are

Pin photographs of famous people or objects around the room. Give each guest a piece of paper and a pencil and let them guess what or who the photographs are of. This is a game which could be done in pairs, especially if there are shy children.

Props: Photographs from magazines or newspapers; Blu-tack; pencil and paper per guest or pair.

Musical Knees

This is an ideal game for using your pairs, but only suitable for older children, who can support the weight of their partner. Dance in pairs. When the music stops one child has to sit on the other's knee. Those who move are out.

Props: Music.

Tray Game

This is an ideal game for playing after tea, especially if the children have outgrown Pass the Parcel. Before the party place about twelve objects on a tray. Select your objects and the number according to the age group you are catering for. Use objects such as spoons, combs, pencils, and so on, that the children will be familiar with. This game can be played in pairs if the children are younger and need reassurance, or individually. Let the children look at the tray for a few minutes, then remove it, and give the children five minutes to write down the names of all the objects they can remember. Collect in the papers, and whoever has remembered the greatest number of objects is the winner. Be prepared for a few ties here, and have enough presents for more than one winner.
Props: 12 different objects; tea towel to conceal objects from prying eyes; tray; pencil and paper per guest or pair.

Musical Islands

Place pieces of newspaper on the floor, and have one less than the number of players. Let the children dance around to the music. When the music stops everyone has to find an island and stand on it with one foot and one hand and whoever cannot keep still is out. Don't expect the children to stay still for long. Remove one (or however many are out) island from the sea, and start the music again. Continue until one island is left, and two people are also left. The winner is whoever claims the last island first and balances there.
Props: Newspaper pieces 2 feet (60 cm) square per guest; music.

Musical Chairs

Substitute chairs for cushions (page 102).
Props: Chair per guest; music.

Musical Statues

The children dance around and when the music stops, they have to keep very still. Whoever moves is out.
Props: Music.

Also see Musical Bumps, etc, in section for younger children.

Treasure Hunt

Children usually find it more enjoyable to play this game in pairs. Make your preparations in advance, and have a certain amount of supervision in the house. Don't play it at all unless you are prepared for the whole house to be used during the game. Write out ten cards giving the names of different parts of the house, or pieces of furniture. A typical set of cards might read:

Upstairs mirror
Under cushion
Around tap
Behind radiator
Under upturned bucket
Under bed
Under chair
In atlas or large book (but sticking out)
Under rug
Behind curtain

Then write out ten (depending on the numbers of pairs of children) pieces of paper with the figure 1 on them, then ten with 2 on, and so on up to the number 10. (This is a job

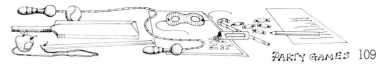

your children can do, but don't let them help with the hiding.) Keep one clue back and hide all the others in the appropriate places, together with the numbered slips of paper, all the 1's with the first clue, 2's with the second and so on. The last hiding place contains the last set of numbered pieces of paper and a little pile of wrapped sweets – one for each child. When the game begins, read out the first clue. Each pair of children then finds the first hiding place, and reads the next clue, but before looking for it, brings back one of the number 1 pieces of paper to you (this is to prove they are following the treasure hunt in the right order and to keep a check on their progress, in case some of the children need help). You then send them off to the next clue and so on, until they all finally reach the treasure, which is the pile of sweets. You can, if you like, also give a prize to the pair of children who finish the treasure hunt first.

Props: Enough cards (PC's or ordinary paper) per child or pair and same number of pieces marked 1, 2, 3 etc. Sweets.

Button Hunt

An adaptation of the Treasure Hunt. Divide the children into two teams, and let each team choose a captain, or if you have already paired the children, divide the two halves of each pair into two teams, and then let them choose the captain. Place the buttons around the house or, if you are having an outdoors party, around the garden before the children arrive. If the children are older, and you want to make the game more difficult, camouflage the buttons on a similar coloured background, for instance a brown button on a brown table. Then tell one team to shout 'Miaow' when they find a button, and the other team to shout

'Woof' when they do. The captain of each team is the only one allowed to pick the buttons up, as the buttons must not be touched by any team member, so be prepared for a lot of noise. If it is taking a long time to find the buttons, set a time limit of say, three minutes, and then the captain who has collected the most buttons represents the winning team.

Props: Lots of buttons.

Blindfold Smelling

Before the party prepare saucers of chocolate, tomato ketchup, coffee, orange, curry powder, and whatever else you like. Bring the children individually into the room, blindfolded, to see who can identify the most number of smells. Then, when they have had their go, let them sit and watch the others. But they must not call out the answers. This can also be done as a tasting game, or you can let the children both taste and smell. An alternative to this game is to blindfold the guests and then give them a pair of gloves to wear, and a selection of items to feel and identify. Whoever identifies the most is the winner.

Props: Saucers and 'smells'; blindfold; or objects to feel and gloves; or things to taste.

Sardines

Choose one person to go and hide, the rest then count to twenty, and go and search for the missing guest. This can be done in the dark (especially if older children are playing). When anyone finds the missing guest they join him very quietly and wait until everyone else has found the hiding place. The last person to find the tin of 'sardines' has to do a forfeit.

Props: None.

Railway Carriages

Before the party take one newspaper per guest, and muddle up all the pages. Then sit the children in a circle and give each one a jumbled newspaper. The first child to put the paper back into the correct order is the winner. Remember not to use varying sizes of newspapers, because the smaller ones are obviously going to be easier to handle.

Props: Collect enough copies of the same newspaper as number of guests (then they will all have the same size paper to cope with).

Pass the Balloon

Divide the children into two teams. Give each team leader a balloon. The team leader puts the balloon between his knees, and passes it down to the next person in the line, and so on. The team which does this most quickly is the winner.

Props: 2 balloons – 2 spares or more!

Pass the Matchbox

Divide the children into two teams. Give the captain of the team a matchbox cover. The children have to pass the matchbox on their noses along the line, without using their hands. Whichever team finishes first is the winner.

Props: 2 matchbox covers.

Pass the Orange

Divide the children into two teams. Give each captain an orange. He or she puts it under their chin and passes it down the line. A variation of this is for the two teams to lie on the floor and to pass the orange between their ankles.

Props: 2 oranges.

Balloon Running

Divide the children into two teams. Another way of playing passing the balloon if you have enough space, is to have the children running down the room and back with the balloons between their knees, and then passing it to the next member of the team. Whichever team finishes first is the winner.

Props: 2 balloons and spares.

Making Masks

Before the party, make basic masks out of coloured paper, and cut eye holes and mouth holes (see page 22). Attach strings. Have a supply of glue-on bought coloured shapes, and a large supply of felt-tip pens, and allow the children a certain length of time to make their own masks, decorating them with the coloured shapes and the felt-tips. Make sure that this is not done where felt-tips can harm either the children's clothes, or a table cloth, etc, and then let them all run around in their masks, and give a prize to the most imaginative.

Props: Masks; hole reinforcers; coloured shapes; felt-tips; string, etc.

Funny Hats

Provide each child with a large piece of coloured paper, newspaper, ribbon, pins, paperclips, and some odd bits of coloured tissue paper, and give them a certain length of time in which they have to make a hat. Whoever has the best product at the end is the winner.

Props: Paper; newspaper; paper clips; staples; pins; coloured tissue; shapes (ready glued).

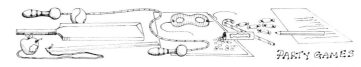

Charades

Divide your guests into two teams. Give each team a list of suitable subjects – book or film titles, etc – and a few minutes to think about them. Then each team acts them to the other team, within a set time limit. Whichever team guesses the most titles is the winner. Doing it in teams avoids the embarrassment of individual people having to act the charades.
Props: None.

Apple Bobbing

A very suitable game for a Hallowe'en party. Play this game in the kitchen, or outside if the party is in the summer. Place a large bowl of water on the floor and float some apples in it. The guests kneel down with their hands behind their backs, and pick up the apples with their teeth. If your bowl is large enough you can have more than one person kneeling beside the bowl at a time. See who can pick out the most apples within a particular time limit.
Props: Large bowl; apples; something water resistant to put bowl on (a PVC cloth); towel to wipe faces.

Apple Variation

Using a skewer, pierce the apple through the core and thread a piece of string through the hole. Knot at the bottom and attach the string to a pole (eg, a broom handle balanced between two chairs). The children kneel down, with their hands behind their backs, and see which of them can eat an apple first. This may also be played using rolls or doughnuts, instead of apples. Push a skewer through the centre of the roll or bun, and thread the string through, tying the end of the string back on the broom handle.
Props: Broom stick; string; apples; skewer or similar. Poultry or upholstery needle for threading string.

Smarties in a Dish

Place some Smarties in a large bowl, give each guest a straw and a small plate. Have a time limit. The idea is for them to transfer the Smarties from the bowl to the plate without using their hands, by sucking the Smarties up one at a time, at the end of the straw. Whoever has the most Smarties on their plate at the end of the time limit is the winner. A less expensive version of this game can be played with dried peas or beans.
Props: Smarties, dish; straws; plates.

Jar of Smarties

Place a certain number of Smarties or other sweets in a glass jar before the party. The children have to guess how many Smarties are in the jar, and whoever guesses the nearest to the correct number wins the Smarties.
Props: Lots of Smarties (you can buy giant tubes); jar; pencil and paper to list names and guesses.

Shopping List

Sit the children in a ring. The first child says, 'I went shopping and I bought . . . a cabbage.' Number two says, 'I went shopping and I bought a cabbage and some toothpaste.' Number three adds to the list until someone forgets the correct list, and they are out. The game continues until a winner is found.
Props: None.

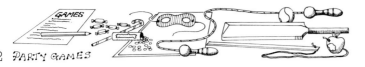

Bun Fight (not really!)

Take a long piece of string or garden twine and a piece per guest of a smaller length of string. Allow half a currant bun per guest, and make a hole in each half. Thread the buns with the short pieces of string and knot underneath. Then tie each of these pieces, leaving about 1 foot (30 cm) between, to the long string. Two helpers hold either end of the long string, and the children try to eat the buns as they dangle there. The helpers can jerk the string about a little while the guests are trying to eat.

Props: Long piece of string or garden twine; small pieces of similar; half currant bun per guest; 2 helpers.

Shoeing the Horse

Divide the children into two teams. Place a chair in front of each team, and by it four washing powder measuring cups. Blindfold one member of each team, who then has to try to put the cups underneath the legs of the chair. Each member of the teams has to do this, and the first team to finish is the winner.

Props: 8 washing powder cups, or similar; 2 chairs (NB, with legs that will fit in the cups); 2 blindfolds. Have plenty of extra cups in case any get broken.

Jigsaw Game

Allow three Christmas cards per guest. Cut each card into four pieces, and keep one piece of each card back, but hide the rest around the house. The children are then given the piece you hold, to find its lost parts. Once they have found one complete card, give them another single piece and repeat. Whoever gets most cards wins the game.

Props: Old Christmas cards.

Around the World

Using about fifteen place names, have pieces of paper around the room, with different cities or countries in the world written on each piece. Have one 'Home'. Each guest is given a list containing the names of these places, but each list is written in a different order. The children start from Home and have to run to each place according to the order on their list. When they go to each place, they tick that one off. The first child to complete the list and run Home wins.

Props: 15 place names; Blu-tack; a list of the names for each child (NB, in different orders); pencil per guest.

Pass the Parcel with Forfeits

Have a list of forfeits, one per person. Wrap up the parcel with as many sheets of paper as there are guests (but without sweets between the layers). When the music stops, whoever is holding the parcel has to perform a forfeit – kiss his or her neighbour, do a head stand, hop around the circle on the outside, eat a biscuit in one minute, say your eight times table (do be kind though – it's agony if your mind goes blank), sing a song.

Props: 1 parcel wrapped in many layers of paper; list of forfeits; music.

Team Tickles

Divide your guests into two teams. Have two very long pieces of string (the length depends on the number of your guests) with a dessert-spoon tied to the end of each piece. The first team member has to 'thread' the spoon through their clothes, downwards, and pass the spoon to the next member, who threads it through their clothes upwards. NB, the first person has to hold on to the end of the piece of string so that it doesn't get pulled through and out. The first team to sit down, all joined together, is the winner.

Props: 2 very long pieces of string; 2 dessert-spoons.

Hearts, Diamonds, Clubs, Spades

Each corner of the room is named by a card from each suit. Play some music and everyone must run around the room to the music. When the music stops, the children run to any corner that they choose. An organizer cuts a pack of cards and if a heart, for instance, is turned up, then the children in that corner are disqualified. Continue until a winner is found.

Props: Blu-tack; a pack of cards; music.

Chocolate Chopping

Children sit in a circle. Place in the centre one large bar of chocolate, on a plate, with a knife and fork. Also place by them a pair of gloves, a hat and scarf. The guests throw a dice (one turn each). Whoever throws a six rushes to put on the clothes and attempts to chop and eat some of the chocolate with the knife and fork. This operation must take place before another six is thrown, otherwise the turn is forfeit and the clothes are grabbed by the next child in an attempt to chop the chocolate.

Props: 2 large bars of chocolate (unwrapped); plate; knife and fork; hat; scarf; 1 pair of gloves.

In-between Games

We hope that you will have sufficient games here not to have children hanging around and getting bored, and waiting for the next game to start. However, when the children are 'out', here are some thoughts for games to keep them amused, until the main game has finished. Have plenty of Pocketeers on the side – pocket games, electronic games if you have them. A game of Bagatelle or table football is always popular, so long as you have sufficient room. There is a very amusing game you can buy called Twisters which any number can play. Again you need space. If you have sufficient help, as we suggested for the younger children, perhaps someone could be organizing the straw and Smartie game, or guessing the Smarties in a jar (page 111).

Outdoor games for older children

The former games can of course be played outside, but the following are specifically for outdoor parties. For most of these games you need either 2 long pieces of garden twine, string, or washing line as start and finish lines.

Boys' Adventure Dash or Assault Course

This is a very good game for energetic chaps to play before tea. It needs to be prepared before the party, and will depend very much on the size and shape of your garden, and also on the play equipment you can provide. Prepare a course with about ten obstacles to be tackled. You could either play this as a team event, having two identical courses, and whichever team completes the course first in the right order wins; or using a stop watch, time each individual child and whoever is fastest wins. Have a few adults around in case any of the children get into difficulties. Here are some suggestions for the course:

1. Throw a ball into a bucket. (2 balls; 2 buckets)

2. Climb through a tyre (hanging up) or an open ended barrel. (2 tyres or barrels)

3. Score a goal. (2 balls; 2 goals made with 4 bean poles)

4. Run along a board, balanced on two lying-down tyres, or two bales of straw. (2 boards, straw or tyres)

5. High jump. (3 thin bean poles for each jump: and 2 clothes pegs. Attach pegs to 2 of poles to make 2 rests. Use third pole to lie across)

6. Long jump. (4 pieces twine or plastic covered line etc)

7. Jump a set distance in a sack, or with feet tied together with a duster. (2 dustbin liners or 2 dusters)

8. Run with an egg and spoon (potato and dessertspoon) a long or short distance, and back again to place the spoon ready for the next member of the team. If anyone drops the potato they have to start again.

9. If you have an assault course rope ladder, then up and down once.

10. Climb a rope ladder, and touch a specific point.

11. Stepping stones – place several bricks or breeze blocks in a line as stepping stones.

12. Dribble a ball around bending poles. (2 balls and several bean poles)

13. Run on stilts. You can buy mini stilts or make them yourself before the party. For each pair of stilts you will need two identical sized cocoa or other cans (do not use ones which have been opened by a can opener, in case of accidents with jagged edges); 2 pieces of thick string or washing line, each about 2 feet (60 cm) long; a skewer or similar piercing instrument. Make two holes on either side of each can, thread your string through the can and join it to make a large loop. The children can then balance on the can and use the loop part as the stilt.

14. A somersault at the finishing post.

Throwing the Wellie

You need a lot of space for this game. Have any number of old tyres or hoops, and number these 10, 4, 2, etc. The children throw the wellies from a starting line into the tyres or hoops. Whoever has the highest score wins.
Props: Markers for points; tyres/hoops etc; lots of boots; score sheet.

Matchbox Hunt

Let the children either play in pairs or as individuals. Give each child or pair a match-box. Tell them to find as many things as they can fit into the matchbox in 2 minutes. Whoever collects most is the winner.
Props: 1 matchbox per guest or pair.

Pitch and Putt

This is a surprisingly difficult game, and suitable for older children only. Allow two children to have their turns together (or play as a team game). The children stand behind a line and chip golf balls into the following: a tyre, box, paddling pool, or a circle painted on the ground. Don't put these too far away. Each target must have a score marker by it, with different scores. Whoever gets the highest score wins. Allow one or two shots at each target. Children retrieve their balls after their turn and the next guest has a try.
Props: Golf balls and suitable clubs; targets and their score markers – old bamboo sticks slit with paper markers; score sheet and pencils; washing line for base line; short grass (that's not too precious!).

Shipwreck

Choose a child to be 'He'. The 'He' chases the other children who are only safe when off the ground, on straw bales, rugs, newspapers, etc, which serve as islands. If a child is touched by the 'He', while not on an island, then that guest takes over and chases the others. There is no real winner to this game, it can go on until you think the children have had enough.
Props: Depends on how you want to play the game.

Dressing-up Game

Before the party prepare two hats, two jackets or large shirts, two skirts or baggy trousers, and two pairs of grown-up size wellington boots. Divide the guests into two teams and have them queue up behind the starting line. For each team lay out, first, the hat, then a few yards further off the shirt, then the skirt or trousers ending up with the boots. Mark the end of the course with a stick or beanpole. The children have to run up one by one, put the clothes on, run around the end of the course marker, back again and take the clothes off in the opposite order, boots first, then the skirt or trousers, and finally the hat. Each member of the two teams does the same thing, and whichever team finishes first is the winner.
Props: Clothes as noted above.

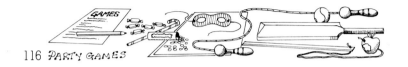

Sack Race

Have one sack per guest, or use only two sacks, and divide the guests into two teams, making it into a team sack race.
Props: Sacks – if real sacks cannot be found, use dustbin liners (but they're not so durable).

Three-legged Race

Have plenty of large men's handkerchiefs or dusters, and pair the children off. Tie their inside legs together.
Props: Hanky or duster per pair of guests.

Wheelbarrow Race

Play this game before tea, or not until well after tea. Again pair the children off. One acts as the wheelbarrow, walking on his or her hands, and one as the 'pusher', holding the 'wheelbarrow's' legs.
Props: None.

Tug of War

This is particularly good fun when you have a tug of war between boys and girls. You can mark a line over which one team has to pull the other to win, but usually it's just the energetic pulling that's appreciated! Use a washing line for the rope.
Props: Washing line.

Slow Bicycle Race

Divide the guests into two teams. Each team needs a bicycle. Individual members of the team bike to a certain point in the garden and back, as slowly as possible. The team to finish last wins.
Props: 2 bicycles; 2 markers.

Balloon Race

Allow two blown up balloons per child, and slip an elastic band securely round the knot so it forms a loop. Children attach a balloon to each ankle with the elastic band. When the whistle blows they race to the winning line – without falling over or bursting their balloons.
Props: Two balloons per child; elastic bands.

French Cricket

There is no winner with this game, but children enjoy playing it. Someone stands with either a tennis racket or a cricket bat. Using a tennis ball the other children try to get the batsman out, by hitting his legs below the knees. If the batsman hits the ball he can turn to face the way the ball will be coming back at him. If however he has missed it, he is not allowed to do this.
Props: Always use a soft tennis ball; a tennis racquet or cricket bat.

It's a Knock Out

(Girls' version of the assault course, page 114). The course needs to be prepared before the party, and as with the assault course will depend very much on the size of your garden, and the equipment you can provide. Play this as a two-team event. Here are some ideas for the course:

1. Throw tennis ball into bucket.
2. Climb through a tyre.
3. High jump.
4. Long jump.
5. Sack jumping (a dustbin liner).
6. Dressing up in huge wellington boots, a skirt and a hat, then getting on stilts in fancy dress.
7. Stepping stones in fancy dress.
8. Ping pong balls into plate, in fancy dress. They have to suck with a straw to lift a ping pong ball on to a plate.
9. 5 skips in fancy dress, with skipping rope.
10. Undress, run back to team, with egg and spoon.
Props: See page 114 for stilts and stepping stones; 2 pairs of wellingtons (large); clothes, etc; tennis balls; buckets; tyres; etc.

Garden Hunt

This is an outdoor version of the Treasure Hunt (page 108). Prepare and play it in the same way, the only difference being that as cards or pieces of paper are likely to blow away out of doors, you should make sure that the clue cards are firmly secured (to a branch, under a pot, etc) and, instead of numbered cards, use lengths of different coloured thread, wool or string (red for the first clue, blue for the second and so on), which the children bring back to you. Suggestions for clues:

In sand pit
Around garden tap
Under bucket
Beside bicycle
Under flower pot
On branch of tree
Under greenhouse door
Under stone
Under garden seat
Beside steps

Props: Pieces of wool; cards etc.

5.OTHER PARTY IDEAS

If you want a change from the conventional tea party, give either a lunch, barbecue, picnic, high tea or supper party instead. You can have these in tandem with treats for older children – visits to the theatre, films, seaside or a conjurer at home. Whether you want large or smaller numbers of guests these parties will be great fun, and at the end of this section we give ideas on appropriate types of food.

Barbecues

If you have a portable or in-built barbecue in your garden this is an ideal way to entertain older children in the summer – children love to eat out of doors and barbecued food is wonderfully easy to cook and serve. Arrange to have at least two adults around – one to cook and one to supervise the children – and of course it goes without saying that none of the children should go near the lighted barbecue.

It is very important to light the barbecue at least one hour before you need to start the cooking as this will give the charcoal plenty of time to heat up so that the food will cook quickly without burning. The flames should have died down leaving a mass of red embers before you start the cooking. There is nothing worse than chicken drumsticks or sausages that are raw in the middle, unless it is hungry children standing around while you prod the food! It is quite acceptable to use a firelighter to light the barbecue, but again be sure to allow plenty of time for the smell to wear off. Just before you start the cooking sprinkle some fresh or dried herbs or a spray of sage or rosemary over the charcoal – this smells delicious and gives the meat a lovely flavour. You can pre-cook the food indoors, earlier, and just finish off on the barbecue, especially if you are catering for larger numbers.

Food

Keep the food simple; in any case all food tastes twice as good when cooked out of doors. Have everything prepared in advance, so that you can get straight on with the cooking when the time comes. Aim to provide a selection of food so that each guest can have one or two or three of the following ideas. Cook some extra as well in case seconds are needed. Sausages, chicken drumsticks, beef-burgers, spare ribs, small lamb chops, kebabs made of lamb or pork with mushrooms or sausage pieces in between the meat. Kebabs made with turkey meat are an excellent idea now that turkey is available in pieces. Brush oil over the meat before and during the cooking. Season the oil, if you like, with finely chopped herbs and salt and pepper. Many children like garlic, so if you decide to use it, press it through a garlic crusher and mix it with the oil before starting the cooking.

With the meat serve some simple salads

which you will have made before your guests arrive, small baked potatoes (to be cooked in your oven unless you have a very large barbecue and masses of time) or garlic, herb or peanut bread, prepared in advance, wrapped in foil and put in the oven 40 minutes before you plan to eat. Serve a simple barbecue sauce or just tomato sauce.

When it comes to puddings, again keep them simple and prepare them in advance. If your barbecue is a birthday party, then try one of the ice cream cakes on pages 73–75. Strawberries or raspberries when in season would be a special treat served with ice cream or a meringue. A simple fruit salad or ice cream served with Mars Bar sauce (page 120) would be a popular way to finish the meal – be prepared for lots of seconds.

Lunch, High Tea or Supper Parties

When your children reach the age of, say, eight and upwards you might find it more convenient to provide a meal other than a tea party. Perhaps you are planning a visit to a zoo, a pantomime or a cinema, and want to combine this with a meal that can be prepared in advance and served up quickly. In this case lunch or high tea is the best answer. Or, again, if you have older children who might dominate the little ones, then give a lunch party for the tinies while the others are at school, but remember to save some of the party food for when the older ones come home so that they won't feel left out. In this case it can be just as much of a party as a tea party if you organize games before and after the meal (see the games chapter) and use some of our ideas from the rest of this book on decorations, prizes, going-home presents and so on.

High tea is a simple meal to prepare and serve, and if you have been out on an expedition the children will probably want a rapid 'warm-up', so have everything prepared beforehand and the table set so that you won't be in a muddle on your return. If you decide on, for instance, a stew as a main course then you could leave this with jacket potatoes in a slow oven while you are out. Don't plan to have a meal that takes a long time to heat through on your return with the starving masses. Beefburgers in rolls or with oven chips are popular; so too are sandwiches made with a sandwich maker if you have one – add some chutney for extra flavour – but keep this for small numbers.

Use flapjacks, shortbread, etc, from the tea party food section, and leave on the tea table covered with cling film, but don't bother with ordinary sandwiches. If it has been a freezing afternoon, or early evening, some children may like hot chocolate to drink, but ask before preparing gallons as some do not like hot drinks. Otherwise, large 2 litre bottles of Coke and a soft alternative would be fine, or try a more adventurous drink (pages 95–97). Have a cake to fit in with your outing and having had a good warm through maybe an ice cream cake as a pudding would be fun – a Mars Bar sauce (page 120) served hot on the ice cream would make it even more delicious.

Whilst you are getting everything organized why not have the children playing some games – plan suitable ones beforehand – so that they are not around your feet.

When little girls are about eight, a real treat is to give a later party – say 5.30 to 8.00 pm, or if at a weekend, 7.30 in case parents are themselves wanting to go out – and make it a supper party instead of tea. It is best done in the winter, as darkness is important: a candle-lit dinner makes them feel extremely grown-

up! Above all else it is important that everything looks very pretty. Use paper plates and cups, etc, and keep a colour theme for your table: 'pink party' would be effective with pink candles, little posies of pink and white flowers (keep them tiny) on the table, pink paper napkins, pink and white streamers around the room etc. Keep everything dainty and small – to girls of this age, small is beautiful! Use tiny flowers, give tiny presents to go home – little scented rubbers or tiny little lavender bags you could make out of remnants. Have some games or perhaps a little home-made disco when the children arrive, followed by supper – which we found took them hours, they ate masses, and we were amazed! – and then you could have a conjurer or film show to end the evening off. This may sound as if it is a lot of work – it actually isn't and they love to feel sophisticated, some arriving in their long dresses. Whatever soft or fizzy drink, you serve, it must be called 'wine!'

Food

As far as food is concerned children like what they know, so keep it familiar. You don't want the party spoilt by your guests refusing to eat your food, but as it is a party make it just that bit more special and take extra care in preparing and serving it so that it looks both appetizing and attractive. Some of these ideas are more suitable for lunch-time parties, some are better for high teas or supper parties, but you can make your choice accordingly. Most of them can be prepared in advance, and need only last minute final touches.

First course

Shepherd's Pie – top with a layer of sliced or grated cheese to make a crunchy topping
Chicken and Mushroom Pies – to add a special touch why not make individual pies

Potato Moussaka – layers of cooked mince, sliced cooked potatoes, and cheese sauce
Savoury Pancakes – filled with chicken and ham in sauce
Grilled Gammon and Pineapple
Roast Chicken and Chipolatas – make it a roast turkey for large numbers
Chicken in Sauce – served with mashed potatoes piped round the edge of the dish
Turkey and Ham Croquettes
Spaghetti Bolognese
Beef Stew
Sausages in a Bacon Blanket – grill sausages, wrap rashers of streaky bacon round sausages, secure with a skewer or cocktail sticks, put under grill, turning once
Baked Potatoes – scoop out the insides, mash them with butter, cheese and chopped ham, and brown under the grill
Vols-au-vent.

Serve these with simple vegetables, for instance, oven chips, peas and baby carrots, coleslaw or a salad full of chopped dates, raisins, cubes of cheese, orange segments, hardboiled eggs, etc (children love lots of these).

Puddings

An ice cream cake – see pages 73–75. Make it in advance, keep in the freezer and take it out when required.
Apple Meringue – colour both the apple and the meringue pink
Fruit Salad in a melon basket
Pineapple – cut lengthways, served in its skin and decorated with glacé cherries
Chocolate Lemon Cups – see page 81
Chocolate, lemon or orange mousse
Ice cream and Mars Bar sauce – just chop Mars Bar into pan with a little water, and stir constantly over a gentle heat

Knickerbocker Glory
Cheesecake
Meringue Pavlova – filled with strawberries or raspberries and decorated with whipped cream
Mandarin and melon balls – this could also be a starter for the supper party.

Picnics

Organization is the key to a picnic party. If you are planning a visit to a castle, zoo or adventure park, check the opening times – and the open season! A trip to the seaside would be lovely, but don't go so far afield to make the day too long for all concerned. Plan to play a few games in the car and organize a few outdoor games to fill in any gaps, when you arrive at the destination. You cannot afford to leave things behind, and to avoid an irate husband, make a careful check list of all the food, drink and etceteras, you will need. Only ask numbers that can be seated comfortably. You can just take a party to the local park or woods for a picnic tea – it will save a lot of mess at home. Have sufficient helpers, especially if you are walking there, crossing roads clutching the picnic basket and a dozen little hands.

What To Take

Kitchen towels or paper napkins, damp J cloths in plastic bag; plastic bag for rubbish; basic first aid kit; Waspeze or insect repellant spray (incense sticks help too); sun tan cream; rugs to sit on; bottle opener (cork screw if required!); a spare set of children's clothes; ball, especially if taking boys; whistle to round up the troops. Collect these things in a washing-up bowl, which itself could be invaluable if someone feels carsick. Take a telephone number of a parent who could let others know if you are delayed and will be home late.

Food

The easiest way to give a picnic meal is to pack a 'nose bag' for each child. You may find bits of food are wasted but it takes all the hassle out of saving the 'bits and bobs' of a picnic. Collect up plastic margarine or ice cream $\frac{1}{2}$ litre boxes or similar and pack each with the food.

For picnic, take (per child): lunch

Packet of crisps; cold chipolata sausage; cold chicken drumstick (you can buy frozen drumsticks in packs very reasonably); a few sticks of carrot and cucumber; small tomato if firm (but can be messy); small roll (buttered); small apple or banana; mini Mars or similar, or mini box of raisins. If you want to do a pudding, take in addition individual pots of yogurt or lemon mousse for each child in old yogurt pots and take plastic spoons. Simplest of all buy an ice cream each.

For tea

Two sandwiches (make two sorts and give one of each); flapjack; brownie; chipolata; sausage roll; packet of hula hoops; avoid melting chocolate biscuits and give a KP chocolate dip to each; if not taking a large birthday cake why not give each a separate cup cake (perhaps piped with the child's name); small apple; mini packet of Smarties, Twix, or similar.

As far as drinks are concerned take a flask of plain water (can be very handy if only to give the dog a drink); fizzy drinks can cause fizzy 'tums', so avoid in large quantities. Buy individual cans or cartons of juices plus straws. Take extra flasks of soft drinks and use old yogurt or cream pots for glasses.

Index

PARTIES

FOR OLDER CHILDREN

Angela Hollest

Penelope Gaine

To David, Edward and Clare
and Michael, David and Daniel

Acknowledgements

We would like to thank Christine Curzon, who typed the manuscript (again and again!), as well as our very generous friends and their children, who gave us so much vital information, especially Anna, Nick and Vivienne, Rosie, Delia, Cherry, Melissa, Maggie, Sue, Pam and Trish.

Contents

Introduction

'I am never giving another party!' We know the feeling! But if you use this book, it should help you through all the minefields so that you can give a party which *everyone* can enjoy. Between the ages of eight and fourteen, children begin to grow up (and parents to grow old!), and if this means a delicious new taste of independence for children, it should mean the same for parents too. However, it's not quite so simple, and there are problems ahead, which is why we decided this book was needed. We have only been able to write it because of our own experiences and because so many generous friends, children and adults alike, have passed on their tips, traumas, and triumphs! It is, we hope, a comprehensive and well-tried guide, and all our suggestions can be adapted to suit your lifestyle.

We have included in the first part of the book many ideas for different types of parties. If you are holding a disco party – don't be appalled at the thought – follow the plan of campaign and you will come through with flying colours. Discuss with your children how your ideas and theirs can sensibly be reconciled, and remember *both* sides must be prepared to listen and be reasonable. We give hints for large-scale party venues, invitations, decorations, plus ideas for food (with shopping-list quantities) and drinks, including the to-be and not-to-be of alcohol for the older age group.

Smaller supper and dinner parties can be quickly organised. If you want to have a theme, there are suggestions on suitable invitations, decorations and mad party food and drink (from pink chicken to green cocktails!). Incorporate a mini disco or play some of the hilarious games that we describe.

Daytime events can be just as enjoyable. Have a match party – football, cricket, rounders, tennis, swimming, etc – or play outdoor games, including an assault course or bike gymkhana. The competitive spirit need not be too obvious – run the party efficiently and it will be great fun even for the less games-minded children. Provide one of our scrumptious teas and lunches or give a sizzling barbecue.

Take a group of friends on an outing party – skating, swimming, etc – or you could go to watch soccer, horse shows, a performance at the theatre, or the animals at a safari park. We give you masses of suggestions, together with do-it-yourself menus for picnics and snacks, or where to go if you want to stop off with a crowd of children. There are plenty of car games to keep you all busy en route.

Another form of party is a family get-together, and you should always involve the children: they can help to set the table or choose and even cook the food – nothing grand, our motto being 'Keep it simple'! Use Hogmanay, Hallowe'en, Guy Fawkes, the Grand National, half-term – anything as an excuse for a party with your own or with other families.

All the recipes for food and drinks are in the second half of the book. Always try and prepare as much of the food as you can ahead of the party. There is a huge choice – decide from the menu in the text what you want to serve, and then turn to the back of the book when you come to the nitty-gritty of cooking. Don't panic! We keep it simple – we are mothers too.We also have a huge section on fun drinks, obviously mostly non-alcoholic. However, there are some others for older children's parties if required. There are also a few ideas for home-made sweets, which could serve as prizes or going-home presents.

Children's parties need not be an extravagant luxury. They can be organised without vast expense, and they do have a function. They teach children to socialise easily, to relax with adults and contemporaries, and to have a giggle, letting their hair down, but still under control. As children get older they will learn to introduce friends to one another, to make sure everyone is enjoying themselves, and not to be hyper-sensitive if they are not invited to a party down the road! You can't always invite everyone.

Keep a party file and include information re addresses and ages of guests, ideas you used for parties, and food you have served. It will be invaluable for future reference, especially if you want ideas for younger children. It's so hard to remember what you did, when, and for how many, etc – and if a friend of ours had not kept such a file some important hints would not have been included in this book.

Our aim has been to give you all a practical, diverse and economical, but above all, *fun* party book. Have a great time!

Angela Hollest
Penelope Gaine
May 1986

Disco Parties

If you are thinking of giving a large party, why not share the strain and give a joint one with friends? You can then pool ideas, skills and guests. This is particularly helpful if you want to have boys and girls but don't know too many children of the opposite sex to your child. So long as the hosts and hostesses all get on together, and are the same age group, it is actually great fun for them too. Giving this type of party is not particularly cheap, however, and dividing the cost is another incentive for sharing the occasion. However, if you want to hold a smaller disco party for younger children, incorporate it with a supper party (see page 21).

Party Preparations

VENUE

One of the main drawbacks of sharing a party is deciding on a venue. In many ways a totally independent hall or club that you could use is the ideal if the party is to be a large one. However, if you are planning to use one of the hosts' homes, then remember that it is inevitable that the guests will tend to think of the party as being given by those whose home it is. To help the others feel involved, why not let the replies to the invitations be sent to their houses? But *do* make sure that there is no confusion as to where the party will eventually be held by wording the invitation very clearly.

If you are giving the party in a hired hall you will probably need to book it very early, so find out who is in charge of running the place and contact them before doing anything else (see also page 11). It is probably best to avoid weekends and hold the party on a week night in the holidays, as your hall will be more likely to be available in the week, and it may help also to avoid gatecrashers.

Other points to remember are to check that the electrics are suitable for a discothèque, and also to ensure that the heating or ventilation (if the party is in the summer) are both adequate. Look at the kitchen and equipment, and especially the hot water supply. Make a list of the things you will need to bring with you (see page 19 for check list). Check the cloakroom facilities too. Don't forget to ask the caretaker at what time you will be able to get into the hall to prepare the decorations, transport food, etc. Also enquire about insurance for the hall.

We do not suggest that you put up large notices advertising that your party is being held in the building, as gatecrashers can be a problem. If you are in the country and people are coming from a long way away, why not photocopy an Ordnance Survey map. Or simply send diagrams to show your guests exactly where the party is being held.

If possible, choose a hall that is not too near a pub. If you do have to, then make sure a father can 'police' outside the hall to avoid gatecrashers and boys going from the party to the pub to buy drinks. It's amazing what they can get up to!

In many ways it is preferable, and of course

cheaper, to have your party at home, depending on the numbers you have invited. Even garages and barns can be transformed with some imaginative decorations, although you can still hit problems. Is the room large enough to accommodate equipment, children and noise? Is the electricity supply suitable for whatever form of music you are using, whether a group, disco or someone's hi-fi, and lighting? Similarly, can you heat whatever room you choose if necessary, and if it rains, is it feasible to transport food, plates, etc, etc? Remember you will need space for serving tables (for food and bar) as well as the disco.

If you don't have outside lighting to show the way to the party room, night lights in jam jars (see page 57) will be perfectly adequate, so long as you have someone available to replenish them if necessary and so long as it doesn't pour with rain! Have some torches to hang up if necessary. Also, you can buy (but they are expensive) very effective garden flares.

Another problem which might arise by having your party at home is that of neighbours being disturbed. This can probably be overcome by a diplomatic warning and perhaps a small box of chocs being presented prior to the event. Give some truffles or fudge (see page 122) made by the children – very endearing.

When it comes to teenage parties, many people experience problems if they hold the party in their house. The larger the party, obviously the more difficulties there can be. This is not to say that every party is going to turn into a disaster, far from it. However, it is only fair on both parents and children to face the fact that sometimes guests get carried away and do not respect other people's property and homes as parents expect they should. There is no point in causing mammoth rows and frustrations between children and

parents over something which should have been great fun. So get together before the party and really discuss with your children what has happened at other parties they have been to, and what opinion they have of giving the party in their own home. We think it is up to the parents to remember what they got up to when they were young and be tolerant, and up to the children to understand that parents are only expecting reasonable behaviour and not trying to be fuddy-duddies. If holding the party in the garage saves a wrecked carpet, frayed tempers, and means everyone wants another party next year, then forego the comforts of having it in the sitting room.

This is not meant to sound all gloom and doom! Be prepared and it will never happen!

THE DISCOTHÈQUE

If your children have been to plenty of local disco parties, they will probably know who will provide the very best music. Maybe some elder brother runs a disco as a hobby. This would no doubt be a lot cheaper than a professional, but don't forget that it will be the music and the disco that make the party and it would be a false economy to spoil the event by choosing the wrong one. Check the following points when initially booking:

1. If you are holding your party at home, you may find that a room you thought was perfectly adequate in size might be quite unsuitable – for example, the ceiling might be too low, and the noise of the discothèque might therefore be unbearable. Do discuss the size of the room and the amount of space the actual equipment will require, to see whether it is feasible or not.
2. Check that the electrics you can provide are suitable. If the venue is in a garage, for instance, then it is probably best if the disc jockey comes and inspects the system to

check everything is correct, well in advance of the event.

3. Ask what he will be bringing in the way of extras – a strobe, a bubble machine etc – and what the extras will cost.

4. Discuss the age group you are entertaining. The disc jockey is the one who will have to keep the party going, and when the children are young, up to the age of about ten, it may be worth including the odd game like Disco Knees or Islands (see page 18).

5. Check on the time that the disc jockey will arrive before the party starts.

6. Check that he knows the way. Give him a map if there is *any* query.

7. Write everything down that you discuss and send a letter confirming the arrangements, having taken a copy first.

8. Query whether you may have to provide a deposit on booking the disco. Also check his insurance.

PARTY THEMES

Having organised your venue and the disco, probably the next most important thing to do is to decide whether you are having a theme for your party. This can affect the invitations, decorations and food. It seems that the older the children get, the less likely they are to enjoy any sort of dressing-up at parties. However, you can have themes which involve whatever degree of dressing up they want – a Black and White party, Razzle Dazzle, Dress to Impress, Dress to Dazzle, St Trinians, Glitter and Gleam, Outrageous Dress, Funky Punk, Shimmer and Shine, Down and Outs, Red, White and Blue, Multicoloured, 1920s, 1950s, Gender Bender, Horror party, etc . Don't forget seasonal parties, for example a Red and Green Christmas party, Dress to Sparkle for Guy Fawkes, Spooky Spoofs and Ghosts and Ghouls for Hallowe'en; Valentine parties are good as well.

Up to about the age of eleven, children will not mind dolling themselves up but will want to know what everyone else is wearing, so do make that clear on your invitation. Remember what you would have felt like if you had been sent off to a party in the wrong clothes at that age!

After about eleven you will probably find that they will not 'dress up' in the same way. This is up to you and your children to organise between you – the children will know what's what! They will keep you up to date on what's new; ideas date so quickly that you should always be prepared to take advice from the young.

INVITATIONS

If you are giving a large party don't forget how time-consuming it is to write out all the invitations. Remember how long it takes to do all those Christmas cards! If you are sharing this party then maybe you will all decide to take on a certain number each, or perhaps one person who isn't very good at making decorations, say, could organise all the invitations and someone else do the decorations, etc but that is up to all of you to decide. Obviously the children can be roped in and may like to undertake the invitations themselves. If they have time, then that is fine, but do all of you go through the shortlist and check the envelopes off, before final posting. Make sure that, if the venue and the RSVP addresses are different, this is very clear. You don't want half the party arriving at an empty house.

Even if a lot of the invitations will be handed out at school, have all the addresses and, if possible, telephone numbers written down in case of a drama. One small point: when we have shared parties, we did agree that if one of the hosts (children that is) was ill, the others would carry on with the party. This obviously depends on the venue and circumstances, but do discuss it between yourselves beforehand so that there are no misunderstandings.

While preparing your guest list, remember not to mix the ages too much. You would probably find that twelve-year-olds would not be pleased to find masses of nine-year-olds at the same party! Think back – you would not have invited many three-year-olds to a six-year-old's tea party. The principle still applies! Keep two separate lists of boys and girls with clear columns to tick who is coming and who is not. You can see quickly and clearly how numbers are going. Always invite some extra boys anyway.

DATE PITFALLS

The decision of when to hold the party will probably dictate how many children will be on your initial guest list. For example, giving a party in the summer holidays can be a real problem and you may want to ask extra numbers to allow for many children being away. August is obviously the worst month of all – there could be a one-third refusal rate – so if possible it is best to plan for a date near to everybody going back to school. There is quite an exodus too in the Easter holidays, now that so many schools and families go skiing then, so check carefully before choosing a date. The Christmas holidays have a natural party atmosphere and in many ways it is the best time to give a party, but remember that *you* will have Christmas to cope with too, so unless you are ultra-efficient or going away for Christmas itself, we suggest you hold the party at the very beginning, or end, of the holidays.

Always try and check as best you can that there isn't going to be another major school or local event that would coincide and diminish your numbers. It's always better for a disco to

seem a bit crowded, so do invite enough people to fill your room.

THE INVITATIONS THEMSELVES

Perhaps your children have specific ideas as to what they want their invitations to look like. Do persuade them to be practical. An elaborate design done by hand may be fine for the smaller event, but if you are contemplating inviting well over 100 children the exercise will become tedious! One way around that problem is to design a single invite and then photocopy it. (Local libraries or office stationers offer this service.) If the photocopy paper is flimsy then make it into a stand-up card rather than a single piece of paper, and remember to allow for this when taking your photocopies. The children could either draw or stencil designs on the corners, or wherever they choose. After the invitations have been printed they could

David & Tim invite you to a
Tennis Party in the park at 4.30
Bring your kit

CLARE CLARKE AND EDWARD JAMES
invite you to a
SPARKLING PARTY
at 1, The Priory
on Thursday 1st September
7.30 pm until 11.30 pm
Dress to Dazzle
Supper
RSVP
4 St Helen's
Trumpington

come to Janet's
VALENTINE PARTY
14 February 7.30   RSVP

TIMING

It seems easiest to plan your party timing backwards, so that if it ends early it should start sooner, and vice versa. Deciding on the time a party ends is a very personal matter, and if it is an oldest child's party one is somehow more aware that it is long past bedtime! (As the eldest often moans, life is much easier for the younger children as parents' attitudes soften!) If the party is for young children – say ten-year-olds – and especially if it is in term-time, then you will probably feel that 10 o'clock is late enough, so start at about 7 pm. Once the children are older, it can be later; as you are bothering to have the party at all, you might as well make it a late night, starting at 8 pm, say, and going on until midnight. Children hate to feel different and while we must not be governed by what others do, we should be sensitive to a child's feelings. If you are worried that it will all end too late, then leave the idea until next year and give an 'outing' party instead (see page 44).

either cut the edges with pinking shears or put some clear light adhesive (Bostik) on the paper and sprinkle it with glitter.

Printed invitations are obviously the least trouble, but more expensive. Go to local printers or phone up through the Yellow Pages and get quotes. Go down with your children to decide what typeface, colour and type of card you require (if you have a colour theme to your party, try to marry up the colour here). Take with you an ordinary postcard on which you have formulated all the information you wish to include. It is possible to have a rough copy printed, so that you can look at it and double-check that everything is correct before the final print is run off. It costs a bit extra but might save you having to alter every invitation. Obviously, you will be asking more children than you expect to come to the party, but order more invitations than guests you intend to invite: whoever writes the invitations will probably make the odd mistake, and you might also think of some extra guests after the other invitations have been sent out.

Check that the size of the card will fit a POP (Post Office Preferred) standard envelope so that you can buy envelopes easily, and at a reasonable price.

DECORATIONS

No doubt you will have your own ideas about decorating your party room but here are a few general hints and ideas as guidelines. Don't forget that once the disco lighting is in full swing the decorations will not be as important as they appear in the cold light of day. However, your venue can be made to look attractive and fun without too much hassle. If you are having a theme to your party then tie in the decorations with this.

Make your decorations well in advance and have them sorted out ready to put up on the day, or the day before the party. It takes a lot longer than one imagines to plan, design and construct decorations, so leave yourselves sufficient time.

In general, if you are having your party in a hall, then consider the following:

1. How long beforehand will you have to decorate the room? You can't go mad if you only have two hours before the party starts.
2. Don't worry about the lighting if you are hiring a professional disco; they will provide their own lights and can hire extra ones if you think you need them.
3. If the hall is large remember that small decorations will not show up effectively.
4. The wall surface of your venue will determine what you can or want to put on it. Consider the size of the walls and the height of the ceiling when planning your decorations.
5. Have plenty of Blu-Tack, which is good as it does not damage wall surfaces if treated correctly. Double-sided sticky tape is very useful but do not use this on wall surfaces which would be damaged by the tape as it is extremely strong (although it does not stick well to wooden beams). Depending on whether or not it is appropriate to use them, have good strong drawing pins to hand. Remember to take a couple of pairs of scissors when you are putting your decorations up.

Posters. Maybe you could find suitable posters that are appropriate to your party theme. Or there is fantastic wrapping paper around which you could use instead.

Balloons. You can hang balloons around the room in clusters. Spray them with glitter for extra dazzle. Tie these clusters together with

pieces of parcel ribbon with strands hanging down (about 2 feet or 60 cm). Take a pair of scissors and run the back of them down the long strands, one at a time, very firmly, and the ribbon will go into curls and twirls. Suspend the clusters wherever you want.

If the ceiling is high and you want to make the atmosphere more 'cosy', see if it would be possible to string up vegetable netting as a balloon net and fill this with balloons. If you wish, and depending on the floor surface and the type of party, mix some balloons with water in them amongst the ordinary balloons. The balloons will all be stamped on at the end of the party, and our children thought it was very amusing when they went to a disco where this had been done! Do *not* fill the balloons with water too soon before the party as they sometimes burst more easily with the water in them. Be prepared for some wise guy to let down the balloons before the end of the party – either you mustn't mind, or make the net so difficult to undo that only you know the combination lock!

If you have a party shop near you (see Yellow Pages), you may be able to get hold of helium-filled balloons. These will be quite expensive but they are fun and if you have them as a centre piece floating up from a crossbeam they can look very attractive. They are usually foil on one side at least, so reflect the light well. If you are having a Valentine party then try and get hold of heart-shaped ones – remember them flying behind the Prince and Princess of Wales as they went off on their honeymoon?

Streamers. Don't ignore good old streamers, especially if you are having a colour theme. To save buying expensive streamers, you can easily make them out of crêpe paper. This is a very cheap way of decorating a large room, and the children can have great fun making them. Buy packets of crêpe paper – the amount and colour depending on your plans – and keep the paper folded as it is. Cut it across into 2 inch (5 cm) strips, then frill the edges by running the back of a pair of scissors down either side. Unwind the strips, join ends with double-sided sticky tape (expensive, but extremely strong and durable). Twist the strips and fasten around the walls and across the ceiling with Blu-Tack. (Try to put these decorations away carefully after the party – they may come in handy next time.)

Why not throw the very thin (and cheap) streamers which curl when you throw them over the streamers crossing the ceiling? You can buy these in packets of about eight from stationers' shops.

Coloured Card or Foil Shapes. These can be cut out into whichever shape you feel appropriate to your party, and Blu-Tacked to the walls and, if possible, the ceiling perhaps. A friend's daughter cut out huge hands and feet and stuck them all over the walls; as you can imagine, the footprints looked marvellous on the ceiling! If you were trying to decorate a very large hall this could be quite time-consuming and expensive to execute, and would be more appropriate, perhaps, in a garage or similar-sized room. However, use your imagination and choose whatever shape marries in with your theme, if you have one: for example, stars, moons and witches' hats for Hallowe'en; hearts for Valentines, etc.

If you are going to try and suspend foil shapes from the ceiling you would have to stiffen the foil because otherwise it would curl in the heat of the disco. Do this by gluing the foil to thin card. Alternatively, cover one wall completely with foil (if it's not too big) as this looks wonderful with the lights. Some dairies are happy to lend you the long strips of foil left over from making bottle tops, if you promise to return them the next day. With their cut-out holes, these are very decorative (and free!) and glitter in the lights.

Painted Branches or Twigs. It is very easy to emulsion-paint or spray-paint bare branches or twigs. If you wanted to fill an empty corner, put a branch (painted in whatever colour your party theme requires) into a tub, and use bricks to hold it in position. Fill the tub with sand. If the branch is very tall and still not 100 per cent secure, tie fishing line to it and attach to the wall on both sides to hold it in position.

Your branch can be decorated in any number of ways. Foil shapes can be made: cut two identical shapes from foil and glue these on to card of the same shape to avoid them curling in the heat. Make a hole at the top and thread cotton ties through to suspend it from the branch. You can also cut kitchen foil into strips long enough to tie into bows – the length will depend on the size you want the bows to be. Tie these bows all over the branches. You can use your Christmas tinsel on the 'tree' plus lights if you want and, of course, if you're giving a Christmas disco you must have a decorated tree in the room – it really adds to the atmosphere.

Food and Drink

The age of the children determines the type and amount of food you will provide, as well as its method of serving. Younger children will

Menu for the Youngest Age Group (per plate)

4 cocktail sausages
1 small packet crisps
A small handful nuts
1 satsuma (if Christmas time)
Half mini bridge roll
1 cheese straw boat with sail
1 cube cheese on stick
1 mini eclair
1 mini filled meringue

Break-time   Ice cream in cornet

B. Menu for the 'In-Betweens' (per plate)

1 chicken drumstick
2 cocktail sausages
3 cucumber sticks (3 inches or 7.5 cm long)
4 carrot sticks (3 inches or 7.5 cm long)
1 ham roll
1 packet crisps
2 cheese squares
1 finger pizza (cold)
Container of apples, bananas, seedless grapes
or satsumas
1 chocolate mousse

Break-time
Vanilla cornet with flakes

C. Menu for the Older Group

From about the age of twelve there is a change of atmosphere at parties, and instead of giving the children individual plates they like to help themselves to finger food from a main table, which they will want to wander up to as and when they choose. As with the other menus, check first with your children to see what sort of things they want. From about fourteen onwards you will find that the children want very little food indeed. You will have to be guided by them. Hopefully guests will have had supper beforehand, but if you are serving any alcohol it is wise to have nibbles available in case anyone has not eaten.

Cheese and pineapple on sticks (2 per person)
Twiglets (2 large bowls)
Tiny meringues (2 each)
Cocktail sausages on sticks (4 each)
Crudités (carrots and celery sticks,
cauliflower florets)
Ritz biscuits
Dips: Tomato, curry, horseradish
Pizza fingers (1 finger each)
Pitta bread and pâté (1 small piece each)
Crisps (2 large bowls)
Chocolate praline cake (1 square each)
Container of satsumas (winter)
Large bowl of strawberries (summer)

eat more and stop for supper, while older ones will eat far less but will nibble away throughout the evening. The amounts we give can be adapted easily to whatever size of party you are planning. (And don't panic at the thought of large-scale catering: it is *not* horrendous, as you will see!) Remember that the disco organiser and your helpers will want to have some sustenance too, so include them when you calculate your requirements.

We suggest Menu A or B for younger children up to eleven, and Menu C for an older party. For the younger age groups we also suggest including a break – when you serve ice cream cornets to everyone. The older children will definitely *not* require this.

It is so difficult to be specific about age so ask your children what they would like. Older teenagers really are not interested in food, but as fussy mother-hens we recommend you always provide something, especially if there is any alcohol being served.

Up to the ages of eleven to twelve, the children should stop for a supper and to give everyone a breather. We think it is far easier to give each child a paper plate with their food already on it. This avoids long queues building up as each child chooses what he or she wants to eat. You may have some waste, but it's worth that for the ease. The main problem is that you may well not have sufficient space to lay out all the plates, but so long as you have a certain number ready, helpers can be assembling others while you are serving. If you are organised, it will all go smoothly.

You will need tables on which to lay out food, whatever the age group. Place your tables where you — and the guests — can get at them easily. If the party is taking place in one room (which is best so as not to split it up), then put the tables along one wall. Make them look attractive with brightly coloured coverings — tablecloths, plastic cloths or coloured sheets. If the table surfaces are likely to be damaged, cover them first with a polythene or plastic sheet (dustbin bags sticky-taped together will be fine).

These disco party menus have been tried and tested and proved popular, but obviously your children may have a particular favourite which you would like to include. The lists on the previous page are what we suggest you put on each plate. In the recipe section (pages 74–78) we say what quantity you will need to buy for fifty guests, and give individual recipes for anything that needs cooking. Think small in everything — the eclairs, for instance, should be tiny two-mouthful ones. This means that

food is easier to handle and the plate doesn't look over-loaded. You can have some plates at the back with extra sausages, cheese straws or whatever for the odd child who might not feel like eating much at suppertime but who, as confidence grows during the evening, suddenly regains an appetite!

DRINKS

Children get through a lot of drink at a disco party and you should always provide plenty. Obviously you will serve non-alcoholic drinks to the younger children. It would be easy to say, 'Right, no alcohol at *any* children's party, and that's it', but life is never that simple! Older children see their parents drinking, and so know that drink is part of the adult world which they feel they are ready to join. It depends on how you feel about alcohol as to what your opinion is on serving children even mildly alcoholic drinks. However, if you are having a party, the following tips should help you cope with this dilemma. Recipes can be found on pages 116–122.

1. Never give a party without adults in attendance — even if they are not always in the room. If you are serving alcoholic drink it is a good idea for a father to run the bar, to keep control of how much is served, to see, and to be seen.

2. Serve a 'cup' type drink, where you can control the content. If you are including alcohol for older children, you can cut this down after the first drink and it won't be noticed. (One friend kept lots of empty wine bottles on view!)

Have plenty of cut fruit in it – apple, orange, cucumber, lemon slices etc – and, depending on the time of year, mint leaves and strawberries. If you are having a very big party use either large plastic containers, preserving pans or new plastic buckets to mix your drink in. Have a large bowl to serve it in and use ladles to spoon it into the glasses. If you are having a small party, serve from a jug.

3. Always serve Coke, lemonade and orange squash as an alternative to a concoction. Put fruit in the orange jug to make it look more fun.

4. Buy a non-alcoholic sparkling wine, and either use this on its own in a wine-cup, or half and half with ordinary wine. Non-alcoholic drinks are becoming increasingly popular, whether wines or lagers.

5. In the interests of the party spirit, give your drinks intriguing names: we have used names for our recipes which are usually given to more alcoholic drinks (everyone will enjoy the sophistication even if they are not entirely convinced!) Adapt names for your concoctions to fit your party – Disco Dazzler or Super Spritzer, for instance.

6. Have masses of ice prepared. If your freezer is full of party food get a couple of friends to make you plenty and keep it for you in their freezers until the evening. Use a cold box if you are in a hired hall and have no freezer available. Have one or two ice containers on the 'bar' with some tongs for children to put their own ice in their drinks. If you are giving a large party, four large plastic carrier bags full of ice should provide enough for fifty.

7. You may find the following information useful. At a disco party for sixty-four eleven-year-olds recently, the Harvest Punch recipe was served, and approximately $112\frac{1}{4}$ pints (64 litres) of drink were consumed! The amounts were for the following mix. First of all, it was 1 cider to 2 apple juices and 5 lemonades;

followed by no cider, 3 apple juices and 5 lemonades.

The total quantities were: Lemonade, 24 bottles ($1\frac{1}{2}$ litres); Cider, 1 bottle ($1\frac{1}{2}$ litres); Apple juice, 15 boxes (1 litre).

In addition: Coke, 6 bottles ($1\frac{1}{2}$ litres); Orange squash, 2 jugs.

Far more drink was available (on a sale or return basis), and we would certainly advise you to have more than the above. However, it is interesting that drink averages $2\frac{1}{2}$ pints (1 litre) per child for an all-evening, energetic party. When they are older they will probably drink even more.

8. If you have older children coming, even if you think they are totally reliable, lock away *all* your own bottles of drinks (especially the spirits) and try to let the word be circulated that anyone bringing their own drinks will be sent home. Yes, we know it would be difficult to frisk them for hip flasks but keep an eye open. The most common way of trouble starting at teenage parties is when drinks *you* provide are laced with drinks that *they* provide. Give them a good cup to get them going, then lessen the alcohol and serve carefully with a very watchful eye from the barman, Dad. Have Coke and squash available as well of course.

9. Always have drinks delivered at least a day before your party, especially if you are having a large party when drinks will be heavy and bulky to move about. If you are hiring a hall or whatever, see if they can be delivered there on the morning of the party, depending on security at the venue. Remember that you can hire glasses from wine merchants if necessary. The advantage of using a wine merchant is that you can have everything on a sale or return basis, very useful for a large party. You don't want to run out of drinks or have to buy far more than you use. Confirm your order when you know the numbers.

Dancing Games

These are *not* for the consumption of older groups; leave them well alone to do their own thing! When the children are young and go to disco parties, it may help to break the ice if you have the odd game with mini Mars bars, or similar little treats, as prizes. We feel you should have an experienced disc jockey to cope with the younger age group; he will know if games are necessary and when to introduce them. Let him be in charge of the evening. He may well have suggestions of his own for games, so discuss this aspect of the party beforehand and supply him with the prizes. However, don't worry if you feel more should be happening and it isn't. The children will enjoy being left to their own devices, and will let themselves be guided by the disc jockey.

The children will probably stand around a bit. Don't panic! You will also find that they dance without having a 'partner' when they're younger. If you want to pair people up before playing a game, have a Paul Jones or a Shoe Dance first. Some games don't need the children to be paired off.

For the youngest group you may want to incorporate a few ordinary party games while the disc jockey has a breather. Choose from the selection on page 61, and don't forget to include the 'props' you will need for these on your checklist.

SHOE DANCE
Every girl puts one of her shoes in the centre. Each boy chooses a shoe and has to dance with whoever is his Cinderella.

DISCO DANCING COMPETITION
Just play a few disco records and the winners are the couple dancing the best according to the disc jockey.

PAUL JONES
The girls make a circle on the inside and the boys on the outside. The two circles move around in opposite directions to the music. When the music stops the boy and girl facing each other dance together.

DISCO KNEES
Everyone dances around and when the music stops the girl has to sit on the boy's knee without her feet touching the ground. If they do, or if she falls over, that couple is out.

MUSICAL ISLANDS
You will need to have a newspaper per couple for this game. Put the newspapers on the floor; when the music stops each couple has to jump on to an 'island'. Take away a newspaper each time, as in musical chairs.

NEWSPAPER GAME
You will need to supply a newspaper per couple. Get the boy to carry the newspaper while he is dancing. When the music stops, each couple stands on their own newspaper, which at that stage should be folded in half. The next time the music stops they have to fold the paper in half again before getting on to it. Each time the music stops they have to fold their paper into a smaller and smaller piece. The couple who wins are the last to stand on their paper without falling off.

TORCH DANCE
Give your disc jockey a torch. He can suddenly turn it on to someone, and they will be out.

FORFEIT DANCE

Prepare a list of forfeits prior to your party and give this to the disc jockey who can then make a forfeit dance as and when he wants. Forfeits can include anyone wearing a safety pin, anyone whose Christian name begins with a G, etc, etc. Those who are 'guilty' are out.

THE HOT POTATO

Give the disc jockey a balloon. The balloon has to be thrown about between the dancers as they are dancing. If the music stops and they have the balloon in their hands they are out. You will have to insist that they catch the balloon if it is thrown at them. If you see them deliberately not handling a balloon they will have to be out in any case.

STATUE DANCE

When the music stops the children have to stand absolutely still. Those who move are out.

DIAMONDS, HEARTS, SPADES AND CLUBS

Have four corners labelled as one of the four suits; have an adult standing at each one holding up a large home-made card, or pin up a card at each corner. When the music stops, the children go to whichever corner they choose. The disc jockey turns his back when the music stops and then shouts out one of the suits. The children in that corner are out. The game continues until there's only one child left on the floor.

Checklist

If you are having your party away from home you will need a checklist. Obviously you can discount some of the items given below if the venue is well equipped but it is probably worth flicking through the list anyway, just to check that you have thought of everything.

Decoration	Chopping board
Blu-Tack	Washing-up bowl
Food	Washing-up liquid
Drink	Towels
Corkscrews	Drying-up cloths
Can openers	J-cloths
Cutlery	Kitchen roll
Crockery	Paper napkins

Ice, tongs and ice bucket
Cold box – to keep spare ice in
Scissors – for cutting cartons, etc.
Dustpan, brush and broom, bin liners
Matches, if gas stove or heating system
Large jugs, bowls, etc, for drinks
Large bucket for slops if 'bar' not near sink
Ladies – for serving drinks
Glasses (can be hired, or use plastic)
Polythene covers, if necessary to cover table surface before putting on cloths (sellotape dry cleaning bags together, PVC tablecloths, groundsheets, etc, for either bar or serving tables)

Disc jockey's telephone number

For younger children's disco parties only
Props if needed, and prizes for the games; camera and flash.

Items for girl's loo

Tissues	Cotton wool
Perfume	Spare loo rolls
Hairspray	First-aid kit
Comb	

Supper and Dinner Parties

Evening parties take over from tea parties as children get older. Supper or dinner parties are greatly enjoyed by girls on their own from eight to about eleven years old: they appreciate the details of candles, flowers and pretty food. A vital ingredient is darkness, so when they are younger it is probably best not to plan this for summertime. Give a barbecue instead (see page 67). Older children would prefer a more sophisticated mixed party. (Before going on to late discos or teenage balls, it would be fun to invite some friends for dinner and then go together to the party.)

When discussing how many to invite, remember that you will have to fit everybody in without too much squash. Smaller parties can be just as much fun, and sometimes children may prefer to invite just their closest friends. When you come to the mixed dinner party, numbers will no doubt be decided between you and the children, but try and make sure that at least one 'life and soul of the party' is invited to get things going from the start!

For the eight-year-olds we think 6–8 or 8.30 pm is an ideal time span – and helpful if parents have to collect children before going out themselves. As they get older, 7.30–10 or 10.30 pm would be a suitable length of time, or make it an 'all-night' party: ask them to bring sleeping bags and stay the night with collection time at, say, 10 the next morning! Once they are into mixed parties then timing is up to you and the children to sort out together.

The recipes we give (see pages 78–101) serve eight, but it is simple enough to double the quantities if required. We have given lists of possible starters, main courses and puddings so that you and your children can choose anything that appeals to you, in whatever combination you require. If you feel, for example, that the younger children won't manage a starter *and* a main course, then adapt the ideas to whatever you and your family decide is appropriate. Only small amounts of a starter need be served; it is there to make the children feel they are having a proper dinner party. You may think that some of our starters sound rather sophisticated, but as children get older they will appreciate this. If in doubt, experiment on your own children first – and always discuss it with them anyway.

The drinks you provide will depend on the age group you are inviting. We give plenty of suggestions for 'concoction' recipes and for drinks to carry through your party themes (see page 117). Give whatever drink you serve a suitable name. Make coloured ice cubes for extra fun – remember they will melt so marry up the colour with your coloured drink. Add a few drops of food colouring to water before freezing the cubes.

Strike a sophisticated note with frosted glasses. To prepare these, beat up an egg white until it has lost its sticky quality, dip the rim of the glass first in the egg white and then immediately into a container of caster sugar and leave to dry. If you want to have coloured frosting, mix the sugar with a food colouring before dipping the glass – for example, add cochineal for the pink party. (The only problem with these glasses is that they are quite difficult to wash up!)

Buy little cocktail trimmings (from good stationers or party shops); mini paper sun-shades; little plastic animals to hang on the edge of the glasses; plastic freezer shapes, like pink elephants, which you can use instead of ice cubes.

No doubt the children would like to organise a seating plan, and would enjoy making individual place cards for the guests. The design and colour of the cards could be tied in with the party theme or decorations. Perhaps they could do some fun menus to go on the table too.

Themes and decorations depend on the age group you are inviting. Always look around and utilise what you have at home – it is amazing how you forget what is tucked away at the back of a cupboard. This is particularly applicable if you decide to have a colour theme for your party.

For a supper party you will need helpers – the number will depend on how many you are inviting. Don't think you can organise games, be cook, waitress, disc jockey and cloakroom attendant all by yourself. No matter how organised you are beforehand, it is amazing how serving the food, doing the drinks and bringing in the next course becomes a real chore if you are on your own! Enlist some friends or older children to help. For the older children's mixed parties, they will serve and

clear themselves: all you have to do is leave them to it!

Don't forget that if an older mixed group don't know each other well, conversation may be a bit sticky. Try odd tricks to get them chatting: serve the Meat Fondue (see page 113) or finish off a meal with the Fruit Fondue (see page 101). Everyone has a giggle together then. And afterwards suggest a few games, such as the Dictionary Game, Charades (girls versus boys), Team Trivial Pursuits (see pages 64–66). Discuss this with your teenager in advance. As a last resort, show a video!

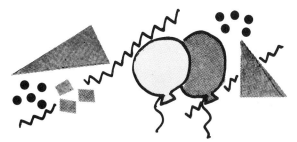

Candlelit Dinner Party

The younger age group are very appreciative of being allowed to feel sophisticated and grown up, so let them have a candlelit dinner. Make the table look pretty with candles and flowers. Serve uncomplicated food which most children would like a little bit of. Have a mini-disco, or play a few games before supper (see page 61) whilst everybody is arriving. After the meal you could continue playing games, or have a video, magician or another mini-disco to finish the evening off. Alternatively, make it a fancy-dress occasion like Hallowe'en.

If you want to give a small disco party for younger children you will need a clear area for them to dance in, and some good pop discs or tapes. Incorporate games with the dancing

MENU
CANDLELIT PARTY

Melon Balls or Cubes with Orange Juice
Cocktail Vol-au-Vents

★★★★★★★★★

Spaghetti (or pasta curls and
shells) Bolognese
Shepherds' Pie Special
Chicken Pie
Mock Moussaka

★★★★★★★★★

Vegetables

★★★★★★★★★

Snow Princess Cake
Pavlova with Cream and Fruit
Ice Cream Bombe
Chocolate Mousse
Lemon Mousse

Christmas fairy lights on a time switch so that they go on and off like disco lights, or simply change your ordinary electric light bulbs for coloured ones. Always keep your decorations in tune with your party theme if you have one.

Don't forget that with this age group you will need prizes for the games, and presents to take home. So be prepared (buy little novelties, mini Mars Bars, or make some sweets, see the section on presents at the back of the book).

As far as the food is concerned, try to have everything prepared by the afternoon. Remember these recipes are for eight, so adapt accordingly. Clingfilm will be invaluable to prevent everything drying out. Anything to be served hot can be heated up at the last minute. Avoid having to carve anything. Keep the food simple and choose dishes that can be 'doled' out, so that you can then help serve the vegetables. Always cook a few sausages, no matter what main course you have chosen, just in case there is a child who doesn't like it!

and the children will feel less inhibited and everyone can join in.

Decorate your room with streamers (see page 14 on how to make them) and balloons. Once you have blown up the balloons use a felt tipped pen and draw a funny face and write a child's name on each one. Tie a piece of string, wool, ribbon or parcel ribbon to each. Mix the balloons into bunches, tie the strings together into a slip knot. If the children are still young enough to appreciate taking a balloon home after a party you can easily free the balloons by pulling the end of the knot. If you want the balloons for decoration only, use parcel ribbon and then run the back of a pair of scissors firmly down the individual strands to form curls. Maybe you could rig up your

Pink Party

A pink party is probably more appropriate for girls on their own. You can really go to town making everything look extremely pretty and delicate. Obviously, you could change this slightly to become a pink and white party, and the advantage of a two-colour theme is that someone with very little in the way of pink clothing will probably have something white to which they can add pink ribbons or tights. Tell everyone to wear pink and send pink invitations using pink writing paper. Alternatively, use white paper and decorate and write it with pink felt-tip.

Pink and white crêpe streamers can be used to decorate the room: buy pink and white crêpe paper and make your own (see page 14). You could go to town and make some tissue paper flowers and decorate the table or part of the room with them. They are quite time-consuming to do but so pretty they are worth the effort! To make them you will need pink tissue paper, cake doilies (size depends on the size flowers you want) and thin wire, perhaps florists' wire. Cut the tissue into different-sized circles, place three or four layers on top of each other and put the doily underneath. Make a 'nob' with the end of a piece of the wire and push the other end through the paper layers. Form the paper layers into a cup or flower shape, and hold in place with the twisted wire or sticky tape.

Carry the theme through to the table decorations with pink candles, napkins, plates, etc. You can dye salt pink with some drops of cochineal and then dry it out in the airing cupboard (it will go a bit hard at first so just mix it up). Put it in an open salt cellar plus little spoon: use an egg cup if you've nothing else so that the salt can be seen!

If you can run to the expense, put a few little pink and white flowers as a posy on the table: it need not be very big. Try to make the flowers

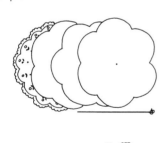

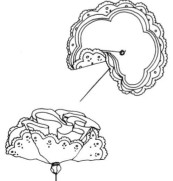

MENU
PINK PARTY

Wild Cherry Soup
Pink Prawn Pâté
Taramasalata
Pink Tomato Dip with Crisps or Crudités

★ ★ ★ ★ ★ ★ ★ ★ ★ ★

Gammon with Redcurrant Jelly Sauce
Chicken with Pink Mayonnaise and Pink and White Pasta Shells
Simple Pink Salad Selection
Tuna Mousse

★ ★ ★ ★ ★ ★ ★ ★ ★ ★

Pink Mashed Potato
Red Cabbage and Orange
Red Cabbage Salad
Pink Pasta Salad

★ ★ ★ ★ ★ ★ ★ ★ ★ ★

Pink Apple Snow
Pink Meringues
White Meringues with Strawberry Cream
Strawberry Ice Cream with Pink Meringues
Vanilla and Raspberry Ice Cream Bombe
Rhubarb Fool
Raspberry or Strawberry Sorbet with Lemon Sorbet

look as dainty as possible. Give little pink presents and prizes (a rubber, a tiny soap, etc.) and wrap these in pink tissue paper. When you serve the pudding put little bowls of mixed pink and white sugared almonds on the table, or pink and white peppermint stars (see page 123). Another idea is to give these as little presents. Put a few in some clingfilm and tie up as a little bundle, with pink parcel ribbon. Leave enough ribbon – about 3 inches (7.5 cm) for each strand – to make into curls (see page 13).

Green Party

As with the pink party, you may find it easier to make this party dual-colour for older children, to allow more flexibility re clothes, decorations and so on: it could be a green and white party, a green and yellow party, or green and red for Christmas.

Send out green invitation cards. You can buy bright emerald-green writing paper and envelopes which are sold loose, so that you don't have to buy more than you need. If you want to use a two-colour theme, have the envelope in one colour and the invitation in the other. The party-givers could cut the writing paper into half and send single sheet invitations decorated either by cutting the edges with pinking shears or putting fun green stickers on. Or fold the writing paper in half and send it as a stand-up card, shaped perhaps as an apple. If you want your guests to come in green clothes, or if you want to have a dual-colour theme (green and white or green and yellow), then state it here.

Decorate your party room with greenery from the garden, or if it is winter time use any green cactus or houseplants – green and cream poinsettia, for instance – to help carry the

MENU
GREEN PARTY

Spinach Soup with Tiny Croûtons
Watercress Soup
Avocado and Oranges with
Green Herb Dressing
Eggs with Green Mayonnaise or
Salad Cream
with
Brown Bread and Green Butter Pinwheels
Heart-Shaped Bread with Green Butter
Hot French Stick with Green Herb Butter
Rolls or French Stick with Green Butter

★ ★ ★ ★ ★ ★ ★ ★ ★

Green Tagliatelli with Ham and
Chicken Cream Sauce
Spinach and Ham Pancakes
Cold Chicken with Watercress Sauce

★ ★ ★ ★ ★ ★ ★ ★ ★

Green Salad
Broccoli, Peas, Beans, Spinach
New Potatoes with Chopped Parsley
Anna's Green Duchesse Potatoes

★ ★ ★ ★ ★ ★ ★ ★ ★

Green or White Meringue with
Apple Cream Filling
Gooseberry Fool
Apple Sorbet
Green and White Fruit Salad

★ ★ ★ ★ ★ ★ ★ ★ ★

Sage Derbyshire Cheese
Herb Roulé
Celery

theme through. Make green tissue flowers (see page 23). Put up green streamers (see page 14), green balloons, etc; carry on the theme with candles, napkins and, if you are planning to use them, paper plates. A friend who gave such a party placed on the centre of the table a bowl of green fruit, with Granny Smith apples, green grapes, greengages, green pears, etc, even including green bananas! After the meal offer little bowls of green and white peppermint creams (page 123.) If the children are still at an age for going-home presents then make them green and wrap them up in green tissue. Similarly if you are having games, try and find some suitably coloured prizes.

Try to prepare as much of the food in advance as possible (see pages 89–94), and don't worry if some of our suggestions seem a little outrageous: the children will love them!

Black and White Buffet Supper

We have included a black and white supper party for older children for a more sophisticated evening – possibly before going on to a black and white disco. Maybe you are planning to give one yourself. If you are, remember that probably not much will be eaten at a disco, so serve only finger food – dips, meringues, eclairs, black and white grapes, cherries, for instance. The quantities on page 95 are for eight; adapt the recipes to suit your numbers.

MENU
BLACK AND WHITE BUFFET

Curry or Horseradish Dip
with White Cauliflower Florets and
Mushroom Slices
Prunes Stuffed with Cream Cheese
Celery Sticks with Stilton and
Cream Cheese Filling
Black Grapes Stuffed with Cream Cheese
and Walnuts

★★★★★★★★★★

Chicken Salad with Black Grapes or
Cherries
Egg Salad with Mock Caviar
White Rice Salad with Raisins and Almond
Chinese Leaf Salad

★★★★★★★★★★

Lemon Syllabub with Black Cherries
Profiteroles (or Eclairs) and Chocolate Sauce
Chocolate Roulade
Yoghurt Cream Surprise
Blackcurrant/Blackberry Sorbet and Lemon
Sorbet

★★★★★★★★★★

Chèvre Blanc
Tomme aux Raisins
Rambol au Poivre
Brie

If your children would like to send out black invitations, you can now buy excellent silver pens which will show up on black card. As far as dress is concerned, while we appreciate that as children get older they are less likely to dress up, the sophistication of black and white seems to continue to appeal to the young.

Bare twigs can be painted with white emulsion. Leave some plain, or if they are not 'black' enough paint them with a black paint too. Alternatively do a zebra effect! Arrange these in pots in the party room to look like small trees (see page 14). If this is a party where you are giving out presents, wrap them in black and white paper and suspend them from the trees. Hang up black and white twisted streamers (see page 14). Black and white balloons (obtainable from party shops), and black and white candles will all help to create the right atmosphere.

As far as the food is concerned, the first section of the menu is for bits to serve with drinks; the second for the main-course buffet, and then just choose a couple of the black and white puds. However, this menu could also be adapted for a more formal sit-down dinner party.

Mixed Dinner Parties

We are only giving two alternative menus here as by this stage the young will know what they want to eat. These suggestions illustrate alternatives that can be easily prepared, are reasonably priced and are not difficult to serve up. For instance, consider whether you could make life easier by handing round individual ramekins rather than serving a large bowl of something. If the children are choosing alternative menus do remember various points:

1. Plan your menu so that the courses provide a variety of colours.
2. Make sure the textures are not all the same: for example don't start and finish with a mousse.
3. Don't repeat ingredients with, say, mushrooms in the starter, main dish and salad.
4. Always try and include something that is a little bit original. For example, if you want to give bread and butter, cut it out with a heart-shaped pastry cutter. It may be wasteful but it does look attractive (see page 100).

Perhaps the children could make the starter and/or the pudding and you the main course? Or you could simply do all the work together!

SUMMER MENU
MIXED DINNER PARTY

Chilled Cucumber Soup

★ ★ ★ ★ ★ ★ ★ ★ ★ ★

Cherry Chicken Salad

★ ★ ★ ★ ★ ★ ★ ★ ★ ★

Lemon Mousse or Fresh Fruit Salad (see pages 83 and 94)

WINTER MENU

Haddock Mousse with Heart-Shaped Bread and Butter

★ ★ ★ ★ ★ ★ ★ ★ ★ ★

Lasagne and Salad
Baked Potatoes

★ ★ ★ ★ ★ ★ ★ ★ ★ ★

Pavlova (see page 81) or Fruit Fondue

At the end why not serve Chocolate Truffles (see page 124) with the coffee, or iced coffee if it is summertime?

Match Parties

In this section, as well as suggestions for match teas or lunches and hints about organising your event, we have included a brief resumé of how to run various matches, such as football, cricket, rounders, tennis and a swimming gala! Everyone forgets! The matches can be shared between two or three families, which is fun, economical and less of a strain. All you need pray for is fine weather! (But if it does rain, see our Bad-Weather Contingency Plan on page 42).

Usually match parties take place away from your home. It is essential, therefore, that you make a list of everything you need to take with you. If you are feeding the children after the game, in the pavilion, then you will need to check what equipment is there: drying-up cloths, washing-up liquid, etc. Don't forget to take a dustbin liner with you for your rubbish.

Have enough helpers to allow you to leave everything neat and tidy. It may be the first time that a private party has been allowed to use the facilities, and it would be a shame to spoil opportunities for others by not having sufficient time to clear up properly. Also make sure you have enough transport available to ferry everyone and everything to and fro.

Depending on how elaborate a party you want, you could round the treat off by having a film show, barbecue, or perhaps a small disco. If you are embarking on these 'optional extras', then ensure that you have plenty of assistance.

Do remember to take a camera for a team photograph.

Football

First of all you will need to organise the venue. If you live in a town, why not ask your children's school whether or not it would be possible for you to hire their pitch? On the whole we have found people very encouraging to youngsters, and only too pleased to put themselves out to accommodate a game of this nature. If you are using a local pitch, you will have to choose a weekend when the team is not having a home match. Sometimes groundsmen will allow you to play on the morning of a match – but this would obviously depend on the state of the pitch and the attitude of the groundsman.

If your son is only nine or ten, playing on a full-size pitch will be very tiring for him and his guests. Make allowances for this, by having half-time after twenty-five minutes instead of the usual forty-five, and perhaps inviting a few extra boys to fill up the pitch! It may also be a good idea to have two people in the goal mouths – these look huge with just one eight-year-old standing guard! Unless you have budding goalkeepers in your teams, you may well find this is not a popular place to fill when you come to select who plays where. By selecting *two* people for goal duty you may solve the problem.

Try to keep your teams even in their ability. If you are sharing the match with a friend who has invited the entire junior team of the local school, whilst your son's friends are less able, then try to be fair and have a flexible team-allocation system. We have found that organising the team placings in advance can avoid a complete walk-over by one or other of the teams and a lot of fuss at the time. It is important to keep the ages of your players as similar as possible – it is amazing how much a year's extra experience and strength makes at this stage.

You will need to have eleven players on each side but it is wise to have a couple of substitutes available in case anybody drops out at the last minute. An ideal way of getting round this is to choose, say, two younger brothers of team members who can, even if they do not play, have the responsibility of taking the oranges to the teams at half-time.

Tell your guests to come in whatever coloured strips your sons have chosen for the two teams. You will probably find that the colours will be determined by their favourite league team. T-shirts, sweatshirts, etc will be fine, so long as they are the right colour. Football boots should be worn for protection and to help stop slipping. If you can get hold of a qualified referee who will arrive in his black uniform then this adds prestige to the game. If not, don't forget a whistle. If you are really serious, employ a few fathers or brothers as linesmen (and don't forget a coin to toss with).

You will need to have about eight oranges, cut into segments with the skins on, for half-time refreshment. And as little prizes as they come off the pitch at the end of the match, why not give mini Mars bars to the winning team and Milky Way bars to the losers?

FOOTBALL MATCH FOOD

You will have to serve a lunch rather than a tea following your football match if the pitch is only available in the morning. If this is the case, you are going to be out for most of the morning and unless you can use any of the facilities that are near the pitch you must have everything prepared before you go. If twenty-two players are all descending on your house for lunch, then provide simple food, which you can leave cooking gently in the oven all morning. Just serve some ice cream and hot chocolate sauce for a pudding (see page 104 for recipes).

You will find that the children will be extremely thirsty, so give them all a squash-type drink as soon as they get in (have this prepared before you leave). You can then safely serve the fizzy drinks during the meal, but gulping the Coke on an empty stomach might prove unfortunate!

For starters, have $\frac{1}{2}$ gallon ($2\frac{1}{4}$ litres) of orange concentrate ready to mix up. For the meal they may get through eight large size ($3\frac{1}{2}$ pint/2 litre) bottles of Coke or lemonade.

After a drink they will be ravenous. Forget the dainty teas of tiny tots, they will be wanting something far more substantial. It is unlikely that they will have changed, so be prepared for them to be muddy, hot and hungry!

No doubt the team captains will have their own ideas as to what they want for their team lunch or team teas, so we are just giving you a few suggestions.

FOOTBALL TEAM LUNCHES

Oslo Steak Stew
Sausage Moussaka
Cheesy Meat and Potato Pie
Sausages

★★★★★★★★★

Baked Potatoes
Quick Cooking Frozen Peas

★★★★★★★★★

Ice Cream and Sauces

Cricket

If your son is a keen cricketer, you could share a match with another friend. However, you might find it quite hard to muster eleven for each side during the summer holidays when friends are away. Make sure that you have a sufficiently long list of possible players before you actually book anything. The next problem is finding a local pitch available for a suitable date. It is probably best to choose a weekend as you will need help from the dads for this match. You must have two competent scorers so that one can have a break, and at least two umpires. (It is preferable to have four people available to umpire so that *if* it is a very hot day they can have a break after the first innings.)

As far as equipment goes you will need to provide the ball, two bats, two pairs of pads, two pairs of gloves, plus a pair of pads and gloves for a wicket keeper, two sets of stumps and bails and a score sheet, not to mention the coin to make the toss with! Most boys who are keen on cricket seem to have their own equipment, but it is probably sensible if between the two teams you have the basic essentials supplied. As the boys get older they really should wear cricket boots so that they have more protection and do not slip. If they do not have these then it's a good idea to suggest that trainers rather than tennis shoes be worn.

You will have your own ideas as to how the match should be run, but do try to make sure your teams are as evenly matched as possible – it will result in a much better game. In our experience we have found it best if everybody has an opportunity to bat. Either arrange for each boy to have a certain number of overs, or to retire once they have made, say, twenty runs. You may feel it is not such a good idea

FOOTBALL TEAM TEAS

Sandwiches or soft rolls	1½ each

Fillings:
Sainsbury's soft pâté
Marmite and cucumber
Hard-boiled egg with salad cream
Ham and lettuce
Peanut butter
Cream cheese and chutney
Honey
Chocolate spread

Sausages	4 each
Bella's Cheese straws	2 each
Sausage Rolls	1 each
Cheese Scones	1 each
Biscuits	3 each

    Selection of bought biscuits
    Chocolate Shortbread Treat
    Shortbread Sandwich Biscuits
    Chocolate Crunch Cakes
    Meringues (see page 88)
    Nutty Chocolate Treat
    Cornflake/Ricicle Specials
    Quick and Easy Fabulous Flapjacks
    Peanut Cookies

Cakes	1 piece each

    Iced Cup Cakes
    Praline Cake
    Match Cake

to have everybody bowling – a feeble over might give the opposing team too much of an advantage.

It is a good idea to run this sort of match according to a time schedule, so if you start at 2 pm, have tea at 4 pm, and end the match at 6 pm. If the teams are ill-matched and you find it is a complete walkover for one team, then have a second match with rearranged teams. Another idea if the match is over too early is to play tip and run, where if you hit the ball with the bat you have to run no matter what.

Remind both captains before the match that it is very boring fielding all afternoon on the boundary. Try to ensure that every boy who has not bowled feels that he has played a part in the match by, for example, fielding near the wicket.

CRICKET TEAS

You may find that the mid-match tea is not devoured as hastily as you expected. The adrenalin is still flowing and match nerves can take away some boys' appetites. However, you will need plenty of drink, especially if the weather is hot. Then if you leave the teatime leftovers out in clingfilm, you will find that they will disappear rapidly once the match has finished.

Don't forget that you will need to feed and water the helpers, and you may well find that several of the parents will stay and watch the match. Provide enough tea for everybody to tuck into! No doubt your child will have his or her own ideas as to what they want for the team tea, but look at some of our suggestions on page 105. Make a cricket pitch match cake if it is a birthday celebration.

Drink. You will need a lot of drink throughout the afternoon, so have plenty available. We suggest half a dozen of the largest $3\frac{1}{2}$ pint (2 litre) bottles of Coke or lemonade; a $\frac{1}{2}$ gallon (2.25 litres) of orange concentrate ready to mix up; and lemon concentrate (you could mix the lemon and orange as it makes a very refreshing drink). If you have a suitable container then freeze bags of ice prior to your match day and, keeping it in the cold box, put some into each jug as you make it up.

Rounders

Anyone, whether sporty or not, can enjoy a game of rounders. You really need nine players a side, but if you have either less or more that is no problem at all. In fact, this is what makes rounders such an ideal party game. It can have a flexible number of participants, and you use very little equipment.

Players, divided into two teams, will include a bowler, backstop (a kind of wicket-keeper to stand behind the batsman), four 'posts' who are fielders, and three outfielders or deep fielders. Additional team members can be extra outside fielders, standing behind and between the posts. The posts must not hinder the batsmen as they run. The four posts are marked by objects such as paint cans, bean poles, or whatever you have to hand. The batsman uses either a proper rounders bat, a cricket bat, a tennis racket (the only problem here is that a tennis racket can hit the ball far too far), or simply the batsman's hand. The ball can be a proper hard rounders ball if playing with a bat, or use just a tennis ball (particularly if you are using hands to hit it with!).

In case you have forgotten how to play rounders, here is a brief rundown of the rules. The batsman tries to hit the ball, but if he misses he can still run to the first post. If he

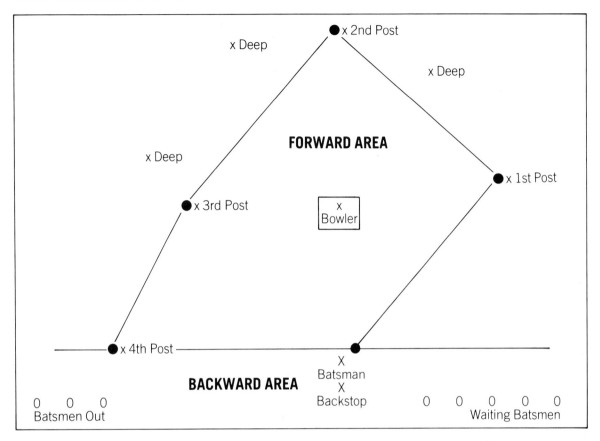

x 2nd Post

x Deep

x Deep

FORWARD AREA

x Deep

x 1st Post

x 3rd Post

x
Bowler

x 4th Post

BACKWARD AREA

X
Batsman
X
Backstop

0   0   0
Batsmen Out

0   0   0   0   0
Waiting Batsmen

does hit the ball he can try to score a rounder by running round all four posts, while the other side tries to get him out by stumping him with the ball. If you haven't played rounders you can easily get hold of a copy of the rules from a library. If you don't actually have anyone scoring the number of rounders made, then make sure that the team captains remember to make a tally.

The match (playing time) will be an hour if you allow fifteen minutes per innings, and give each team two innings. Have a little practice time if you have guests who have not played before. Take some squash and biscuits for a half-time break. Remind guests to come with a sweater or sweatshirt in case of need.

Tennis

TENNIS PARTY FOR SIX CHILDREN

If you want to organise a tennis party do wait until children are experienced enough to play the game at least moderately well! If you book one court for the six children, the actual tennis will take almost 2½ hours to play. Don't be put off by this, because it will be organised so that every child plays every other child (each playing five matches).

As usual, the secret of success is to organise everything efficiently beforehand, and you should make a match chart (see page 33). Each match will consist of three games and the number of games won goes on the chart. To discover the overall winner you simply add together the number of games won: whoever has achieved most wins is the *victor ludorum*. We suggest you award six prizes: a first, second and third graduated prizes, and then three identical smaller prizes to those left. In this way it is not so obvious who achieved least.

Whilst a game is going on, there will be four children left over, two of whom can ball-boy. The other two can sit on a ground sheet watching the match, with puzzles and cards, etc, available to play with if they wish. It will work out that sometimes a child will have to go from playing to being a ball-boy instead of having a rest, but everyone will be able to sit down at some point. It is a good idea to play tennis for $1\frac{1}{4}$ hours, say, and then have a complete break. Your timetable might be as follows:

Everyone comes at 3 pm, and you give them a biscuit or piece of cake and a drink, followed by tennis for $1\frac{1}{4}$–$1\frac{1}{2}$ hours. Then have a break for about 15 minutes doing something totally different, and again have something small to eat. An inventive friend who had a tennis party at her home hung doughnuts on string from her whirlygig washing line, which amalgamated something to eat, a fun game *and* a break from

---

The timetable would look like this:

3.00	Arrive	**6.30**	End games
3.15	Tea (light)	**7.00**	Barbecue
3.45	Tennis starts	**7.45**	Games
5.00	Refreshments	**8.30**	Go home
5.15	Tennis		

---

the tennis! Have plenty of soft drinks available all the time, as everyone including yourself will probably be very thirsty. You then continue the tennis for about another $1\frac{1}{4}$ hours. Afterwards, perhaps have a simple barbecue supper.

We suggest that you umpire for the younger age group (take a light folding chair). For a tournament for six children you will need to have fifteen match score sheets, plus the final score chart and a pencil or pen. Remember how easy it is to forget the score even when you are playing. It is even easier to lose count if one of the other guests asks a question which distracts you for a moment. So be prepared and mark a simple score sheet (see below) with dots as points are won. Put the servers on the top row each time.

If the weather is cold but still fine, check that everybody has some warm clothing to put on while they are not playing (remember

---

SCORE SHEET	HOLLY v REBECCA															
SERVER															Rebecca	Holly
Rebecca	•	•	•				•		•	•					1	
				•	•	•		•								
Holly		•	•		•	•										1
	•			•												
Rebecca		•	•													
	•			•	•	•										1

Individual Match Scores

1.	Julia Michelle	0 3	**2.**	Susan Rebecca	0 3	**3.**	Holly Kirsty	3 0
4.	Julia Susan	2 1	**5.**	Michelle Holly	1 2	**6.**	Susan Kirsty	3 0
7.	Julia Rebecca	2 1	**8.**	Kirsty Michelle	0 3	**9.**	Holly Susan	2 1
10.	Julia Kirsty	3 0	**11.**	Michelle Susan	1 2	**12.**	Rebecca Kirsty	3 0
13.	Julia Holly	3 0	**14.**	Rebecca Michelle	0 3	**15.**	Holly Rebecca	2 1

FINAL SCORES

	games won	matches won	Place
JULIA	10	4	2nd
HOLLY	9	4	3rd
SUSAN	7	2	5th
KIRSTY	0	0	6th
REBECCA	8	2	4th
MICHELLE	11	3	1st

something for yourself as well). If the weather is so appalling that you can't play, have a contingency plan already worked out.

LARGE MIXED DOUBLES TENNIS PARTY

The key to the number of people to invite lies in the number of tennis courts you can use, and the length of time for which they will be available. Remember that children will be slower than adults playing their games: for example, their serving takes much longer, and

an average set will last about 25 minutes. The number invited must be divisible by four. Twelve or sixteen are ideal numbers. You could manage with twelve on one court, but it would take the whole afternoon. Sixteen to twenty people on two courts, and twenty-four to twenty-eight on three courts works well.

If you run the party from, say, 10 am to 4 pm you can give guests individual picnic lunches (see page 51) which they can eat at whatever time they choose, rather than have everybody stopping for a meal which takes up valuable time. The way this party is devised allows everybody to play with everybody else, until after a certain length of time players may start playing with somebody they have already played with.

Here is a list of things you will require:

1. Some other activity to keep people occupied when they are not playing: swing ball, table tennis (if at home), etc, or organise an extra court for practising. If facilities are limited, take plenty of electronic games.

2. Score sheet and chart, see below.
3. A red and blue pen, and a pencil – *very important*. Blackboard stand and boards, if possible. If not, hardboard to pin charts to.
4. Plenty of soft drinks. Collect large plastic bottles in advance of the event and fill with diluted squash, and take yoghurt pots or similar for glasses. It is also a good idea to have some biscuits as well as the picnic.
5. Prizes.
6. Plenty of tennis balls.
7. Remind everyone to bring warm clothing for when they are not playing.
8. The picnic itself. See pages 51–52 for suggestions.

With younger children we suggest you play five games for one match, changing ends after the first game, and thereafter after every two games (someone gets two serves). If the children are playing very good tennis, you may want to play a complete set for a winner.

Our tournament structure may seem complicated, but it works extremely well and is very fair. Usually the problem with running a doubles tournament is that people can get stuck with one player for the morning and one for the afternoon, and this can cause a very unfair result at the end of the day. By this method the players change partners every match, with a boy always playing with a girl, and this has the added advantage that the children all meet and mix with each other.

Study the chart carefully. In the winning

TOURNAMENT CHART				TO BE COMPLETED BY ADULT
Round 1	Round 2	Round 3	Round 4	Round 5
3 Edward/Camilla v Nicholas/Clare 2	4 Nicholas/Alison v James/Clare 1	James/Lucy v Sam/Clare		
1 Sam/Kate v James/Jane 4	3 Sam/Camilla v Charles/Kate 2	Charles/Alison v Jonathan/Kate		
2 John/Susan v Charles/Julia 3	5 Jonathan/Susan v John/Jane 0	John/Camilla v Edward/Jane		
5 Jonathan/Alison v Tom/Lucy 0	1 Tom/Julia v Edward/Lucy 4	Tom/Susan v Nicholas/Julia		
WINNING BOY MOVES UP WINNING GIRL MOVES DOWN Losers stay same level but play each other				

A sparkling disco party (see page 8).

Fun on the football pitch (see page 27).

SCORE SHEET

Children complete this sheet themselves

Name	Round 1	Round 2	Round 3	Round 4	Round 5	Round 6
Edward	3	4				
Nicholas	2	4				
Sam	1	3				
James	4	1				
John	2	0				
Charles	3	2				
Jonathan	5	5				
Tom	0	1				

	Round 1	Round 2	Round 3	Round 4	Round 5	Round 6
Camilla	3	3				
Clare	2	1				
Kate	1	2				
Susan	4	0				
Julia	2	5				
Alison	3	1				
Lucy	5	4				
Jane	0	4				

partnership, the boy always moves up a game, the winning girl always moves down a game. The losing boy and girl partnership then move across on the same level, but are playing opposite each other.

Always fill in the losing pairs' next round position first – this is *very important*. It also helps to underline the boys' names in red, the girls' in blue. Pin the chart to the board. When each game finishes the children come and tell the adult in charge of the chart the score. The adult must then move the children to their next appropriate game, and fill in the next round on the chart.

On the other side of the board will be the sheet on which the children record their own scores – simply the number of games they have won with their partner. During the match the children will score for themselves. Have one person by the blackboard at all times, just checking that the information put down is correct!

Swimming

If you are lucky enough to have your own swimming pool make the most of it and have a swimming gala and a barbecue. Otherwise try and borrow your school's pool or see if your local pool could be available. Do make sure the swimming pool is warm enough for this particular occasion – your family may be used to it freezing cold, but it is so much more pleasant if you have it around 80°F (27°C) just this once!

Really you need not organise too many games as the children will enjoy themselves anyway. Bear in mind that some children will not be experienced swimmers and may not be confident in the water: watch out for this, and encourage them. If some cannot dive, let them start in the water for races. Say that if there is anyone who does not like diving they must get into the water first (although children hate saying they cannot do things). If you find that someone turns out to be a complete beginner let them splash around at the shallow end when everyone is mucking about, but once the races begin whisk them out and ask them to help you organise the games – without giving them any option!

The timing of the party rather depends on when you want to feed the children. If you want to do a barbecue lunch, then you might prefer to have the swimming in the morning, rather than waiting for half an hour until their food is digested and they are able to swim.

Otherwise have them arrive mid-afternoon and prepare a barbecue high tea or supper, depending on their ages (the barbecue recipes are for eight, so adapt to fit your numbers).

Don't invite too many children – that is when accidents happen. Always have an adult in swimming things in attendance, doing nothing else but keeping an eye on the children from the safety point of view – not organising games. Make sure someone knows mouth-to-mouth resuscitation. Tell the children not to run around the sides: it is all too easy for accidents to happen when there are a lot of children getting in and out of the water and making the edge of the pool wet and slippery.

Below are a few suggestions for games and races to play in the pool if there's room.

SIMPLE STROKE RACES
Crawl, backstroke, breaststroke, relay-team race, etc.

NOVELTY HAT RACE
Provide a funny hat – nothing precious – for each team. The race will start and the hand-overs will take place in the water.

MUSICAL BALLOONS
This is the same idea as musical chairs, but if it is a windy day you will have to use balls (that can't be blown out of the pool) instead of balloons. When the music stops everybody has to swim for a balloon and if they don't get one then they are out. Remove one balloon each round. Whoever grabs the last balloon is the winner.

HOT POTATO GAME
The children all swim around with the music playing. One child has a ball which they throw to a neighbour, shouting out their name. Whoever is named has to pick up the ball and throw it on to somebody else. Whoever has the ball when the music stops is out.

BALLOON RACE

The children must swim a length with the balloon in their mouth and hand the balloon to the next person in their team, who repeats the performance. When the last member of the team finishes, the balloon has to be burst before the race is won.

OVER AND UNDER RACE

This is really only suitable for older children to play. One member of the team jumps in the pool and the next one follows him and swims between his legs to take up a position just beyond him. The third member of the team jumps in, goes through the legs of the first one, and then has to swim over the top of the second one who goes down in the water. They then stand in their position with their legs open for the fourth person, who jumps in the pool through the legs, over the next, through the legs again and is ready and waiting for the next person to go over the top. It rather depends on the depth of the pool as to how long this race can go on for. If necessary, divide the teams into small numbers and either go across the pool widthwise or, if the children are large enough, do it going towards the deeper end. In either case, you will probably need to run heats.

FOLLOW MY LEADER

This is not a race, just a game where the children have to do whatever a 'leader' does. Get various children to have a go as the leader, but don't allow them to run in and out of the pool in case of accidents.

READY STEADY AND ALL GO

You will probably have to do this race as a timed heat, with each team swimming individually. The fastest team is the winner. The number in each team would be dependent on the width of the pool. The children stand in a line holding hands and jump in at the deep end. They then have to swim the length of the pool, holding hands all the time. When they get to the shallow end they have to clamber out, still holding hands. The children at either end can obviously help most because they·have one hand free.

HELPFUL HINTS

1. Twenty children would be enough for this kind of party. And for that you would need four adults to help organise, one of whom must be there simply to be ready to jump in if necessary.
2. Depending on the age of the children, the actual swimming time should not be more than two hours. If you are thinking of making it an evening party, remember that even in the height of summer it will be cool for the children.
3. Check before everybody (the 'lifeguard' too) goes in the pool that they are not wearing watches, unless they are waterproof.
4. If you are giving a single-sex party in a private pool and do not have a changing room outside, place some chairs in a corner of the garden where the children could change to avoid twenty pairs of wet feet paddling through the house.
5. Tell the children to keep their towels nearby as they will need them while they are standing about – if they are out of a game, or while the rest of their team are swimming.
6. Plan the barbecue timing carefully.
7. Have some games planned – not too active! – to play when the children have finished their meal.
8. If you want to show a video film after the party instead of playing games this can be a useful in-built contingency plan in case the weather changes.

Lunch and Activity Parties

There comes a time, around eight years old, when children have grown out of the conventional tea party, but are still too young to play matches. They are at an age when they will enjoy an outdoor 'fun-day' party. They can ask as many as your garden – and you – can cope with! Invite guests for a lunch and arrange to have a Dad around to help organise and control. You will certainly need some helpers anyway. Depending on the weather, you can get the children out of the house and doing something active to work off a bit of steam. Have the party from 12.30 to 3 pm which will give you half an hour of activity before lunch at about 1, and probably an hour and a half of activity following lunch – which disappears amazingly quickly!

Food

As far as the food goes, if the weather is good, provide a barbecue (see pages 67–73). If not, it is best to keep everything simple. We have included a few ideas to make conventional menus a bit different (see pages 110–111). Don't bother with a starter, but always cook some sausages (allow two per person); if there are children who don't like their main course, then you have a pretty safe alternative to offer them (and you can serve a sausage each,

anyway, with any of these main courses). The recipes are for eight so adjust them to suit your numbers.

Arrange to have someone organising arrival games so that you can be putting final touches to lunch. It is so much easier to be thoroughly organised beforehand and to keep everything very uncomplicated – all our suggestions are deliberately so!

MENU I
Barbecue (see pages 67–73)

★★★★★★★★★★

Ice Cream with Butterscotch Sauce (see page 104)
Bananas au Chocolat (see page 73)

MENU II
Home-made Beefburgers
Devilled Chicken Drumsticks (hot or cold)
Bacon Jacket Potatoes
Sausage Moussaka (see page 103)
Pigs in a Blanket
Bowls of Tomato Sauce

★★★★★★★★★★

Plum and Apple Crumble with Vanilla Ice Cream
Lemon Pudding
Chocolate Mallows

Assault Course

If the weather is being kind, younger children will relish the challenge that an assault course brings. Let them divide into teams, or give individuals a time score – the *victor ludorum* will be the one with the fastest time (you will need a stopwatch for this). Organise a practice run before lunch, and afterwards allow a suitable length of time to allow their meal to go down. (Play a quieter game in this period – a garden treasure hunt, for instance, see page 42.) Be prepared for English weather to ruin your ideas and have a contingency plan to turn to in case of need (see page 42).

We found that a points system worked the best, so that if you win you earn five points, and losers still score some points, say two. Hopefully this will avoid the losing team becoming very disheartened. Have a scoreboard of some sort to keep the tally. Use either a washing line lying straight on the ground or bean poles to mark the start and finish. The size of your garden and the type of equipment you have to hand will dictate what sort of course you wish to run. Once the children have used an item – the egg and spoon, say – either make them take the articles back for the next person before they move on to the next obstacle, or have them doing so in a reverse form on the way to the finish. Alternatively, have enough helpers to organise this for the children.

POSSIBLE OBSTACLES

Always organise your props well ahead.
1. Going through a tyre (hanging up or on ground), or through an open ended barrel.
2. Dressing up – huge wellingtons, skirt and hat.
3. Running in a sack (dustbin liner will do).
4. Throwing a ball into a bucket. If the

children are older you could substitute with a pitch and putt alternative.
5. Egg and spoon (use potatoes).
6. Stepping stones (use concrete blocks or whatever you have to hand, but if the children are getting older why not make them go backwards over these?). Or run along a board balanced on two tyres or straw bales.
7. Bending in between bean poles, kicking a football, and then shooting at a 'goal' – two bean poles making each goal.
8. Picking up six Smarties with a straw and dropping them into a bowl.
9. Bobbing for an apple.
10. Climbing a rope ladder, and touching a certain point.
11. Long jump or high jump.
12. Running on stilts. You can buy mini-stilts or make them from two identical cocoa-cans or similar (do not use cans opened by a can opener because of the sharp edges). Thread a thin piece of string or washing line, about 4 ft (120 cm) long, through two holes on either side of the can. The children balance on the cans and use the loop as the stilt.
13. Throwing a wellington into a hoop which is lying on the ground.
14. A somersault over the finish line. If a relay race, when one team member has completed the requisite number of obstacles, the next member then sets off. The individual's time can be recorded, and the victor is the one who is the fastest.

Bike Gymkhana

If you have a suitable garden or access to a nearby flat open space, you can hold a bike gymkhana. (Don't let them ride on soggy grass, however, as it could mean a wrecked lawn!) You can either ask your guests to come equipped with their own bikes, depending on the numbers involved and the space you have, or run two teams and just have two bicycles which everyone uses. This saves problems of transporting bikes any distance. If everyone brings a bike, include a fancy-dress class. Everyone arrives togged up and the fancy dress is judged before lunch. All can be normal then for the serious stuff of racing after the meal. You need not have races all the time, and you can play other games (see page 41) as well, but make the theme of the party the bicycle 'bit'.

If your guests all bring bikes, you can have race heats and then a final, depending on numbers. In either event, team or individual racing, keep a scoreboard and record points for winning, coming second, etc. The ultimate overall winner will have most points at the end of the day. You should be in charge of the scoreboard – pin up a large piece of paper on which to write the points. Have this organised well in advance, and have some little prizes ready.

Remember you will have plenty of props to organise. If you have to go to an open space, pack the car in advance ready to go straight after lunch. Have a checklist of props! Even if you are at home, be well prepared before everyone arrives. The following are a few ideas for games.

BENDING RACE

Place bending (bean) poles between which the riders have to go. It can either be the fastest rider who wins or the slowest, or do both – but separately of course!

COLLECTING THE CAN

Place empty yoghurt pots or similar on top of each of the bean poles. Place a bucket by each 'start'. The riders have to collect the pots off the bean poles and bring them back to the bucket one by one. If doing this as a team race, have the next member taking the pots back one by one and replacing them, and carry on in this way, turn and turn about.

OBSTACLE RACE

The rider bikes to a point where he has to get off and put on a hat and scarf and gloves. He gets back on and goes on to the next point where he has to bike round a circle of bricks which are laid on the ground. He bikes back, takes off his hat, gloves and scarf, and then bikes back to the start.

APPLE BOBBING

Bike to a bowl with water and apples in and bob one out. Race back to the start.

SPEEDWAY

Whoever is fastest wins!

SLOW BICYCLE RACE

Whoever is the slowest wins.

Hiring a Bouncy Castle

Children seem to adore bouncy castles – you will have seen them at local events. We have an amazing friend who hired one privately for her daughter's party, and it was the greatest success. Shop around and ask about hiring if you see one being used anywhere – a local council, a zoo or safari park or even Yellow Pages might be able to help. The charge is quite high, but comparable to hiring an entertainer or magician.

Obviously this is for a fine weather party, and you will need to have sufficient space in your garden to accommodate the castle. They come in various sizes, but if you can't find a small one, ask your school if you could hire their playing field. Share the cost and the party with a friend, then you could give a picnic tea and have additional outdoor games on the field.

NB: Children are not allowed to wear shoes when bouncing.

Outdoor Games

This is a selection of outdoor games which you can include with any outside party.

THROWING THE WELLIE
You need a lot of space for this game. Have a number of old tyres or hoops and number these 10, 4, 2, etc. The children throw the wellies from a starting line into the tyres or hoops. Whoever has the highest score wins. Have a score sheet.

MATCHBOX HUNT
Let the children either play in pairs or as individuals. Give each child, or pair, a matchbox. Tell them to find as many different things as they can fit into the matchbox in two minutes. Whoever collects most is the winner.

PITCH AND PUTT
This is a surprisingly difficult game. You will need golf balls and suitable clubs; targets and their score markers – old bamboo sticks slit with paper markers; score sheet and pencils; washing line for base line; short grass (that's not too precious!).

Allow two children to have their turns together (or play as a team game). The children stand behind a line and chip golf balls into the following: a tyre, box, paddling pool, or a circle painted on the ground. Don't put these too far away. Each target must have a score marker by it, with different scores. Whoever gets the highest score wins. Allow one or two shots at each target. Children retrieve their balls after their turn and the next guest has a try.

SHIPWRECK
Choose a child to be 'He'. The 'He' chases the other children who are only safe when off the ground, on straw bales, rugs, newspapers, etc, which serve as islands. If a child is touched by the 'He' while not on an island, then that guest takes over and chases the others. There is no real winner to this game: it can go on until you think the children have had enough.

SACK RACE
Have one sack per guest or use only two sacks and divide the guests into two teams, making it into a team sack race. If real sacks cannot be found, use dustbin liners (but they're not so durable).

WHEELBARROW RACE
Play this game before tea, or not until well after tea. Again pair the children off. One acts as the wheelbarrow, walking on his or her hands, and one as the 'pusher', holding the 'wheelbarrow's' legs.

THREE-LEGGED RACE

Have plenty of large men's handkerchiefs or dusters, and pair the children off. Tie their inside legs together.

BALLOON RACE

You will need two balloons per child or per team, plus two elastic bands (buy *more* than you need). Slip an elastic band securely round the knot of the balloon so it forms a loop. Children attach a balloon to each ankle with the elastic band. When the whistle blows they race to the winning line – without falling over or bursting their balloons.

GARDEN HUNT

You will need pieces of wool, card etc. This is an outdoor version of the Treasure Hunt (see page 62). Prepare and play it in the same way, the only difference being that, because you're out of doors, you should make sure that the clue cards won't blow away by firmly securing them (to a branch, under a pot, etc). Instead of numbered cards, you could use a length of different coloured thread, wool or string (red for the first clue, blue for the second and so on), which the children bring back to you. Suggestions for clues depend on ages.

Simple ones might be:

Around garden tap	Under greenhouse
Under bucket	door
Beside bicycle	Under stone
Under flower pot	Under garden seat
On branch of tree	Beside steps

FRENCH CRICKET

You will need a tennis ball and some sort of bat. There is no winner with this game, but children enjoy playing it. Someone stands with either a tennis racket or a cricket bat. Using a tennis ball the other children try to get the batsman out, by hitting his legs below the knees. If the batsman hits the ball he can turn to face the way the ball will be coming back at him. If however he has missed it, he is not allowed to do this, and must keep his feet in the same position (awkward when the ball is being bowled from behind him!).

Bad-Weather Contingency Plans

When you plan an outdoor party of any sort, always have a contingency plan up your sleeve in case the weather lets you down. Don't leave it until the day dawns wet and windy before you decide what to do. Be prepared and it will never happen! Check for example what films are on locally, and the times of performances, or take the children to the nearest sports hall or ice rink. Do your research thoroughly: can you bring food along and eat indoors wherever you are going, for instance, or would it be better to have your food at home? Think about the costs involved, and the transport you will require. Or you may prefer to entertain your guests at home. Look at the indoor games suggested (see page 61). But in any case have your plans formulated well before the day itself.

Another idea might be to run an indoor Olympics. You would need to have organised things prior to the event, and you may need to borrow some games from friends. Operate a points decision – remember to give the losers a few points as well after each contest so that everybody has some score. You can make this a team event, or pair your guests off, or allow the individuals to compete for themselves. The type of games you play will largely be dictated by the size of your house. If it is possible to have some sort of game per pair of guests then everybody should be occupied at least to begin with. Some games will take longer than others to complete, and you should have time limits for longer ones so that everybody has a shot at all of them.

Here is a list of ideas from which to choose: mini-snooker; table tennis; electronic games; television games; cards (Snap, Beggar My Neighbour, etc); board games (put on time limits); Subbuteo or similar; Scalextrix or similar.

You will need:

1. Sufficient adults to help organise the score sheet and to referee the games.
2. To have checked that you have no dud batteries in the games.
3. Sufficient table tennis balls to allow for breakages.
4. To try to avoid games which you know will take a very long time to complete (Monopoly, for instance).
5. To draw up a points table, listing your guests' names, and with headings of the games you decide to play. There will be no ruffled feathers at the end of the day as the points earned will show clearly and will be indisputable!

Presents and Prizes

You will still be requiring presents and prizes for younger age-group parties – the older ones will not need them – and we suggest that you ask your children to help you choose the little goodies. Last year's fashions will be dated this year so you'll have to be guided. But be warned – the smaller the gift, often the more expensive it is!

If you are giving out prizes for games throughout the party, it is a good idea to provide each guest with a little bag to put them into. You can write each child's name on an ordinary paper bag, or carry on your party theme: decorate a piece of card with a bicycle, for a bike gymkhana, print the child's name on it, and staple it to a bag. Some party shops actually sell suitable bags marked 'loot', which are great fun, but obviously the cost quickly mounts up!

Bought presents can include items like:

Pencil sharpeners
Little pencils and notebooks
Small packets of sweets, Smarties, etc.
Mini soaps
Fun stickers
Little selections of sweets (put a few different sweets in pieces of clingfilm, twist the top of the film and tie with a pretty ribbon)
Jokes and nasties (trick fly, trick sugar lumps, etc.)
Fun-shaped rubbers
Coloured marker pens

However, if you want to save the pennies and give home-made sweets as presents, we give some ideas on page 122.

Outings and Picnic Parties

First of all, discuss with your children where they would like to go. We and our friends have visited swimming and wave-machine pools, ice- and roller-skating rinks, been to a football match and horse events, and taken groups to a leisure centre, cinemas and the theatre. For an outing that couldn't be nearer or cheaper, but is still extremely popular, try camping out in the garden (after a barbecue supper).

If you have just arrived in your area, or simply want to find somewhere new to take the children, make use of your local museum or library. They both have a fund of information which they are only too glad to share. They will provide an exhaustive list of local galleries, country houses, castles, mills, forts, nature reserves, country and wild-life parks: even if you think you know your part of the world well we're sure you'll find that you haven't been to half of them!

Check out exactly what you are letting yourself in for well in advance, by either writing for a brochure or maybe even doing a recce first. Check the opening and closing times, and that wherever you are going is open on the particular day you have chosen. Check your costings and what extra costs you may incur when you get there. Plan to play a few games in the car (see page 52) and have a couple of outdoor games organised to fill in any gaps when you arrive at your destination.

We have included plenty of advice about picnics if you wish to provide the food yourself. However, if you are travelling far, and the weather might be a problem, we suggest that you stop at a restaurant chain – which the children will love even if you don't! – and they are quite reasonably priced.

When organising an outing, invite your guests half an hour earlier than the time you plan to leave. This allows for the one who is going to be late! If your outing is to be an all-day affair – and you don't want to have the aggravation of being back at a certain time – either arrange to drop everyone off at their homes, or invite guests to stay for an early supper, or even the night. Remember, though, that it will be an exhausting day for *you* before you commit yourself to too much! Always take a telephone number of one parent who could let the others know if you are going to be delayed.

Be well organised in advance, and you will be less likely to leave the picnic food or anything else behind. Have a checklist – and remember to check it. If you have large numbers of children to cope with, take a checklist of the children's names and do occasional head counts throughout the day! Only ask numbers that can be seated comfortably in the car – or cars, as it is a very good idea to organise a party with a friend so that you can take *two* cars. It is much better to ask fewer guests than have an uncomfortable journey; even if you have an estate car, don't think of it as a mini-bus! (You could hire a mini-bus, but that is an expensive exercise.) Don't plan to go too far – it will be a tiring day. Always have a contingency plan ready if the weather is really unpleasant (see pages 42–43). Whatever the weather, you should ask your guests to bring a waterproof of some sort with them. Most important of all, choose a meeting place or instruct children to find a policeman if anyone gets separated.

If you want, you can plan a surprise party and devise a mystery outing, not telling the children where they will be going.

Swimming Pool or Wave-Machine Pool

There are no two ways about it, taking a group of children to a swimming pool is a great responsibility. When you visit a wave-machine pool, you must remember that the wave created is quite strong, so do make sure that all your guests really can swim. Unless you really have a lot of helpers, try not to take children under the age of nine.

Always have helpers – one helper to four children, depending on the children's age and ability. A friend who organised this treat for her daughter tied markers of ribbon on the girls' swimming-costume shoulder straps. She imagined that this would make it easier for her to keep an eye on her 'brood'. However, in the mêlée of children in the pool there was no way that these properly singled out her group. What we are saying is that it is going to be difficult for you to have your eyes everywhere, and you don't want to be too restrictive in what you tell the children they can or cannot do or you will spoil the party. Perhaps a good hint is to find out from your local pool which is their quietest day, and plan your treat around that.

Remember that you may need change for locker keys in the changing rooms, so check that at the same time. When you organise the event, stress that no watches nor jewellery should be brought. We would also suggest that you put a dustbin liner in the car so that all the wet things can be put into it.

Even if *you* do not feel like swimming, it is a good idea for you – or your helpers – to be in a swimming costume in case you have to jump in quickly.

Scheduling really depends how long a day you want to make this treat. You could go to the wave-machine pool in the morning and come back for lunch, in which case you would probably ask everyone to be at your house at around 9.30 am and be collected at 2 pm. Or you could have a lunch at home with everybody coming at about 12 pm, then take them to the pool (allow half an hour after eating before they swim) and give them a picnic or hot snack afterwards, in which case they would be picked up at about 6 pm. Don't forget that whenever you go, the children will be extremely hungry immediately after their swimming, so either be prepared to fork out and buy something at the pool, or take some goodies with you.

If you want to find out if there is a wave

machine pool near you, look in the Yellow Pages under swimming pools and public baths. Your local pool will tell you if they know of one nearby. Check opening times before fixing the time of the party.

Ice Skating

At the moment, ice-skating rinks are few and far between. Check in the Yellow Pages or ask at your local library or town hall to see if there is one in your area. Organise this do with a friend and, depending on the numbers involved, take two cars.

Make sure you know the way to the rink; most provide a brochure with instructions, if requested. It is best to go at the quietest time of day if you are taking a group of children, particularly if some of them have not skated before. Telephone the rink when you are first planning the outing and you will find them very helpful. If you want coaching for the children this could be arranged at the same time. If the children are beginners, then tell them to come with gloves, and the girls to wear jeans not skirts. This is to protect them if (or when) they fall over.

When you arrive at the rink the children may have to queue for their skates and similarly at the end for their shoes. This can take quite a time, so allow for it in your calculations if you want to get off home promptly. When the children ask for their skates they have to give their shoe size. It is important that you check that their laces are done up sufficiently tightly, particularly around the ankles. Indeed, you may find yourself doing up everybody's skates for them. If you are not skating yourself, go with warm clothes – it is a bit chilly! You can sit by the side of the rink and keep an eye on everybody – and buy hot drinks to warm

yourself up. A friend will give you an extra pair of hands if there is any problem, either on or off the ice. Having experienced this, we know it *can* happen!

When the children have finished skating they will be thirsty and probably peckish. If you don't want to spend more money buying refreshments, take a basket of sustenance with you in the car (biscuits, crisps and drink).

If you were planning this activity as a birthday treat for an under-twelve, and if it involves a long motorway drive, it might be worthwhile contacting a quick food restaurant en route and asking them to organise a birthday meal for you. Happy Eater, Pizzaland and Little Chef will organise parties if they have sufficient warning.

Roller Skating

Roller-skating rinks are also few and far between, so you may find yourself driving miles. Once again, we suggest that you organise this event with a friend. As many children can roller skate at home, try to take a group who are roughly the same standard. Otherwise, the ones who cannot skate will probably feel rather left out.

You can hire or use your own skates. Telephone the rink and check which times would be the best for your group: you will find, for instance, that there are disco periods when the skating can be fast and furious. So, if you are taking beginners, ask the rink to suggest the best, least busy, time to go. As with the ice skating you can ask for private tuition.

Some roller rinks cater for birthday-party groups of all ages so, if that was your plan, ring up and ask for full details. If you do not want to skate, there are spectator facilities, and if some children come off the rink earlier than the others, there are usually video games provided.

The children will come off thirsty and probably quite hungry, so either come equipped with your own drinks and nibbles in the car, or be prepared to buy them refreshments.

Football Match

With all the recent problems at football matches you can't be blamed for not being very enthusiastic about this idea. A football outing needs careful organising. The best thing to do is to ring your local team (see Yellow Pages under Sports Clubs and Associations) and ask what they would recommend. Do not go when there is a local Derby on as these are the most likely trouble times. It is best to book seats for your group, and again be advised by the club as to where is the best place to sit. You will need to ring well in advance to find out when a suitable home match is being played. Don't try and take too many children in any case, and always go with sufficient number of helpers.

When you get into the vicinity of the stadium you will probably find that you have to park quite a distance away and walk to the entrance. It might be worth doing a recce before you park in order to discover where your particular entrance will be. You can then park as near as possible to that side of the stadium.

If the sun is not shining on your part you may find that sitting under cover in the shade is quite cool, so ask the children to come with suitably warm clothing which they can always take off if they get too hot. If it is a chilly day we would recommend that you take a couple of travelling rugs, which could alternatively be used to soften the seating! It might be worthwhile taking a bag holding a few refreshments for during the match – if it were a freezing day you could take a flask of hot drink. When the match ends, depending on the number of spectators, it might be advisable to wait until the bulk of the crowd has disappeared before you start to move.

Always arrange with the children either a meeting point, or a contingency plan, if anybody gets separated from your group.

What you provide for tea following the match rather depends on how near the football stadium you live, and also on the weather. Perhaps you could plan to take a picnic (see pages 51–52) or wait until you get home, and have tea there (see pages 105–109). If it is a birthday treat have a football match cake (see page 108).

Horse Events

There are sure to be keen riders among your children, and friends who would relish a trip to a major three-day event, a point-to-point, or a horse show.

The best way to get information regarding dates of events is through horsey publications. Look out for point-to-point fixtures in the January edition. For summer events you will have to buy the March numbers. If you need a copy of a specialist magazine you'll have to book it in advance from a newsagent. Sometimes isolated newspaper orders never materialise, so if you want to be 100 per cent sure of getting a copy, write to the magazine's editorial office.

Take a picnic to any of these events and you'll have a good day out – weather permitting. If it is very cold, you will have to eat the picnic in the car – bring a thermos of hot soup, but don't be surprised if it is drunk by the adults and not the children.

There is always plenty to see even if you are not particularly horsey. Even the very young are catered for at our local point-to-point with a bouncey castle as the main attraction. Make up a party and go with another family or two. Always take waterproofs and, depending on the weather, rugs to sit on. If you don't arrive early you will have to be prepared to queue to get in, and also remember that it takes a while to leave these events too. Allow sufficient time in your schedule to cover possible delays.

Specific Shows

If your child has a favourite hobby or particular interest, you could use this as a basis for an outing party with a couple of similar minded friends: for example, to an air show (check with plane mags for dates and venues), science museum, safari park, tennis tournament. Or plan a day in London, Edinburgh or your nearest city, choosing two particular venues to visit – plus a trip to McDonald's, of course!

Leisure Centres

Most leisure centres are very good at organising children's parties, and it is certainly a wonderful way for energetic youngsters to let off steam. The usual arrangement is for the party organiser to get the children involved in activities such as trampolining, roller skating or football for perhaps half an hour. Then they get changed into swimming gear and swim for half an hour (but allow about 20 minutes for changing before and after). Then tea, which might be hamburgers and chips, Coca Cola and ice cream, usually provided by the leisure centre. Of course, you would be very welcome to provide your own cake if it is a birthday party.

Get in touch with your local leisure centre to see what they can organise and how much it will cost, then book your party well in advance. You may well find that there is more than one party taking place at the same time – but there is plenty of room in a leisure centre and this never seems to matter.

When you send out invitations to the party, enclose a short note explaining what the party will consist of and what the children should wear, for instance: 'Please come in a track suit, as we shall be roller skating and trampolining. Also please bring swimming things and towel (and arm bands if you can't swim) in a marked bag. NB: Please leave your watches at home.' Bring a list of your guests with you, so that you can check when everyone has arrived.

Be prepared to take an active part in the party – one party organiser won't be able to cope on his/her own. Wear track suits to help with the roller skating, etc, and change into swimming things with the children. It goes without saying that taking children swimming is a great responsibility, and you should be on the look-out for possible trouble the whole time. You may find that you can keep a closer eye on them from the edge of the pool, but if they are good swimmers you could enjoy a swim yourself and perhaps help organise a race or two.

Finally, if there are any gaps in the party (for instance while the children are waiting for their tea), it is better to organise a simple game or two, or perhaps running races, than to let them get over-excited by roaring round on their own.

The Cinema or Theatre

When you are planning a trip to a theatre or cinema, you will obviously want to choose the right level of entertainment for the age group you are catering for. Films are easier to choose than plays, as you will probably have heard about them anyway, or your children will have. Also you have the age restrictions on the films to go by.

The choice of a play will also be dependent on the ages of the children involved. Don't expect teenagers to enjoy a marionette theatre, for example – some may, but most won't. Find out from the theatre if you are not sure what the plot, is, and discuss the childrens' ages with them. We were once disappointed taking some little girls to a ballet, which although it was entitled *Sleeping Beauty* turned out to be some rather way-out modern ballet, and not what any of us had bargained for. If there is any query, do a little research and then you won't be disappointed.

Some theatres are only too pleased for you

to go backstage after a performance. You would have to enquire whether this was possible, but it is a great thrill if the staff are agreeable. When making your enquiry always state that it is for children and a birthday treat, or whatever. (Some theatres – the Royal Shakespeare Theatre, Stratford on Avon, for instance – organise backstage tours, but not necessarily after the performance.)

If you are thinking of taking a group of your child's friends to the cinema or theatre for a party treat, do remember before you ask half the class that it will be a costly exercise. Check with the box office whether they have any cheaper times – weekday matinees, perhaps – which you could take advantage of. If you are offered cheaper seats, check that there isn't a post in front of you all obscuring the view. Explain that you want seats that children will be able to see from – the staff are very helpful usually.

Consider what expenses you may incur when you get to the performance. You will want to buy a programme for each guest, and have something for them to nibble. Instead of buying expensive boxes of sweets, go armed with a polybag of goodies per child: a medley of little sweets, not sticky ones, which they can pick at during the performance. You will probably have to buy at least one drink per child in the interval. You could take individual fruit drinks or whatever, but children need to get up and stretch their legs, so they might as well go and buy a lolly or ice cream. Anyway, that is all part of the treat. (It might be a good idea to have a damp J-cloth for sticky fingers in a plastic bag in your handbag.)

When planning what meals to provide you will be governed by the time of the performance. If you are not taking many children, make it a special treat and turn it into a whole-day party. Keep the food simple, especially if you are having a supper at home after the performance. If you are going to an evening performance – and as the children get older, they would obviously prefer this – invite your guests to stay the night. It is so much easier than asking parents to turn out in the middle of the night, and also much more fun for the kids.

Camping Out

One of the greatest treats of all for younger children is to camp out for the night in your back garden. This could be organised with a few friends – if there is room in the garden for all their tents! Give them a barbecue supper and organise some games before they turn in for the night.

Be prepared for your night's sleep to be disturbed, though. This is partly because you may be sleeping lightly anyway – half keeping an ear out – and partly because, as sure as fate, someone will come in during the night. However, it is worth it as they do really enjoy themselves!

Tell your guests to bring tents, pillows, sleeping bags and torches, and have some spares available. Ideally, the tents should have attached ground sheets, but if there is one without you must put down some sort of waterproof base to prevent the sleeping bags going directly on to the ground. There probably won't be room in the tents for camp beds so you could offer eiderdowns, duvets or whatever you have available to go under the sleeping bags for added comfort – some may refuse

such luxury! We would also advise you to spray the children with insect repellent before they finally go to bed!

Make sure each tent has a torch. You will have to leave your back door open, and of course leave some lights on. Do make sure your garden is secure so that the children can't wander off. Tell them to leave their shoes or slippers by the tent entrance – then they won't find themselves lying on them and it will remind them to put them on when they go out.

Before you say goodnight stress that you won't mind at all if someone wants to give up half way through the night. (It's probably best if the tents are large enough to have two in a tent anyway.) Don't attempt this enterprise with children who are too young – probably not below the age of eight. And don't attempt it with boys and girls who are too old, either! With the eight-to-tens you should be all right. They must be really keen or they will be indoors in two seconds! If the children are still quite young perhaps Dad could be persuaded to sleep out there too . . .

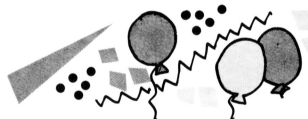

Café Parties

Many chains of restaurants – The Happy Eater, McDonald's, Wimpy Bars, Little Chef, Pizzaland, as well as lots of local eating places – have now jumped on the party bandwaggon and will provide all you need in the way of food and decorations for your children's party. Sometimes they'll even lay on the cake and entertainment too. It does, of course, cost more than doing it at home, but if you have taken a fairly small group to, say, a swimming pool or football match, it can be a wonderful way to round off the day. Look up in the Yellow Pages (under Restaurants) for the address of your nearest eating place, and discuss the party with them. Not unreasonably, they usually like several days' notice.

Food for Outings and Picnics

Organisation is the key to a successful picnic outing. Make a careful checklist of all the food and bits and pieces you will need as you can't afford to leave anything behind. The following list is pretty comprehensive and would cover most eventualities, but some things you would obviously not require if you were just popping down the road. Whether you are taking a party on one of the outings discussed, to the local park or woods, or further afield, have sufficient helpers. This is especially relevant if you are walking there, crossing roads and clutching the picnic as well as a dozen little hands.

Food, itemised
Kitchen towel or paper napkins
Damp J-cloths in plastic bags
Plastic bag for rubbish
Basic first-aid kit, Waspeze and insect repellent spray
Sun-tan cream (depending on the weather!)
Rugs to sit on

Bottle opener (corkscrew if required!)
A spare set of children's clothes
Towel
Ball (especially if taking boys)
Whistle to round up the younger troops
Food, drink (and cutlery if required)
Washing-up bowl (could be useful in car journeys if someone feels ill, or just for giving the dog a drink!)
Bottle of plain water (for anyone feeling ill or dog to drink)
Telephone number of a parent to be contacted if you are delayed.

We found that the easiest way to cater is to pack a 'nose bag' or individual picnic for each child. You will find some food is wasted, but it takes all the hassle out of serving up the bits and bobs of a picnic. Collect up enough large plastic margarine or ice-cream boxes beforehand. Put a piece of kitchen roll at the bottom of each and pack with the food. Discuss with your children what they think would be the most popular food to include in this 'nose bag'.

Alternatively, if you are going with other families each could bring a separate part of the meal. Plan the whole thing together so that one person takes the main course, someone else puddings, someone else the drinks (if it is freezing weather, perhaps include some soup to warm everyone up). If you are leaving early, you will have to prepare your picnic the night before. This is fine, but just make sure that everything is cold, clingfilmed and refrigerated for the night.

Popular picnic food would include a selection from the following:

LUNCH

Chicken drumsticks. Frozen drumsticks can be bought in packs very reasonably. Cook them with butter and dried herbs for flavour, or roll in beaten egg and then breadcrumbs and fry for crunch! Try the devilled chicken drumstick recipe on page 110. Place a little clingfilm at the end of the bone – it will avoid those very greasy fingers.

Sausages. Chipolatas are easier for young children to eat than large sausages.

Pigs in a blanket (see page 110) are excellent served cold.

Scotch Egg or plain hard-boiled egg.

Slice of favourite bought pizza.

Soft roll, pre-buttered if required. See Match Party Food for some filling ideas.

Salad. Sticks of carrot, cucumber or celery, and quarters of tomato.

Packets of crisps, etc.

Piece of fruit.

Pudding. If you want to do a pudding have individual pots of fruit yoghurt, or make individual chocolate or lemon mousses (see page 83) in old yoghurt pots. Take plastic spoons. (It is probably best if you keep these out of the 'nose bag': if you have an insulated cold bag or box keep them in this, but don't forget to hand them out.) Simplest of all, buy everyone an ice cream.

TEA
2 sandwiches (make two sorts and give one of each)
2 chipolatas or one plus a mini sausage roll
1 packet each of crisps, Hula Hoops, etc.
Biscuits: try and avoid melting chocolate biscuits and give a KP chocolate dip to each with, say, a flapjack (see page 107).
Give each a separate cup cake perhaps piped with the child's name (see page 109).

Pieces of fruit
Mini packet of Smarties or raisins, etc.

See also Match Party Food.

DRINKS
Don't take too many fizzy drinks if travelling far. Try the following instead.

Flask of plain water

Individual cans or cartons of juices, plus straws. It may be more expensive to buy a selection of individual drinks but it is so much easier to hand them out, especially if somebody wants a drink while you are going along in the car.

Flasks of soft drinks. If you prefer to take the drink in flasks, use old yoghurt or cream pots for glasses.

Games for Journeys

Most of us would agree that long journeys, especially car journeys, are not much fun for younger children. Most of them dislike sitting still! Try all the sensible ideas like the odd stop, the occasional packet of sweets or biscuits (but not chocolate-covered ones) and cassette tapes of stories, pop music, etc. When you cannot take any more pop, or they get fed up with golden oldies, see if the following games can help to pass the time. They are all simple to learn and need no special props. The object is not so much the winning or losing, but rather keeping everyone amused. However, you can if you like award points in each game and keep a running total, ending the journey with a championship title. It depends on how competitive you are all feeling.

MAPS
This is not really a game, but does pass the time very constructively. Encourage the children to look at the map or road atlas – it makes the journey more interesting for them if they know where they are going, and where they are on the map. Get them to work out what the symbols on the map mean. Explain how the mileage scale works so that they can see how far they are going. Older children can help you to work out your route and navigate while you are driving.

ROAD SIGNS
Most road atlases have an illustrated page of road signs. Get the children to study these and then have a competition to see who can be the first to call out the meaning of the road signs as you drive past them. Younger children can each choose a particular sign (a 'T Junction' or a 'Stop sign') and see how many they can spot of their own sign.

HOMONYMS
Players have to think of words which are pronounced in the same way but spelt differently – place, plaice; whale, wail; current, currant, etc. Score one for single-syllable words, two for two syllables. This is a game that can last off and on for days.

MY AUNT ELLEN
One person thinks of something that Aunt Ellen hates (words containing the letter P, for instance), and says 'My Aunt Ellen loves cakes but hates pastry', 'My Aunt Ellen loves oranges, but hates apples', until the others guess the answer. They can ask questions if it helps them to guess.

AUNT JEMIMA
The first player starts off with 'Aunt Jemima went shopping and she bought a cabbage', the next player says 'Aunt Jemima went shopping and she bought a cabbage and a tin of shoe polish', and so on. Players who forget one of the items drop out until only one remains.

I SPY
A good game for younger children but don't choose objects such as gates or chimneys that flash past too quickly.

QUICK SPOTTING
Draw up a list of ten things you might see on a journey and award points for each one. For instance one point for a red car, two for a thatched cottage, three for a police car, ten for a Lamborghini, and so on, and the first person to see the object and shout out wins the points.

JUST A MINUTE
Play as in the radio game: a player has to talk on a topic – chosen by the driver who is chairman – for one minute without repetition, hesitation or deviation.

CAR NUMBER PLATES
Use the letters in the number plate of the car in front to make a phrase or sentence, including the names of the people in your car if possible – ELB, 'Edward loves blancmange'. This is another game that can be played on and off for days.

CAR NUMBERS
Call out the number of the car in front and the first person to add them up correctly scores a point: for instance 682 = 16, and so on (or for younger brothers or sisters get them to spot their own age in a number, 4 in 241, for instance. This is especially good in a town with lots of traffic about).

HANGMAN

The object in this word-making game is to avoid being the last person who is obliged to finish the word. The first player says a letter, say, 'L', the next person says 'E', the next 'M' and so on, until the word is formed, in this case LEMON. Any player can challenge, when it is his turn, if he thinks the previous player is merely guessing and not spelling a real word. You are also out if you accidentally produce a shorter complete word within the longer word 'Yes' in 'Yesterday', for instance.

CAPITAL CITIES

The first player thinks of a capital city beginning with 'A', Addis Abbada, the next thinks of one beginning with 'B', Brussels, and so on. An easier version is to play by using the name of any town, not just capital cities. You can also play the game with boys' names, Angus, Bernard, etc, or girls' names, Amy, Bernadette, or invent your own ideas for lists.

BOOM

Everyone can play this. Players take it in turns to count, but the number 6, or numbers where it appears, say 16, are replaced by the word 'boom'. Count as fast as you can and as soon as you make a mistake the next player takes over. A more difficult version is to omit multiples of the number, this would mean leaving out 12, 18, 24, and so on – good practice for learning tables!

LINKED NAMES

Choose one kind of name – boys' names, towns, countries and so on – and then everyone in turn has to think of a name in which the first letter is the last of the one before, for instance, France, Egypt, Tunisia, Austria, and so on. Anyone who can't think of a name is out.

MESSAGES

Think of a word – not too long – and everyone has to make a sentence using the letters of the word (in the same order). For instance the word 'flower' might make:

> 'Fred loves outings with elephant rides'
> or 'Fetch Lucy our wooden-eared rabbit'

It's always hard to decide on a winner as everyone likes their own effort the best!

SONGS

These songs all go on for a long time and can be sung over and over again, and so help shorten the journey. They are all old favourites, easy to learn and great fun to sing. Try taking a verse each in turn, and award points for the one who sings it best – or worst.

One man went to mow

One man went to mow
Went to mow a meadow
One man and his dog
Went to mow a meadow

Two men went to mow
Went to mow a meadow
Two men, one man and his dog
Went to mow a meadow
Etc, etc.

Ten green bottles

Ten green bottles standing on the wall
Ten green bottles standing on the wall
If one green bottle should accidentally fall
There'd be nine green bottles standing on
  the wall

Nine green bottles standing on the wall
Nine green bottles standing on the wall
If one green bottle should accidentally fall . . .
  Etc, etc.

Green grow the rushes-o

I'll sing you one-o!
Green grow the rushes-o!
What is your one-o?
One is one and all alone and ever more
  shall be so.

I'll sing your two-o!
Green grow the rushes-o!
What is your two-o?
Two, two, the lily-white boys, clothed all in
  green-o
One is one and all alone and ever more
  shall be so.

I'll sing you three-o!
Green grow the rushes-o!
What is your three-o?
Three, three the rivals,
Two, two, the lily-white boys, clothed all in
  green-o
One is one and all alone and ever more
  shall be so.

The following verses are:

Four for the gospel makers
Five for the symbols at your door
Six for the six proud walkers
Seven for the seven stars in the sky
Eight for the April rainers
Nine for the nine bright shiners
Ten for the Ten Commandments
Eleven for the eleven who went to heaven
Twelve for the twelve apostles.

There's a hole in my bucket

1. There's a hole in my bucket, dear Liza,
      dear Liza,
    There's a hole in my bucket, dear Liza,
      a hole.
2. Then mend it dear Henry, dear Henry,
      dear Henry,
    Then mend it, dear Henry, dear Henry,
      mend it!
3. With what shall I mend it, dear Liza . . .
      with what?
4. With a straw, dear Henry . . . a straw.
5. The straw is too long, dear Liza . . . too long.
6. Then cut it, dear Henry . . . cut it.
7. With what shall I cut it, dear Liza . . .
      with what?
8. With a knife, dear Henry . . . a knife.
9. The knife is too blunt, dear Liza . . . too
      blunt.
10. Then sharpen it, dear Henry . . .
      sharpen it.
11. With what shall I sharpen it, dear
      Liza . . . with what?
12. With a stone, dear Henry . . . a stone.
13. The stone is too dry, dear Liza . . . too dry.
14. Then wet it, dear Henry . . . wet it.
15. With what shall I wet it, dear Liza . . .
      with what?
16. With water, dear Henry . . . with water.
17. In what shall I get it, dear Liza . . . in what?
18. In a bucket, dear Henry . . . in a
      bucket
19. (All together) 'There's a hole in my
      bucket, dear Liza . . . A HOLE!!'

She'll be coming round the mountain

She'll be coming round the mountain when
  she comes
She'll be coming round the mountain when
  she comes
She'll be coming round the mountain
Coming round the mountain
Coming round the mountain when she
  comes

She'll be wearing pink pyjamas when she
  comes . . .

She'll be riding six white horses when she
  comes . . .

Make up your own additional verses.

Family Parties

Midsummer, Hallowe'en, Guy Fawkes or Hogmanay parties could be the excuse for small or large family gatherings, but you don't need any particular reason for an informal meal followed by some fun games. There are many occasions when it's a nice idea to invite a couple of other families (or more, if you have space) for a lunch or supper: for example, the boat race, FA Cup Final or the Grand National.

Don't worry too much about the children's ages coinciding exactly – obviously there must be some who are comparable with your children but you will be surprised how the teenagers will have a giggle with the six-year-olds in this sort of atmosphere. These parties are a good way for you to entertain easily and casually, and for the children to experience and learn to socialise – great for family togetherness. You can get everybody involved in the preparations, but keep things simple as it is not a grand lunch or dinner party you are planning, but a family get-together! If you are likely to be pushed for time, the children can make a fruit salad or simple mousse for pudding. And if you cannot face the messy kitchen following that exercise, ask the other families who are coming to bring something. Share the work load, and everyone can have fun.

The menu we provide is for a gathering of about fourteen people for a casual supper or lunch. However, we have included lots of other ideas for larger parties, with page references for the recipes at the end of the book.

The children will want you to join in with them, so don't go and nod off in the sitting room or chatter exclusively amongst yourselves. You must prepare to have family entertainment. The children can help organise. Here are a few ideas for you to work on.

Sporting Events

If the party is planned round a sporting occasion, run some sort of a sweepstake. For example, if you were having a Grand National party cut the names of all the runners out of a newspaper and put them in a hat. Everyone then has an interest in the race, and those who pick out the winner, second, third or fourth could either be given a little present, or perhaps some money. If there are more runners than guests, then give them two chances. For the Boat Race, ask your guests to take either a dark or pale blue ribbon from a hat – allow equal numbers of ribbon for Oxford and for Cambridge. The two teams which result will have some definite allegiance and whichever team loses could pay a forfeit – acting a charade for the others, or doing the washing up! Later, use the team divisions for playing games (see page 64).

In summertime have a family tennis match

– depending on ages, have fathers and daughters against mothers and sons. The others can ball-boy and umpire, and the finals can be between the winner of each group. Finish up with a barbecue at home (see page 67). Look up the tennis-match section to devise a proper tournament if your numbers are large.

New Year's Eve Party

New Year's Eve can be a problem when you have children who are old enough to enjoy staying up, but perhaps not old enough to be left without a babysitter (a rare commodity on New Year's Eve). Solve the problem by inviting in some friends with children of a similar age to your own, and both generations can enjoy bringing in the New Year.

Sort out some Scottish reels. You must have a caller who really knows what they are doing. If necessary ask for information from the dancing teacher at school. You'll need the right records or tapes, of course. Run a disco as well for a break from the reels. Try the cold chicken concoction (see page 114) for a buffet supper, or a lasagne (see page 100) if you have room to sit everybody down.

Hallowe'en Party

If your guests are the right sort of age, they will enjoy wearing fancy dress. Try out the following ideas:

GHOST
Use a small sheet to cover the 'ghost' completely. Cut eye holes and fasten a piece of elastic around the back of the head to hold the sheet in place. If you have any old black net, cover the sheet with this to give a very ghostly effect.

WITCH AND WIZARD
You need long black, purple or red cloaks (old curtains?), tall witches' hats (make these out of black card, and cover with stick-on stars and moons). Colour faces white, and add black lines and red lips with face paints, and black out teeth with mascara. Witches could paint their fingernails with black nail varnish. If you have a small besom broom let the witch carry this.

VAMPIRE
A long cloak (as above), white shirt and black trousers is all you will need. Get a set of plastic fangs from a toyshop and have lips and chin dripping with blood (face paint!)

SKELETONS
Paint white bones on to an old black jersey and tights.

Older children dislike wearing fancy dress, so don't try to persuade them. However, they may be willing to wear long cloaks, which will add to the spooky atmosphere and keep them warm if you are out of doors.

Get your decorations ready in good time. Use pumpkins if you can find them – hollow them out, make holes for eyes and mouth and put nightlights inside. Don't worry if you can't get hold of pumpkins – turnips will do, or even sugar beet, if you live in the country. When you have hollowed them out, turn them upside down so that they have a flat base to stand on. Another idea is to put night lights inside ordinary jam jars: you can stick coloured tissue paper around the outside for extra effect. All these lights can be used in the house or the garden, but make sure they are well out of harm's way. You may well be lucky with your weather and decide to start the party off out of doors with a bonfire. Put a baking tray filled with chestnuts into the embers (prick with a fork first) – but only adults should fish them out, and with long tongs.

In the house, change some of your light bulbs to red, orange or blue, or cover the old ones with paint. This gives a very ghostly light.

Go round the local dress shops well before the party and persuade them to lend you some of the old mannequins used in the shop windows. Dress them up as witches and skeletons, etc, and have them hanging on the walls or sitting in a chair.

Include among your games such traditional ones such as apple-bobbing and doughnut-chomping.

BLINDFOLD FEELING GAME

Each player is blindfolded in turn and led into a separate room to identify a collection of objects by touch: a peeled grape (tell them it is a witch's eye), cold spaghetti (Medusa's hair), avocado pear skin (frog's skin), avocado stone (a Cyclop's eye). We won't give you any more ideas here or the adults will know them all – the children are very clever at thinking up their own. You can extend this game by making it a smelling and tasting game as well: fill saucers with coffee, curry powder, tomato ketchup, chocolate sauce, etc. When each player has had his go, they can sit and watch the others, but they must not shout out the answers!

Make the room for this game very ghostly with dim lights and weird noises, but if any of the younger children are at all frightened, let them help you blindfold the others rather than making them play themselves. Your children will enjoy recording a tape of weird noises in advance to play back during the party.

APPLE-BOBBING

Play this in the kitchen! Put a large bowl or bucket of water on the floor and float apples in it. Players have to pick up the apples with their teeth (hands behind the back). The winner is the one who gets most apples in a particular time limit.

DOUGHNUT-CHOMPING

Thread doughnuts on pieces of string, and fasten string to a broom handle or pole. Attach the pole to the ceiling or across two doors, if you can. If not, balance it between two chair backs. Players have to eat the doughnuts with their hands behind their backs. First to finish is the winner.

Also see page 61 for lots more games.

Serve a buffet supper. Dips and crisps, Devilled Chicken Drumsticks and a profiterole pyramid, for instance. If you want to serve a hot drink, serve the Mulled Mystery on page 119 – it is quite delicious. Otherwise serve a fizzy apple or orange punch, but have a look through the drinks section first. Give all the guests a toffee apple to take home.

Firework Party

You can choose one of two sorts of firework party. Bearing in mind that fireworks are both dangerous and expensive, the first option is to arrange to meet some other families at a local firework display and then come back home for supper. Have some indoor fireworks and sparklers to finish the evening off for the children. The second option is to have a party at home which is so well organised that the risk of accidents is minimal. Make it a 'bring a firework' party to cut down the cost a bit.

If a display is to be worthwhile you will find the cost horrendous, so ask those who are coming to provide a couple of fireworks per person and you will at least have a basis for the display. One or two big fireworks are better than a box of small ones. Ask guests to deliver their contributions a couple of days ahead of the party to allow you time to organise the order of fireworks and devise a good varied display. Order your own fireworks well ahead of the date of the party. Always organise your props – posts for catherine wheels, etc – in the daylight, even the weekend before the party. Don't try to rush home a bit early on the day to organise things. The display will be a disappointment, and the person in charge will be in a flap (this could be dangerous). Make sure that there is one person, with a helper, who is specifically in charge of the fireworks.

Write yourself a plan, and list the fireworks and where they are to be positioned. Don't forget equipment such as torches, matches and a bucket of water or sand. Make sure the guests and children are standing well away from the actual display area and, if possible, have the area roped off. Ask a friend to look after your pets indoors.

Get the children to make the Guy (not out of their father's best suit!), and build the bonfire where the spectators can be warmed by it. Don't light the bonfire before the guests arrive – it's amazing how quickly it will burn out. If you are inviting a lot of people, serve your food and mulled drinks while the display is going on – then with any luck you need not have them indoors at all (thus avoiding millions of gumboots marks over the kitchen floor). The children can help hand everything round. Why not make bowls of popcorn and hand them round too?

When the display has finished give the younger children a couple of sparklers each. This is a good way of ending the evening. Alternatively, once the fireworks are over, have everyone indoors to eat supper. This way they stay longer and perhaps you can play some family games (see page 62). The food you serve will depend on the type of party you plan, and the time at which it is held. Adapt these general suggestions to suit your particular party. The recipes are at the back of the book.

If food is outside:
Hotdogs
Chicken Drumsticks
Beefburgers in rolls
Baked Potatoes cut into manageable pieces
Pizza Fingers
followed by chocolate biscuits.

If food is inside:
Stew
Lasagne
Shepherds' Pie
Baked Potatoes
followed by Chocolate Mousse.

Provide jugs of mulled drinks (for children's recipe see page 119) and have a jug of orange squash in case of need.

Barn Dance

You must have a suitable venue for this party, but even more important is to book an experienced and enthusiastic caller and an equally good band. A party like this could be a disaster if you don't have somebody competent in charge. We heard of an occasion where the caller kept looking at his notes, trying to keep everybody going but failing dismally. Nobody enjoyed themselves.

Ideally you should contact a caller and band through personal recommendation but the Yellow Pages (under Dance Bands) might list a suitable group. Failing all else you could ask a local dancing teacher, or go through an agency – see Yellow Pages under Entertainment Agencies (you will incur an agency fee, though). Wherever you find your band, double check how successful they are, and ask for references and take them up. Make certain, too, that the band can cope with mixed age groups.

Remember to ask your band how long a break they will be taking during the evening so that you can plan the party. You might like to serve supper during the break, or have food available all evening. If you have a running buffet, play some disco music while the band has a break. Perhaps you could rig up a hi-fi system with some tapes, depending on the venue.

DECORATIONS
If you are lucky enough to have access to a real barn for this party, put straw bales around for everyone to sit on (so long as you are particularly strict about no smoking). Otherwise decorate your room, garage or hall with streamers, balloons in a net, etc. If you could get hold of any Western posters these would be fun, but remember that anything too small will not make much impact in a large hall.

FOOD AND DRINK
Serve simple food that can all be eaten with the fingers. The children could label the food with appropriate names, for example, 'Bunk House Burgers' (beef burger in a roll, see page 110), 'Sheriff's Sausages' (sausages on sticks, see page 74) 'Cowboy's Chicken' (chicken drumsticks, see page 110). For very large numbers, see discothèque food, page 110.

Everyone will get very thirsty, so have plenty of drink available. A fruit cup is always popular.

Family Party Food

Throughout the book we have stressed that you should keep everything very simple, whatever kind of party you are holding. If you are having a casual get-together at home perhaps the easiest thing would be to serve finger foods for the children to hand round instead of a starter. Then have the main food in the kitchen as a buffet; take your plates and sit down at one table together if possible. This way you will get more of a party atmosphere. Younger childen will love making place names and organising the seating plan.

MENU
Mini Sausage Rolls
Cheese Straws
Dips

★ ★ ★ ★ ★ ★ ★ ★ ★ ★

Meat Fondue
Cold Chicken Concoction
Beef Casserole

★ ★ ★ ★ ★ ★ ★ ★ ★ ★

Salad
Baked Potatoes

★ ★ ★ ★ ★ ★ ★ ★ ★ ★

Chocolate Mousse (see page 83)
Pavlova (see page 81)
Ice Cream with Various Sauces
(see page 104)

Our recipes are for fourteen, so adapt the quantities to suit your requirements. They are designed for everyone to eat, so they are not too sophisticated in case there are much younger children involved. Whatever food you serve, try to ensure that you have a selection which can appeal to adults and children alike: for example, serve cold chicken which you can dress up with a sauce, or serve plain and simple for the less adventurous. If the weather is fine, the ideal way to entertain one and all in an unsophisticated way is to hold a barbecue.

Try a fondue party. The advantage of this particular meal is that it helps breaks the ice and gets everybody chattering together. Add another dimension by playing forfeits if anyone drops their meat into the cooking oil, for example, kiss the person on their left.

Indoor Games

The games suggested here incorporate some for young children, some for older children and some for all the family to play. You will have to choose what is best for your occasion.

Always plan your games in advance rather than trying to organise them at the time. You will probably find that you will not get through them quite as fast as you did when the children were younger. However, have plenty planned! Have prizes ready for the younger groups. Make a list of the games you intend to play as your mind can go blank so easily – it's not only the children who are getting older, we all are! By each game jot down what props you will need, then you can get the children to organise them for you!

BABYFACE
For this game you will need a piece of board made of wood or hardboard, or a pin board and Blu-Tack. Provide your guests with a piece of paper and a pencil each. Ask everyone to bring a photograph of themselves as a baby. One of your family must be in charge of collecting the photographs when everybody arrives, and Blu-Tacking them on to the board with a number underneath each photograph. Everyone then has to guess who is who. Whoever is in charge of the game then marks the papers, and whoever has scored most wins. Remind everybody to name their papers, otherwise you won't know whose is whose.

MUSICAL CHAIRS (WITH A DIFFERENCE)
Instead of just having chairs, use the odd chair, cushions, bean bags, rug, pillow, anything you have to hand. (If you are having a coloured theme to your party, try to find things in

matching colours.) Put all these objects in the middle of the room and the participants have to dance to disco music around them, and when the music stops grab whatever form of seating they can, and sit on it. You remove one item of seating after each go, and whoever is in last wins.

PICTURE GALLERY

Put photos of famous faces on a board, or Blu-Tack them to a wall having written a number in the corner of each photograph. Give the children a pencil and paper each and whoever guesses the most faces, wins.

JIGSAW PUZZLE GAME

Cut up advertisements from magazines into two or three pieces, depending on the participants' ages, etc. Keep one piece back to give to each person and hide the others around the house. Whoever collects most advertisements wins. Alternatively use old Christmas or birthday cards for the jigsaws.

STATUES, MUSICAL

It is quite fun to play musical statues the wrong way round. Stand still when the music is playing and dance when it stops! If anyone moves when the music is playing they are out, and whoever is in last wins.

PASS THE PARCEL IN REVERSE

Wrap up one small present, and put a heap of paper bags or carrier bags, or whatever sort of mixed bags you want, in the middle of a circle of children. Give one child the wrapped present to pass round. Each time the music stops the child with the present has to put another bag on to it. The person who puts the last bag on gets the prize, which they then have to unwrap! NB. Use smallest bags first.

PASS THE PARCEL WITH FORFEITS

You will need to wrap up a conventional pass-the-parcel parcel with enough layers for each guest to unwrap one and, if you wish, you can tape a sweet to each layer. However, instead of just passing the parcel and grabbing the sweet, they will have to perform a forfeit as well. Make up your list of forfeits prior to the party: for example, imitate Maggie Thatcher at Question Time, say the seven-times table backwards, and so on.

RAILWAY CARRIAGES

You will need to provide a newspaper per guest and, in advance of your party, muddle up the pages of the newspaper. It is only fair to have identical newspapers for the children, as some are so much larger and more difficult to cope with than others. The first player to get the newspaper back into correct page order wins the game.

CHOPPING CHOCOLATE GAME

You will need a plate, a knife and fork, a pair of gloves, a hat, a scarf, a dice and a large bar of chocolate unwrapped. The children have to throw the dice and when a player throws a six, he/she puts on the hat, the scarf and the gloves, and tries to chop the chocolate (which can be eaten if successfully chopped)! In the meantime, the other children are throwing the dice, and if anybody else scores a six the person chopping has to give up all the equipment and the next one has a go. (There is no real winner to this game.)

TREASURE HUNT

You can play this individually or in pairs. Give each a list of items to find. Also give them a pencil with which to write where each item is (keep a 'master' list to yourself). Let the whole house be used as it's so much more fun. Have at least twelve items. Whoever finds them all first is the winner. Examples of what to hide might include:

Piece of Elastoplast	A nut
Piece of sticky tape	An elastic band
A Polo mint	A button
A safety pin	An egg

HAPPY HELMES HOUSE GAME

You can play this game as individuals or in pairs. Give clues, preferably in rhyming couplets, to objects to be found around the house. Each person (or pair) has a photocopy of the clues on which he (or they) writes the answers. The winner is the first person to discover the word which is made up from the first letters of the answers to the clues. To make the game more difficult, muddle the order of the clues so that it becomes an anagram. Adapt your clues to suit the age group of your guests.

As an example, here is a list of nine clues, with answers which make up the word 'Wednesday'.

1. Look behind the yellow curtain
Of the answer, you'll be certain. — **W**indow

2. In a cupboard on the wall
You'll find some help if you should fall. — **E**lastoplast

3. *You must not look –* remember well.
When you came in was there a bell?
A knocker on the door?
A chime?
A trumpet? Banger? Squeaky toys?
What have we put to make a noise? — **D**oorknocker, door bell, etc.

4. Tis now the last day of the year,
What sort of party have we here? — **N**ew Eve's Year

5. Look in the desk and you will discover
Along with the paper a useful cover. — **E**nvelope

6. They have their ups and downs you know,
Eleven standing in a row,
Another four, lead to the floor,
They help you to your bedroom go. — **S**tairs

7. In a room where we feel dozy
These cover us up and keep us cosy. — **D**uvet

8. There was a young lady of Ryde,
Who ate a green . . . ? and died.
The . . . ? fermented,
Inside the lamented,
And made cider in side her inside.
(There's a bowl of these in the dining room) — **A**pple

9. In a cool place you must seek,
These pots will keep at least a week. — **Y**oghurt

TASTING GAME

You will need a blindfold and about ten morsels to taste – jam, toothpaste, carrot, chocolate, etc – a spoon and pencil and paper for each guest. You give each guest a taste of each and they have to go out and write down what they think they have eaten. The winner is the one who gets most correct.

WHAT'S IN ROSIE'S BOX?

You will need one large box, prepared with a hole on top and half of a pair of tights stapled to the hole so that no one can see inside. Inside the box will be eight items – a coin, a piece of string, a piece of ice (put this in just before you play the game), etc. Give each guest a pencil and paper. Each player puts a hand in the leg of the tights in the box and identifies what they can feel inside. They have two minutes (you will be timekeeper) to feel, and then they must write down what they remember. Whoever gets most right is the winner.

TRAY GAME

You will need a tray with twelve items on it – a pen, a paperclip, a rubber, a book, etc. If you are giving a party with a colour theme, again continue this by making sure that all the items are, for example, pink. Give each child a pencil and a piece of paper. Show them the tray with the items on for a certain time, then take the tray away and allow them two minutes in which they have to remember and write down all the items you showed them. Whoever remembers most, wins. Be prepared for a tied win and have several little prizes ready.

FATHERS' KNEES

This is not a team game, it is just good fun. The fathers go into a separate room, the doorway of which can easily be seen by the remaining families. A rug is pinned over the top two-thirds of the doorway.

The fathers take off their trousers and tie beribboned rosettes below their knees. They then, one at a time, parade their legs, incognito, past the doorway. The families guess which pair of legs belongs to each father.

Indoor Team Games

There are many ways of dividing everyone into teams and it is a good idea to organise this when guests first arrive. Pop a 'team' sticker (the children will love organising this) on everybody. They can be bought at any good stationer's, or use coloured labels for a cheaper version. Alternatively make badges, and use different colours or shapes for your teams. Other ideas for team divisions could be animals (pigs, cows, sheep, mice) or TV soap operas (*Dallas, Dynasty, Coronation Street, East Enders*), and so on. If you are having a family party, you could pre-match the teams and make yourself a list: put a parent with his own shy child; a father in each team; split similar aged children. Alternatively have the children versus the adults, in which case give the adults some sort of handicap.

PASS THE ORANGE

You will need two oranges. Give each captain an orange. He or she puts it under their chin, and passes it down the line. A variation of this is for the two teams to lie on the floor, and to pass the orange between their ankles.

PASS THE MATCHBOX

You will need two matchbox covers. Give the captain of each team a matchbox, and then the guests have to pass the matchbox on their noses along the line, without using their hands. Whichever team finishes first is the winner.

PASS THE BALLOON

You will need two balloons, and two spares or more! Give each team leader a balloon. The team leader puts the balloon between his knees and passes it to the next person in the line, and so on. Neither team has won until the last member has burst the balloon. Alternatively pass small balloons under chins.

CHARADES

Give each team a list of suitable subjects – book or film titles, etc – and a few minutes to think about them. Then each team acts them to the other team within a set time-limit. A variation on this game is to let each team suggest a word, for example a three-syllable word, such as candlelit. They then act out each syllable. The team then acts a little play, the first act of which includes in the dialogue the first syllable, and so on. Then the final act must include the whole word.

TEAM TICKLES

You will need lots of string and two dessertspoons for two teams. Have two very long pieces of string (the length depending on the number of your guests). With the dessertspoon tied to the end of each piece, the first team member has to 'thread' the spoon under their clothes, downwards, and pass the spoon to the next member who threads it similarly upwards! The first person has to hold on to the end of the piece of string so that it doesn't get pulled through and out. The first team to sit down, all joined together, is the winner.

TEAM 'TRIVIAL PURSUITS'

If you have the general knowledge game 'Trivial Pursuits', play this as a team game. Each side has a box of questions. Choose two team leaders. The captains keep score cards, so provide two pencils and pieces of paper. All the questions on each card are asked by one team of the other. A member from one team asks the first set of questions of the other team. The team captain gives the final answer to the questions, after a general discussion amongst all the members of the opposing team. Everybody has an opportunity to put the list of questions. After a round (when the questions from one card have all been answered), the opposing team then has the chance to put the questions on their first card to the other team.

GENERAL KNOWLEDGE QUIZ

It is probably kinder to make this a team game in case anyone gets a fit of nerves and can't answer a single question. Have a list of general knowledge questions and pencil and paper for each team.

BARK IN THE DARK

This game is played in the dark with two teams. Before the party, write out two identical lists of animals or birds and the noises they make for instance, horse = neigh, pig = grunt, owl = twit twoo, and so on. Give each team leader a list, making sure that there are enough noises to go round. The leader then whispers the name and noise of an animal to each individual team member.

Take the teams to separate parts of the house, and turn out all the lights. In the darkness each person shouts out their appropriate noise (moo, hiss, meow, twit-twoo, etc) and finds his 'partnered noise'. When the partner is found, hang on to them and stop making the noise. The last two to pair up are then the only ones making a noise and have lost. The lights are turned on and they do a forfeit such as blind man's feast, when two people (both blindfolded) feed each other jelly whilst sitting cross-legged on a table.

DRAWING GAME

Divide your guests into teams. The host lists simple objects or ideas such as cold, happy, light, etc. If there were four teams he would need four lists of, say, twenty objects. He retains the list. Each team sends off to the host one member, who is given the name of an object on his team's list. He returns to his group and without speaking or miming, he draws the object as best he can. As soon as another member of his team has guessed it, even if it is only partly drawn, the next team member runs off to the host to collect the next object. He will first have to confirm that the previous answer was correct, before being given his turn. The first team to guess all the objects on its list wins. Adapt our lists as you wish.

North	South	East	West
Owl	Peacock	Swallow	Parrot
Mouse	Beetle	Bee	Ladybird
Camel	Cow	Giraffe	Elephant
Sun	Saturn	Moon	Star
Sheep	Pig	Cat	Rabbit
Leek	Cabbage	Marrow	Pea pod
Car	Train	Army tank	Ship
Snow	Rain	Fog	Cloud
Spoon	Fork	Knife	Cup
Volcano	Wave	Whirlwind	Bomb
Tin can	Dustbin	Bottle	Sack
See-saw	Swing	Slide	Circus
Parson	Queen	King	Bride
Sickle	Hammer	Nail	Scissors
Violin	Piano	Trumpet	Saxophone

DICTIONARY GAME

One team looks up a very unusual word in the dictionary. Each member of the team then gives a definition of this word. One of the meanings is the correct one. The other team has to decide whose answer is correct. The points are scored when a team guesses the right answer.

LOO ROLL GAME

Choose two captains, and divide the guests into two teams. Give each team a roll of loo paper and whoever can wrap up their captain first in the loo roll is the winner. This is very popular!

TISSUE RACE

This is a team race and you will need two tissues (have some spares in case of need) and give each member of both teams a drinking straw. Have a start and finish line. The object of the race is to blow the tissue along the ground with the straw. Once over the finishing line the next member of the team gets going, and whichever team finishes first is the winner.

SARDINES

This is a good game to finish off with, involving everyone. It must be played in the dark, and it is probably wise, therefore, to restrict the area in your home where the participants can go without doing damage. One person goes and hides, then after a certain length of time everybody else sets out to find him or her, and hides there too. Complete silence should be maintained, although this becomes rather difficult when everyone is squashed up together!

Preparing food for the barbecue (see page 68).

'Pass the Balloon' teams in action.

An occasion for a family party (see page 59).

A giant inflatable or a bouncy castle will always get them going.

Barbecues

Barbecues are becoming increasingly popular, in spite of our uncertain weather. The reasons for this are not difficult to find: food tastes wonderful when cooked and eaten out of doors, and the cooking itself is such fun that everyone wants to lend a hand, especially the men, which is a wonderful break for habitual female cooks. In fact, some mothers have a barbecue practically every weekend in the summer because they find it such a wonderful way to get out of doing the cooking! Older (sensible) children can certainly help with the cooking, but it goes without saying that there must be an adult around at all times to supervise the barbecue itself. A fire which is hot enough to cook food is certainly hot enough to burn over-eager fingers.

The first thing you need is a suitable place for the barbecue. Out of doors, of course, not too far from the house because of all the fetching and carrying, and preferably in a sheltered place so that the wind won't blow the smoke into the house or straight to where you are planning to eat. Have a table alongside for all your cooking utensils, meat, seasoning, etc.

You can buy very attractive fully equipped barbecues of varying sizes, which have the added advantage of being mobile, but they are rather expensive. There is in fact nothing easier than building your own barbecue, either a temporary or a permanent one, for very little cost.

Charcoal is the conventional fuel for a barbecue. Buy it in the form of small briquettes, or as charcoal pieces. You can buy bags from most hardware shops, and it is certainly convenient to use and to store. But you don't need to use charcoal. Indeed, most kinds of wood, dried and cut small, will make a good barbecue – and can be easier to light and hotter than charcoal. Some people prefer the flavour of food cooked over a wood fire.

To light the barbecue, take off the top metal grid, crumple up some newspaper on the lower shelf, arrange kindling wood or a firelighter on top (or both, if you are a pessimist) and then a good layer of fuel, either charcoal or wood, on top. If you prefer you can buy special barbecue firelighters. When you have lit the fire, keep an eye on it until you see that the fuel itself has caught and is burning well. On no account encourage it with paraffin or petrol. Quite apart from the danger, it will make the food taste horrible.

Make sure you light your barbecue a good hour before you need to start the cooking. The flames should all have died down, leaving a pile of glowing embers, but don't forget to add fuel from time to time to keep the heat up. Replace the top metal grid to give it time to heat through. Allow enough time after the ember stage in which to cook the food. There is nothing worse than having hungry guests standing around while you prod chicken legs that you know quite well are still horribly raw in the middle! Get your cooking utensils together before the start, as well. You will need a jug of water (to sprinkle a few drops on the occasional flame), a small bowl of cooking oil and a pastry brush with which to baste the meat as it cooks, a pair of cooking tongs and, if possible, some sprigs of rosemary, sage, thyme, a bay leaf or two, or other herbs to give a lovely flavour to the food as it cooks.

Food

As with all parties, planning in advance for a barbecue is the secret of success. You don't want to be stuck in the kitchen while the family or guests are out of doors (hopefully) enjoying the sunshine.

If you are marinating the meat, then do this the night before and leave it in the fridge, turning it occasionally. Then make the barbecue sauce and leave it in the saucepan to reheat quickly. Then prepare the garlic bread, baked potatoes, etc, and finally the salad (but don't add any dressing until you are ready to serve). If you are entertaining a large number of guests, why not start cooking the meat and potatoes indoors and finish off on the barbecue, so you won't have so long to wait for them all to cook, especially if your barbecue is a small one?

We give the recipes in some detail for the benefit of younger cooks. You can, if you like, plan the whole meal from this section – the meat, the vegetables and the pudding – or you can serve a salad with the main course and ice cream for pudding – try one of the sauces on page 104 to go with it. These barbecue recipes are for eight people.

MARINADES FOR MEAT

If you are cutting the meat up (for kebabs, say) then do this first. Marinate the meat for several hours, or even overnight, turning occasionally. Use what is left of the marinade for basting the meat while cooking.

HERB MARINADE

3 tablespoons salad oil
1 tablespoon vinegar
1 clove garlic, crushed
2 teaspoons chopped mixed herbs, fresh or
  dried (thyme, rosemary, oregano, marjoram,
  etc.)
a pinch of salt and pepper

Mix all the ingredients. Put the meat into a shallow dish and pour the marinade over. Turn several times.

SPICY MARINADE

3 tablespoons salad oil
1 tablespoon soy sauce
2 cloves garlic, crushed
1 tablespoon brown sugar
1 teaspoon ground ginger
½ teaspoon dry mustard

A delicious zingy marinade, especially good with spare ribs. Mix all the ingredients, as above.

BARBECUE SAUCES

These should be made in advance to allow the flavour to develop. Reheat in a saucepan (on the cooker indoors, because it's so much easier) and pour a little over the meat just before serving. Serve the rest in a jug so that people can help themselves. You can also use these to baste the meat while it is cooking. Make a large quantity of the sauces if you like, to use when needed, as they will keep very well in a sealed jar in the fridge.

VERY EASY BARBECUE SAUCE

1 small tin concentrated tomato soup
2 tablespoons tomato ketchup
2 tablespoons vinegar
2 tablespoons pickle
1 tablespoon brown sugar
2 teaspoons Worcestershire sauce

Mix all the ingredients in a pan and simmer gently for a few minutes.

HERB-FLAVOURED BARBECUE SAUCE

5 tablespoons tomato ketchup
1 onion, chopped very fine
1 clove garlic, crushed
1 tablespoon fresh mixed herbs
1 tablespoon vinegar
1 tablespoon brown sugar
1 teaspoon Worcestershire sauce
a pinch of salt and pepper
$\frac{1}{2}$ bay leaf

Combine all the ingredients in a pan. Simmer slowly until onion is soft. Remove bay leaf before serving.

HOT FLAVOURED BREADS

Children love these breads, but don't serve them before the meat is ready, otherwise they will all be gone before the meal has started. Take a long French loaf, and cut it downwards every 2 inches (5 cm) along the loaf, but not right through, then spread one of the following flavoured butters between the slices. Wrap up firmly in foil and heat at the bottom of the oven for half an hour. You can buy herb, garlic or anchovy purée in tubes from most good supermarkets and if you are pushed for time, then these will make very good substitutes.

GARLIC BUTTER

3 oz (75 g) softened butter
3 cloves garlic, crushed
a pinch of salt

Work the garlic and salt well into the butter before spreading.

HERB BUTTER

3 oz (75 g) softened butter
1 tablespoon chopped mixed herbs (fresh if
  possible)
a pinch of salt

Work the herbs and salt into the butter, as above.

ANCHOVY BUTTER

3 oz (75 g) softened butter
$\frac{1}{2}$ tin anchovy fillets

Finely chop or pound the anchovy fillets, then work into the butter.

MEAT

Quantities will depend on the age of the children, but they do seem to eat more out of doors! Have a selection of meats if possible, and allow one item of each per guest. For instance, a good mix would be; one chicken drumstick, one beefburger and 2 sausages or alternatively 2 spare ribs and one lamb chop. If in doubt about quantity, err on the over-generous side – it never seems to get wasted.

BEEFBURGERS

Although you can buy these, home-made ones are much better for the barbecue because, being thicker, they won't dry out. For this reason also we suggest you bind the meat with milk rather than egg, as egg tends to dry out the meat in cooking.

Makes 8

2 lb (900 g) lean chuck steak (or more
  expensive steak if you can afford it)
5 tablespoons fresh breadcrumbs
a little milk
a pinch of salt and pepper
1 onion, finely chopped (optional)

Mince the steak yourself, or ask your butcher to mince it for you. Combine all the ingredients, and shape into eight beefburgers about ½ inch (1 cm) thick. Place on a sheet of foil over the grill and cook until they are brown all over, turning once. Children probably prefer them cooked right through rather than pink in the middle.

CHEESEBURGERS

Turn the beefburgers when one side is cooked and put a slice of cheese on top of each one. This will just be melted when the burger is done.

KEBABS

Allow one kebab per guest. You will need long skewers for kebabs so as not to burn your fingers while cooking them. Choose lamb, pork or turkey and buy half a leg of lamb, a small joint of pork, or a turkey joint, allowing about 6 oz (175 g) boned meat per younger child and 8 oz (225 g) per teenagers and adults. Cut the meat into pieces about 1½ inches (4 cm) square, making sure to remove all sinews. Marinate the meat (see page 68) and then push the meat on to the skewers (the more closely you pack the meat the longer it will take to cook, but it will dry out less and taste better). Grill the kebabs over the barbecue, turning them several times and brushing them with oil or the marinade, until they are nice and brown.

To remove the meat from the skewers put the kebabs on the plate, hold it down firmly with one hand, with a fork in the other, and pull the meat slowly off the skewer with the fork.

You can serve kebabs inside the Greek pitta bread, or inside a piece of long French bread (heat both kinds of bread first). This is a good idea if you are serving large numbers, because you can do away with plates, knives and forks.

Using vegetables alternately with the meat makes it go further, prevents it drying out during cooking, and improves its flavour.

Lamb, Tomato and Mushroom Kebabs

Cut small tomatoes in half, remove stalks from the mushrooms and push on to the skewers, turn and turn about with the meat.

Pork, Pineapple and Frankfurter Kebabs

Use large chunks of pineapple or rings cut into quarters to alternate with the pieces of pork and Frankfurter sausage.

SAUSAGES

These are always popular, but for a change try the following variations. Dip the sausages into milk, and then into flour (best with the skinless variety). The end result is a lovely crisp surface which does not burst. Or wrap a rasher of streaky bacon round each sausage and hold in place with cocktail sticks.

HOTDOGS

8 Frankfurter sausages
8 hotdog rolls

Wrap the Frankfurters in foil making a flat parcel. Cook for about 4 minutes on each side, turning once. Cut each roll lengthways, spread a little tomato or barbecue sauce over one surface, and add the Frankfurters.

SPARE RIBS

These are delicious and not at all expensive.

2 spare ribs per person
barbecue sauce (see page 69)

Cook for about 15 minutes, turning occasionally. Spoon a little of the sauce over each one and continue to cook for another 5–10 minutes. They should be crisp and well browned.

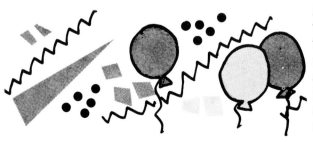

SPICY CHICKEN DRUMSTICKS

Chicken is one of the most popular meats for the barbecue. You can buy packs of frozen chicken drumsticks which are ideal to barbecue, but frozen chicken thighs are very much cheaper. They taste just as good, but they don't look so special, so the choice is yours. We do not suggest cooking whole chicken portions over a barbecue because they take so long that the skin tends to burn while the inside is still pink. It is very important to have them cooked right through. Allow one drumstick or thigh per guest.

2 tablespoons flour
1 teaspoon powdered mustard or curry powder
$\frac{1}{4}$ teaspoon ground ginger
$\frac{1}{4}$ teaspoon ground mace, cinnamon or other spice
a little salt and pepper
8 drumsticks (or thighs)
oil

Combine the flour with the spices and seasoning. Brush each drumstick with oil, and roll each one in the mixture. Cook for 15–20 minutes, turning every 5 minutes and either brushing with oil, or dribbling a little oil over the chicken pieces. Brush with a little barbecue sauce during the last few minutes cooking time.

LAMB CHOPS

Allow one per guest. Buy slightly thicker ones than you would normally. Trim them and leave to marinate overnight. Cook for about 15 minutes, turning them every 5 minutes. They are also good cooked in foil. Prepare beforehand a separate parcel for each one, add a spoonful of marinade, and a little butter. Cook for about 20 minutes, turning once.

VEGETABLES

Hot vegetables make a change from salads, and are very little trouble. You can cook almost any vegetable on a barbecue by wrapping it first in kitchen foil. Make sure you keep the fire up.

BAKED POTATOES

Choose smallish potatoes, as big ones would take too long to cook. Scrub them well, sprinkle on a little salt and wrap each one separately in foil. Cook them in the fire (not on the grid) for about an hour, turning once. When they are done, take them out of the foil, cut them open lengthways and add a knob of butter and some grated cheese. New potatoes also are delicious cooked this way – allow a little less than an hour.

CORN ON THE COB

Defrost if frozen. Spread a little butter on each cob and wrap up well in foil. Cook on the fire (not the grid) for about 25 minutes.

SWEET-CORN RINGS

These are ideal for younger children, if you think they will not eat a whole cob each. Defrost the cobs if frozen. Cut them across making neat rings – you should get about six from each cob. Brush with oil and lay them directly on the barbecue grid. They will cook in 3–4 minutes.

TOMATOES

Season with salt and pepper and wrap whole tomatoes in double foil. Cook for about 10 minutes.

BAKED CARROTS, PEAS, FRENCH BEANS, RUNNER BEANS, ETC.

These may sound unusual but are quite delicious. Use fresh or frozen vegetables. If fresh, cut carrots or runner beans into thin strips. Place vegetables in foil, in as many 8 oz (225 g) packets as you think you'll need, spread plenty of butter (about 1 oz or 25 g) over the vegetables, and add a sprinkling of salt. Wrap them up securely and cook directly in the fire for about 10 minutes. Fresh vegetables may take a little longer.

MUSHROOMS

Wrap whole mushrooms in double foil with a good knob of butter, and salt and pepper. Allow about 15 minutes' cooking time.

VEGETABLE KEBABS

These are ideal on their own for vegetarians, or can be served with the barbecued meat – lamb chops, chicken or whatever. The following quantities will feed eight children.

1 lb (450 g) tomatoes
1 red pepper
1 green pepper
8 oz (225 g) courgettes
8 oz (225 g) mushrooms
1 can pineapple chunks

Cut tomatoes in half, core and de-seed peppers, and cut them into flat pieces. Slice the courgettes. Remove stalks from mushrooms. Thread the vegetables and the cut pineapple on to the kebabs and barbecue for 5–10 minutes, basting occasionally.

PUDDINGS

Hot barbecued fruit is delicious and easy, and makes a change from cold puds. Try serving with ice cream, as the combination of hot and cold is irresistible to children (and grown-ups)!

BAKED BANANAS

These seem to shrink during cooking, so allow two per person for adults. Don't peel the bananas, but wrap them in foil and cook for about 20 minutes on the barbecue. Serve them in their skins with crunchy brown sugar and cream while they are still hot.

BAKED BANANAS AU CHOCOLAT

Split the skin and flesh of each banana lengthways and lay in it a chocolate flake. Wrap up in foil, skin and all, and cook for about 20 minutes on top of the barbecue. Serve in their skins, so that guests can scoop out their own.

TOASTED MARSHMALLOWS

Finish your barbecue with these – children love them. Spear the marshmallows on to a skewer and cook holding them over the grid (but not letting them touch it) for about a minute, turning frequently.

BARBECUED ORANGES

Cut round the orange with a sharp knife, removing all the peel and white pith. Stand each orange on buttered foil and sprinkle with brown sugar. Wrap up well and cook on top of the barbecue for about 15 minutes.

BARBECUED APPLES

Choose nice big apples and remove the core with a sharp knife or apple corer. Put each apple on a double layer of foil, and fill the centre with brown sugar, butter and a mixture of raisins, sultanas, chopped dates, walnuts, glacé cherries, depending on what you have in your store cupboard. Wrap up well, and cook for about half an hour in the fire, or an hour on the grid. Serve with cream or ice cream.

BARBECUED PEACHES

Use fresh peaches if you can – the flavour is so much better. Peel them and cut them in half, removing the stone. Otherwise use tinned peaches. Place one half, flat side up, on a layer of double foil and spread on it a teaspoon of brown sugar and a knob of butter. Lay another half peach flat side down on top and wrap up securely. Cook on top of the barbecue for about 15 minutes.

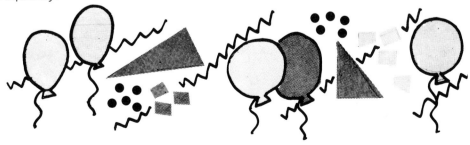

Disco Party Food

The amounts we suggest are for a party of fifty children, but you can easily halve or double the quantities. Always keep portion sizes small.

The Youngest Age Group

If you have any food left over when you've filled the individual plates, keep it back until later on in the evening, so that children can pick at it if they feel peckish.

6 lb (2.7 kg) sausages. You should get roughly thirty-two cocktail sausages per 1 lb (450 g) of weight. Buy either cocktail or chipolata sausages. If using the latter, untwist the skin and squeeze each sausage gently in half, and then retwist – do not cut them apart until they are cooked. Put the sausages on a tray in the oven with a little cooking fat at 350°F, 180°C, Gas Mark 4 for about 30 minutes. Drain off the fat, and leave the sausages to drain on kitchen paper until cool. For this number you will probably find it easier to serve the sausages cold, so cook them the day before the party and put them in the fridge covered with clingfilm once cooled.

50 packets of crisps, Hula Hoops, Monster Munch, etc. If you want a flavoured crisp, try to choose one that is likely to be generally popular, bacon rather than prawn flavour, say.

2–3 lb (1–1.5 kg) salted nuts. Beware: these can provide entertainment if flicked across the room!

50 satsumas. If the party is in the Christmas holiday or term, do try and get a box of these – they are always popular. Leave the children to peel their own.

Mini bridge roll. 25 mini bridge rolls – you will need half for each child. Cut the rolls in half and spread each with the butter – it must be *soft* – filling and a small piece of tomato or cucumber to garnish.

Fillings for mini bridge rolls

9 hard-boiled eggs, finely chopped, mixed with 8 oz (225 g) jar salad cream and some of the soft butter for spreading.

8 large slices of ham – each cut into about 8 pieces with scissors.

Sandwich spread, Marmite, etc.

To decorate mini bridge rolls

8 oz (225 g) firm tomatoes, cut into thin slices and then into smaller pieces.

$\frac{1}{2}$ cucumber cut into thin slices and then into smaller pieces.

Mini bridge roll boats. As above but if you wish to make these into boats you will need also ½ packet (50) cocktail sticks and 2 lettuces. Cut the lettuce leaves into triangular shapes with sides about 3 inches (7.5 cm) long. Use scissors to cut these as it is much quicker than trying to tear the lettuce to shape. Push a cocktail stick through the lettuce in two places to hold the 'sail' upright. Push the end of the stick into the prepared half roll. You can prepare the basic rolls in the morning, and the sails. Clingfilm them separately and refrigerate. Assemble as 'boat' nearer the time of the party.

50 CHEESE STRAW BOATS WITH RICE PAPER SAILS

Oven Temperature: 400°F, 200°C, Gas Mark 6

12 oz (350 g) plain flour, sifted
7 oz (200 g) margarine
4 oz (110 g) Cheddar cheese, finely grated
beaten egg or milk
rice paper cut as triangular sails with 3 inch (7.5 cm) sides
½ packet (50) cocktail sticks

Filling

4 oz (110 g) Cheddar cheese, very finely grated
6 oz (175 g) cream cheese
6 oz (175 g) softened butter

Grease some mini boat-shaped pastry moulds. You will have to bake in batches depending on the number of moulds you have. Make the pastry in a processor, adding enough egg or milk to reach a dough consistency. If you do not have a processor, mix the flour with grated hard margarine until a breadcrumb consistency. Add the cheese. Mix in some egg or milk and knead the dough. Roll out on a floured board and cut boat shapes slightly larger than your mould. Prick the pastry to stop it rising. Bake for 8–10 minutes until golden brown. Cool slightly and turn on to a wire rack to go cold. You can store these in a tin for a few days.

For the filling, process the ingredients in a food processor or beat very well indeed. Pipe the mixture into your boats. Push a cocktail stick into the top and bottom of the 'sail' and place into the filling to make a 'boat'.

Cheese on sticks. You will need 1 lb (450 g) mild Cheddar cheese and ½ packet (50) cocktail sticks. Sometimes a grocer will cut the cheese for you with his wire, but if not you will need to buy a good square piece of cheese to achieve the best result you can yourself. Cut the piece into slabs about ½ inch (1 cm) thick, and mark out the slab with a knife into squares of about ½ inch (1 cm). Then cut these neatly. Place a cocktail stick into each. Of course you can economise by putting the cubes on a plate without a stick. You could prepare the cubes the day before and clingfilm thoroughly, but don't put the cocktail sticks in until serving.

50 filled mini meringues. You need double quantities of the recipe on page 88, about a 100 little halves and not 50, to allow you to sandwich the two meringue halves together with the cream. Make the meringues very tiny, about 1 inch (2.5 cm) in diameter. You could divide your mixture in half and make one half pink, green or chocolate and the other white, etc. Pipe tiny rosettes on to the Bakewell paper and bake as instructed. When cold, you can store in an airtight tin for up to 2 weeks in advance, and assemble with the cream on the afternoon of the party. Whip 1½ pints (850 ml) double or whipping cream until it is stiff, and sandwich the two halves of the meringues together. Cover with clingfilm.

50 MINI ECLAIRS

Follow the profiterole recipe (see page 97) using a 4-egg mixture. Pipe the pastry with a $\frac{1}{2}$ inch (1 cm) plain nozzle on to the baking sheets, as for the profiteroles. Make 50 eclairs – about 2 inches (5 cm) long – and cook for 15 minutes.

Filling and icing

1 pint (600 ml) double or whipping cream, whipped
3 oz (175 g) cocoa, sieved
1$\frac{1}{4}$ lb (550 g) icing sugar, sieved
$\frac{1}{4}$ pint (150 ml) hot water

When cold fill the eclairs with the whipped cream. Pipe the cream in, using a plain nozzle. Mix the cocoa with a little cold water to make a paste. Add the hot water to the icing sugar a little at a time, then add the cocoa paste and mix. Beat to a soft consistency. Quickly dip the filled eclairs into the chocolate icing and allow to set. Refrigerate or freeze for about a week.

The 'In-Betweens'

50 chicken drumsticks (see page 110).
3 lb (1.4 kg) cocktail sausages (see page 74).
50 packets of crisps (see page 74).

2 large cucumbers. There is no need to peel the cucumbers. Cut them into small sticks, about 3 inches (7.5 cm) long, and really quite thin. Allow three per child. Prepare these in the morning. Clingfilm thoroughly and refrigerate.

1$\frac{1}{2}$ lb (675 g) carrots, peeled. Cut into sticks the same size as the cucumber. Allow four per child. Prepare in the morning and either leave in a bowl of cold water or clingfilm thoroughly and refrigerate.

50 ham rolls. 50 soft, and not too large bap rolls; 4 lb (1.8 kg) piece of gammon, cooked until tender and thinly sliced (this will be cheaper than buying ham slices); and 1 lb (450 g) soft butter.

200 cheese squares. 1 lb (450 g) mild Cheddar and 1 lb (450 g) red cheese (Double Gloucester, say). Have contrasting colour cubes (see page 75). Any leftover cheese can be put on the pizza fingers.

50 pizza fingers. 5 Sainsbury's oblong pizzas: add extra topping – grated cheese leftovers (see above), tomato sauce, ham, etc. Cook the pizzas and allow them to go cold. Cut them each into approximately twelve pieces.

BREAK-TIME

50 oblong cornets (buy a few extra in case some break), four 1$\frac{3}{4}$ pint (1 litre) long and narrow oblong blocks of Neapolitan ice cream. These blocks should cut into about fifteen slices for the cornets. An optional extra is 50 mini chocolate flakes to stick into the ice cream. If you can't get mini flakes buy the large size and cut each one into three pieces. You will need seventeen of them.

50 individual chocolate mousses (see page 83). Make them in 50 individual paper cups, bowls or saved-up old yoghurt pots, etc. And, unless you have a very large mixing bowl, we suggest you make them in two batches. If you like, pipe a tiny rosette of whipped cream on to each mousse on the afternoon of the party and place a Malteser on top. Do not leave these sitting around – we did and the Maltesers vanished! For fifty mousses, you'll need about 1 pint (575 ml) double or whipping cream and about two 2 oz or 53 g packets of Maltesers.

The Older Group

200 cheese and pineapple cubes on sticks. You will need 1½–2 lb (675–900 g) mild Cheddar cheese, cubed (see page 75). Make the cubes quite small as you will have the pineapple on the sticks as well. Cut the slices from 2 cans of pineapple slices into cubes. Put cheese cube and pineapple cube on to wooden cocktail sticks (you'll need two boxes of 100), and then stick hedgehog-like into two grapefruit.

Pitta bread and pâté. Use 5 pitta bread, 1 large packet of Sainsbury's smooth liver pâté and *soft* butter. Cut the bread into half horizontally, spread with the butter and the pâté. Cut each half into small pieces about 2 × 1 inches (5 × 2.5 cm).

Dips The following is a good tomatoe dip.

12 oz (350 g) fresh cream cheese
4 tablespoons single cream
1½ tablespoons tomato purée or 3 tablespoons tomato sauce
salt and freshly gound black pepper, to taste

Make sure the cream cheese is at room temperature and beat well with the cream and tomato flavouring. Season to taste, and cover with clingfilm.

For a curry dip and a horseradish dip, see page 114, and double the quantities given.

Crudités. Serve Ritz biscuits as well as crudités to dip. You'll need about two packets.

Carrots: 1½ lb (675g)	All cut into 3
Cucumber: 2	inch (7.5 cm)
Cauliflower: 1, cut into florets	sticks (see
Celery: 1 head	page 76)

Pizza fingers (see page 76). Don't have these too large as they will be difficult to handle and the children won't have plates to put them on.

Chocolate praline cake (see page 107, but double the quantities). Allow 1 piece 2 × 1 inches (5 × 2.5 cm) for each child.

4 large packets of crisps (see page 74).
4 boxes twiglets.
100 tiny meringues (see page 75).
200 cocktail sausages (see page 74).

Supper and Dinner Party Food

The quantities we give throughout this section are for eight, but you can easily increase or decrease amounts as required.

Candlelit Dinner

STARTERS

MELON BALLS OR CUBES WITH ORANGE JUICE

1 medium ripe melon (check by pressing your thumb on the top or bottom of the melon – it should give a little)
1 carton fresh orange juice

Cut the melon in half and scoop out the pips. Using a melon baller, scoop the flesh from the melon, or cut the melon in the normal way and chop into small cubes. Place the melon in a bowl and pour on the orange juice. Clingfilm the bowl and refrigerate; or, if you have enough space, divide into the children's bowls, clingfilm each bowl and refrigerate. Take the melon out 30 minutes before you plan to serve the starter so that it will not be too cold for them to eat, and the flavour will be better too. (The children may need a little caster sugar.)

COCKTAIL VOL-AU-VENTS

Oven Temperature: 350°F, 180°C, Gas Mark 4

8 mini vol-au-vent cases
½ pint (275 ml) white sauce

either
1 small cooked chicken breast, chopped, and 2 slices cooked bacon, chopped

or
4 slices of ham, chopped
chopped parsley
chopped lettuce

Cook the vol-au-vents as instructed and leave on the baking tray. Make the white sauce and allow to go cold, covered with clingfilm. Add the cold chicken and bacon – or the ham – to the sauce in the pan and re-cover with clingfilm. Refrigerate. Just before serving put the vol-au-vents on the tray into the pre-heated oven for 2 minutes. Heat the sauce and check the seasoning. Spoon the sauce into the vol-au-vents, sprinkle with parsley and serve on a bed of chopped lettuce to make it look pretty! This allows one vol-au-vent case per person.

MAIN COURSES

SPAGHETTI BOLOGNESE

We do not think that children would eat the usual 2 oz (50 g) per head of dry spaghetti normally suggested on the packets. However, if you think that your guests would eat more, cook 1 lb (450 g) spaghetti.

The Bolognese sauce can be made ahead and frozen or made the day before and refrigerated.

12 oz (350 g) spaghetti (or pasta shells)

Bolognese Sauce
1½ lb (675 g) good lean beef mince
1 large onion, peeled and diced
1 large carrot, peeled and diced
4 oz (110 g) firm button mushrooms, sliced
  (optional, as some children are not keen)
1 heaped tablespoon flour
2 × 15 oz (425 g) cans tomatoes
tomato purée, to taste
a good pinch marjoram
1 dessertspoon redcurrant jelly
salt and freshly ground black pepper
4 oz (110 g) mild Cheddar, very finely grated,
  served separately

Have a large pan of salted water, preheated, so that when you come to bring it to the boil it will not take very long. Cook and drain your spaghetti and toss with some pepper and ground black pepper. Put on a large serving dish and top with the Bolognese.

Fry the mince in a large pan over a moderate heat. (This will release the fat in the meat so that you do not need to cook the vegetables in added oil and make the Bolognese fatty.) When sufficient fat is available, add the onion and cook gently, stirring occasionally, until the onion is softened. Add the carrot and the mushrooms, and fry these gently until softened. Sprinkle in the flour and cook, stirring for a few minutes. Add the canned tomatoes, tomato purée, marjoram, redcurrant jelly and seasoning. Stir, allow the mixture to come to the boil and then cover and simmer gently. You do not want this mixture to be too runny. Cook for about 30 minutes. Ladle the Bolognese on to the spaghetti and serve. Put the bowl of finely grated Cheddar on the table with a teaspoon for the children to help themselves if required.

SHEPHERDS' PIE SPECIAL

This dish could be frozen if made ahead, or made the day before and refrigerated.

Oven Temperature: 350°F, 180°C, Gas Mark 4

1 recipe Bolognese Sauce (see above)
2 lb (900 g) potatoes, peeled and cooked
milk and butter or margarine, to taste
1 egg
4 oz (110 g) mild Cheddar, grated

Make the sauce as directed above. Mash the potatoes with the milk, butter or margarine, and egg, and check the seasoning (you could add a little grated nutmeg to give the potato more flavour if you think the children would like it.) You can either simply spoon the potato on top of the mince, smooth and mark with a fork, or you can put a covering of most of the potato on the mince and reserve some to pipe little rosettes round the edge of the pie. Sprinkle the grated cheese on the pie before putting it in the oven, for 30 minutes.

If this is a birthday treat, just before serving you could put candles in their holders in the piped rosettes as well as putting them in the next course.

CHICKEN PIE

This pie can be made ahead and frozen, or made the day before and refrigerated.

Oven Temperature: 375°F, 190°C, Gas Mark 5

1 × 5–5½ lb (2.25–2.5 kg) chicken
2 carrots, peeled and sliced
2 small onions, peeled, 1 chopped, 1 sliced
bay leaf
6 black peppercorns
2 oz (50 g) butter
4 oz (110 g) mushrooms, sliced (optional, as
  some children are not keen)
2 oz (50 g) flour
salt and freshly ground black pepper
12 oz (350 g) shortcrust pastry
a little milk or beaten egg, to glaze

Cook the chicken by covering it with cold water, adding one of the sliced carrots and the sliced onion, together with the peppercorns and bay leaf. Cover and bring to the boil, then lower the heat and simmer for 1 hour. Allow the chicken to go cool in the stock and then remove.

Fry the finely chopped onion in the butter, and add the remaining sliced carrot. (If you are including the mushrooms, add them briefly when the carrots are softened.) You may need to add a little extra butter here before you add the flour, which should be cooked for a couple of minutes. Remove the pan from the heat. Measure out 1 pint (570 ml) of the stock in which you cooked the chicken – strain it first – no floating bayleaves, please! – and add gradually to the flour and vegetables, stirring well in. Bring this mixture slowly to the boil and cook for a few minutes. Add the seasoning and cool.

Take all the flesh from the cold chicken and cut into bite-sized pieces. Add this to the cold sauce and pour into a pie dish. Grease the edges of the pie dish and roll out the shortcrust pastry. Cut some pastry trimmings to run along the edge of the dish, brush with water and cover the whole pie with the remaining pastry. Press the edges down well, having cut the pastry to fit. Do not put slits in the pie case until you are ready to cook it. Just before you put the pie in the oven, brush with a little milk or beaten egg. Bake for 45–50 minutes.

MOCK MOUSSAKA

Oven Temperature: 375°F, 190°C, Gas Mark 5

1 recipe Bolognese Sauce (see page 79)
2½ lb (1.1 kg) potatoes, peeled and sliced
3 tablespoons cooking oil
8 oz (225 g) mild Cheddar cheese, grated

Sauce
1½ oz (40 g) butter
1 tablespoon flour
½ pint (275 ml) milk
salt and freshly ground black pepper
1 egg, lightly beaten

Make the Bolognese sauce. Fry the potatoes in hot oil for about 10 minutes, making sure that they are cooked through. When they are golden, remove and drain on kitchen paper.

To make the sauce, melt the butter and stir in the flour. Cook gently for a couple of minutes, stirring constantly. Remove from the heat, allow to cool and gradually stir in the milk. Return the pan to the heat and bring the sauce to the boil for a couple of minutes, stirring constantly. Draw off the heat, add the seasoning and then the beaten egg.

Place a layer of the potato slices in a large ovenproof casserole. Add a layer of meat, topped with grated cheese. Continue this layering, leaving some cheese, and top with the sauce, sprinkled with the last of the grated cheese. Bake for 35 minutes until golden.

VEGETABLES

Serve a selection of vegetables – peas, carrots, French beans and so on – but do not mix them up in the serving bowl, as some children may only like one or other of them. However, it can be effective to put rows of two different vegetables into the serving dish.

If you have a canelle knife, cut down the sides of the peeled carrots with the knife, and then slice them across. Each slice of carrot will look a little like a flower.

DUCHESSE POTATOES

Oven Temperature: 400°F, 200°C, Gas Mark 6

3 oz (75 g) butter
1 egg
salt and freshly ground black pepper
2 lb (900 g) potatoes, peeled, boiled and
  mashed

Add the butter, egg and seasoning to the mashed potatoes, and beat well. Put into a piping bag and pipe rosettes on to a greased baking sheet. Cook for about 25 minutes, near the top of the oven until golden brown.

PUDDINGS

If it is a birthday party, you can put candles on the pavlova or the bombe (try the trick ones that relight). You could also stick sparklers in (buy in indoor firework sets from party shops, if it is not firework time), but only light them when you have put the dessert safely on a table or sideboard. Don't walk with it lit in case one falls off. Put the pavlova or bombe on a tray for the same reason.

PAVLOVA WITH CREAM AND FRUIT

As with meringues, silicon paper is vital for unsticking success! The pavlova base can be made beforehand and either stored in a tin or frozen.

Oven Temperature: 350°F, 180°C, Gas Mark 4
***After 5 minutes,* reduce to 250°F, 120°C, Gas Mark $\frac{1}{2}$**

4 egg whites
8 oz (225 g) caster sugar
1 rounded teaspoon cornflour, sieved
1 teaspoon vanilla essence
1 teaspoon white wine vinegar

Filling
$\frac{1}{2}$ pint (275 ml) double cream
fruit in season (halved strawberries,
  raspberries, 2–3 kiwi fruit, thinly sliced)

Whisk the egg whites until stiff. Add a tablespoon of the caster sugar gradually, as you are beating. When the mixture is nearly stiff, add the rest of the sugar, whisking it in little by little. Then quickly fold in the cornflour, essence and vinegar with a metal spoon. Place a piece of silicon paper on a baking tray, and pour the mixture on to it. Shape it into a round (if you are worried about this, draw on your baking sheet a large 12 inch/30 cm circle, then turn the paper over and use the line to guide you). Slightly hollow the centre of the pavlova. Bake at the higher temperature for 5 minutes, and then lower the heat and bake for a further hour. Turn your oven off, and leave the pavlova in it to go cold.

Whip the double cream quite stiffly, and spread over the cold pavlova. Arrange your fruit in circles on top.

SNOW PRINCESS CAKE
Oven Temperature: 450°F, 230°C, Gas Mark 8

*1 × 7 inch (18 cm) diameter single layer round
  sponge cake (see Match Cake, page 108)
5 egg whites
10 oz (275 g) caster sugar
1¾ pints (1 litre) Italiano Ice Cream (round)
cheap plastic doll, suitable size, and foil for her
  bodice (remove her legs)
sugar flowers
candles and holders (if a birthday celebration)*

Make a 2-egg simple sponge cake. When the
cake is completely cold, whisk the egg whites
until stiff. Add half the caster sugar and whisk
this mixture again until stiff. Fold in the
remaining sugar with metal spoon. Place the
round-shaped ice cream on top of your sponge
cake, and either spoon the meringue mixture
to cover the ice cream, or pipe it around the
ice cream, using a large star vegetable nozzle.
Decorate the top with meringue rosettes, if you
wish. It is vital to *completely* enclose the ice
cream within the meringue mixture.

   Put the Princess's 'skirt' in a pre-heated
oven and leave for approximately 4 minutes.
The meringue should be soft on the inside but
a little crisp on the outside. (If you wish, you
can freeze the skirt at this point. When you
wish to serve you will need to remove it 30
minutes beforehand, and keep in the
refrigerator.) Just before serving the Princess,
position the top half of the doll (use a piece
of foil as her bodice) on top of the meringue.
Camouflage the join with sugar flowers. If the
doll you use has a hollow body with a 'waist'
the same size as the top of a skewer, you could
secure her by putting the skewer in her body
and placing the pointed end into the meringue
and ice cream. Put candles around her waist.

ICE CREAM BOMBE

*1 pint (575 ml) strawberry soft-scoop ice
  cream
1 pint (575 ml) chocolate ice cream
hundreds and thousands, or chocolate
  vermicelli, to decorate*

Take the strawberry ice cream out of the
freezer for a few minutes to allow it to soften
slightly. Meanwhile prepare a mould: oil the
inside of a 2 pint (1 litre) glass pyrex bowl and
line it with clingfilm. Then spoon the ice cream
into the mould, pressing it well into the base
and up the sides. Make sure there are no gaps
(you will be able to check this through the glass
bowl). Smooth the ice cream into an even layer
about 1 inch (2.5 cm) deep all around the
bowl, then return to the freezer for an hour.
Take the chocolate ice cream out of the freezer
for a few minutes, then scoop it into the centre
of the bowl, again pressing well down. Smooth
the top with a palette knife, cover with clingfilm
and return to the freezer for at least 2 hours.

   It is wise to turn the bombe out in advance
so that you can do it at your leisure. Hold the
bottom of the bowl under hot water very briefly
then invert on to the serving dish, tapping it
sharply. Peel off the clingfilm, and smooth the
creases with a palette knife. Return to the
freezer until you are ready to serve it, and then
decorate.

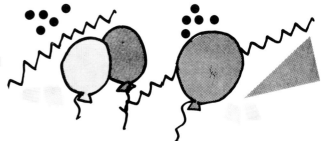

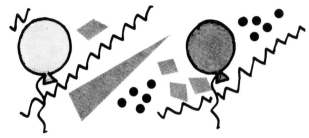

CHOCOLATE MOUSSE

This is a very economical recipe and rather less rich than the usual one. It is also very good for serving in large quantities at disco parties, say.

For 8:

8 oz (225 g) sugar
1 packet (11 g) gelatine
4 heaped tablespoons cocoa
$\frac{1}{3}$ pint (200 ml) milk
1 large can (14$\frac{1}{2}$ fl oz or 413 ml) evaporated
  milk

For 50 (make in 2 batches):

3 lb (1.4 kg) sugar
5 packets (55 g) gelatine
1 large can (8.82 oz or 250 g) cocoa
1$\frac{3}{4}$ pints (1 litre) milk
3$\frac{1}{2}$ large cans (14$\frac{1}{2}$ fl oz or 413 ml) evaporated
  milk.

Stir all the ingredients, except for the evaporated milk, over a low heat until dissolved. Bring to the boil, let it bubble for 1 minute (4 for the larger quantity) then allow to cool slightly. Put the evaporated milk into a mixing bowl and beat until it has increased in volume and is quite solid (this will probably take 3–4 minutes, 6–7 for the larger quantity). Fold in the chocolate mixture, pour the smaller quantities into a serving bowl and put it in the fridge to set. Put the larger quantity into individual pots.

LEMON MOUSSE

A fresh lemony taste and a light texture.

4 oz (110 g) caster sugar
4 eggs, separated
juice of 2 lemons
2 level teaspoons gelatine
$\frac{1}{4}$ pint (150 ml) double cream

Put the sugar, egg yolks and lemon juice into a bowl. Stand the bowl over a pan of hot water which is barely simmering, and whisk until the mixture thickens. Remove from the heat, and whisk occasionally until it is almost cool. Meanwhile, dissolve the gelatine with 2 tablespoons of water in a cup and stand in hot water until the gelatine is dissolved. Pour into the egg and lemon mixture, stirring well. Beat the cream until thick, and stir it in gently. Finally, whisk the egg whites until they hold a peak and fold them into the mixture. Pour into a serving bowl and leave in the fridge until firm.

Pink Party

STARTERS

WILD CHERRY SOUP

1 × 12 oz (350 g) can red cherries
juice of 1 lemon
3 small pots natural unsweetened yoghurt or
  soured cream
1–2 drops cochineal

Stone the cherries and cut them in quarters. Stir the cherries, cherry juice and lemon juice into the yoghurt. Add the cochineal to improve the colour, if necessary. Chill in the fridge for an hour or two before serving.

PINK PRAWN PÂTÉ

4 oz (110 g) butter
2 tablespoons mayonnaise
4 oz (110 g) cream cheese
1 dessertspoon tomato purée
salt and freshly ground black pepper
1 teaspoon chopped chives
8 oz (225 g) peeled prawns, roughly chopped

The secret of this pâté is to have everything at warm room temperature. Beat the soft butter, add the mayonnaise, then beat in the cream cheese and tomato purée. The mixture should be light and smooth. Add the seasoning, the chives and the prawns. Refrigerate. Remove from the fridge 30 minutes before serving to allow the flavours to develop.

TARAMASALATA

You really do need a food processor to make the best taramasalata.

12 oz (350 g) potatoes, peeled
8 oz (225 g) smoked cods roe
1 small clove garlic, peeled and finely chopped
6 tablespoons olive oil
2 tablespoons lemon juice
freshly ground white pepper
1 heaped teaspoon finely chopped parsley

Boil the potatoes, then allow to cool. Take the skin off the roe using a spoon, and place the roe in the processor with the garlic and potato. Process this mixture and then add the olive oil and lemon juice, very gradually. Blend until well mixed, and add the pepper and parsley. Chill. Serve the taramasalata either with rolls, or hot toast and butter.

PINK TOMATO DIP

8 oz (225 g) cream cheese
2½ tablespoons tomato ketchup

It is important to have your cream cheese at warm room temperature for this to be soft enough to beat well with the tomato ketchup. If you find the consistency is not quite soft enough, add a little oil and vinegar dressing. This must be beaten in very thoroughly. You can make this the day before and refrigerate. Serve with crisps or crudités (try strips of carrot, small cauliflower florets etc).

MAIN COURSES

GAMMON WITH REDCURRANT JELLY SAUCE

Oven Temperature: 350°F, 180°C, Gas Mark 4

2½ lb (1.1 kg) gammon joint
1 carrot, chopped
1 onion, chopped
1 bay leaf
6 peppercorns

Glaze and Sauce
4 tablespoons redcurrant jelly
1 tablespoon white sugar
juice of 1 orange
1 teaspoon ground cinnamon
1 glass red wine
1 oz (25 g) raisins
2 teaspoons arrowroot

Soak the gammon joint in cold water in a large pan for several hours. Pour this water away and add fresh water to just cover the joint. Add the vegetables, bay leaf and peppercorns. Bring the pan to the boil and then simmer gently for 1 hour. Lift joint out and place in roasting tin (retain the cooking liquor). Cut off the rind, and mark the fat with a sharp knife into diagonal lines. Pour several tablespoons of cooking liquor over joint and put in the oven for 30 minutes.

Meanwhile, prepare the glaze. Mix together 1 tablespoon of the redcurrant jelly, the white sugar, orange juice, and ground cinnamon. When the joint has been in the oven for 15 minutes, spoon some of this glaze over the meat, a little at a time. Make the sauce by dissolving the remaining redcurrant jelly in $\frac{1}{2}$ pint (275 ml) of the strained cooking liquor (make sure it's not too salty). Add red wine, raisins and any remaining glaze. Simmer to reduce. Add arrowroot, previously soaked in a little cold water, but do not continue to cook the sauce, or the arrowroot will become thin. Carve the gammon before you serve it and pour a little of the sauce over it; serve the rest of the sauce separately.

CHICKEN WITH PINK MAYONNAISE

This is a simple and delicious recipe, but start cooking the day before you need it, so that the chicken will be completely cold.

Oven Temperature: 350°F, 180°C, Gas Mark 4

1 × 5 lb (2.25 kg) chicken
1 carrot, chopped
1 onion, chopped
1 bay leaf
fresh herbs, or 1 teaspoon dried herbs
salt and freshly ground black pepper
$1\frac{1}{2}$ oz (40 g) butter
$1\frac{1}{2}$ oz (40 g) flour
1 dessertspoon tomato purée
1–2 drops cochineal
6 tablespoons real mayonnaise
4 oz (100 g) blanched, split almonds (optional)

Put the chicken, chopped carrot, onion, bay leaf, herbs and seasoning into a large lidded ovenproof dish. Add 1 pint (575 ml) water, cover the dish, and cook in the oven for $1\frac{1}{2}$ hours. Leave the chicken in the stock until it is cool, but not cold, then remove to a plate to finish cooling in the fridge. Strain the stock and put in a jug in the fridge for a few hours until the surface fat has solidified. Remove this carefully.

Melt the butter in a pan, and stir in the flour. Cook for a minute then add half the chicken stock. Cook over a low heat until the sauce is thick and smooth, then add the rest of the stock and a little salt and pepper if necessary. Colour the sauce by adding the tomato purée, and a little cochineal. Cover and leave in the fridge. When it is absolutely cold, stir in the mayonnaise.

Remove and discard the chicken skin, and take the meat off the bones. Chop it into bite-sized pieces. Stir into the prepared mayonnaise sauce, spoon on to serving dish, and decorate with the blanched split almonds, arranged in circles.

PINK AND WHITE PASTA SHELLS

1 packet pasta shells or bowknots (not coloured ones)
a few drops of cochineal
oil and vinegar salad dressing

Cook the pasta shells as directed on the packet, but pour into the boiling water several drops of cochineal food colouring. The water will turn a brilliant pink and so will the shells eventually! You may prefer to cook one half of the pasta shells in the pink water, and the other half in plain water. Drain and plunge into cold water. Drain again and toss with oil and vinegar dressing. Allow to go cold, and serve with your chicken.

SIMPLE PINK SALAD SELECTION

8 slices ham
8 slices salami
8 slices any other pink cold meat, pâté, or
* other type of salami*

Just roll the ham slices, and arrange on a bed of lettuce together with the selection of other pink meats.

TUNA MOUSSE

You really need a food blender of some sort to make this mousse successfully.

1 × 10 oz (275 g) can tuna fish
$\frac{1}{4}$ pint (150 ml) mayonnaise
1 dessertspoon tomato purée
2 tablespoons water
$\frac{1}{2}$ oz (10 g) gelatine
3 tablespoons whipped cream
salt and pepper
1 egg white

White sauce
$1\frac{1}{2}$ oz (40 g) butter
$1\frac{1}{2}$ oz (40 g) flour
$\frac{1}{2}$ pint (275 ml) milk
seasoning

First make the white sauce. Melt the butter, add the flour and cook for a couple of minutes. Remove from the heat and gradually add the milk. Season to taste, and stir over a low heat until the sauce is thick and smooth. Allow to go cold, covered with clingfilm.

Drain the fish and remove any bones. Blend the fish until smooth and add the white sauce, mayonnaise and tomato purée. Put the water in a small bowl, sprinkle the gelatine on it, and allow to soak for 5 minutes. Place the bowl in a little simmering water and dissolve the gelatine. While this cools, fold the whipped cream into the tuna mixture together with any seasoning required. Fold in the dissolved gelatine, whip the egg white until fairly stiff and fold in. Turn at once into a bowl or bowls.

VEGETABLES

PINK MASHED POTATO

2 lb (900 g) potatoes, peeled, boiled and
* mashed*
a few drops of cochineal

Simply colour the mashed potato with a few drops of cochineal and beat well to mix the colour in.

You could make this into Duchesse potatoes as on page 81, but reheat in a cool oven so that they don't brown.

RED CABBAGE AND ORANGE

1 oz (25 g) butter
1 small onion, finely chopped
$1\frac{1}{2}$–2 lb (700–900 g) red cabbage, finely sliced
$\frac{3}{4}$ pint (425 ml) carton orange juice
1 rounded dessertspoon caster sugar
grated rind of 1 orange

Melt the butter in a pan and gently cook the onion until soft. Add the cabbage and cook, stirring, for a couple of minutes. Pour in $\frac{1}{2}$ pint (275 ml) orange juice and sprinkle on the sugar. Cover and simmer for at least an hour until the cabbage has softened and the juice has almost evaporated (you may need to add extra juice if it boils away too fast).

Just before serving, sprinkle on the orange rind.

RED CABBAGE SALAD

1 small red cabbage, thinly sliced
1 small head of Chinese leaves, thinly sliced
a few radishes, thinly sliced
4 oz (110 g) white button mushrooms, thinly
  sliced
2 small cooked beetroot, peeled and chopped
  into small cubes

Mix up the red cabbage and Chinese leaves
and sprinkle the radishes, mushrooms and
beetroot on top.

PINK PASTA SALAD

10 oz (275 g) pasta shells
salad dressing
2 red-skinned apples, cubed and tossed in
  lemon juice
½ cucumber, skinned and cubed
sliced radishes
2 sticks celery, sliced

Cook the pasta shells (see page 85) and
plunge into cold water, then drain and toss with
salad dressing. Make the apple and cucumber
cubes a similar but slightly smaller size than
the shells. Make sure you toss the apple in
lemon juice. Add these and the sliced radishes
and celery to the pasta.

PUDDINGS

With any of these puddings, if you are serving
cream, whipped or pouring, add some drops
of cochineal and before you say 'yuck',
remember that this is a joke party!

PINK APPLE SNOW

You'll need a large jelly mould – about 2 pints
(1 litre) – for this.

3 lb (1.4 kg) cooking apples, peeled, cored and
  sliced
6 oz (175 g) sugar
3 level teaspoons gelatine
6 tablespoons cold water
juice of ½ lemon
a few drops of cochineal
2 egg whites

Put a little water in the bottom of a large pan,
and cook the apples gently. Make sure they
do not stick as they will go brown. Add a little
more water as required. When they are cooked
add the sugar and stir until dissolved. Liquidise
in a blender or rub through a sieve. Prepare
the gelatine by sprinkling it on to the measured
cold water in a cup. Stand the cup in a bowl
of simmering water until the gelatine is
completely dissolved. Add the gelatine, lemon
juice and a few drops of the cochineal to the
purée (be very careful with the cochineal: the
colour to aim for is a soft, not a lurid, pink).
Beat the egg whites until stiff, fold gently into
the pink purée and pour into the jelly mould.
Leave in fridge for 2–3 hours until set. When
you are ready to turn the pudding out, run the
mould *very quickly* under the hot tap, and
invert on to the serving dish, giving it a sharp
tap. Serve with pink meringues, sandwiched
together with whipped cream.

PINK MERINGUES

Makes about 16 halves
Oven Temperature: 200°F, 100°C, Gas Mark ½

3 egg whites
6 oz (175 g) caster sugar
3–4 drops cochineal
¼ pint (150 ml) double cream

Whip the egg whites until they are stiff, then add half the sugar, and cochineal (be careful). Continue to whip until the mixture is thick and glossy and holds a peak. Fold in the rest of the sugar. If you have a piping bag, pipe rosettes of the mixture on to a baking tray covered with silicon baking paper. If not, use 2 dessertspoons to scoop the mixture on to the paper in neat ovals. Cook at the bottom of the oven for 1½ hours, but keep an eye on them to make sure they do not discolour.

When you are ready to serve, whip the cream and sandwich the meringues together with it.

WHITE MERINGUE WITH STRAWBERRY CREAM

Make the meringues as above, but omit the cochineal. Sandwich them together with this strawberry cream.

¼ pint (150 ml) double cream
3 tablespoons fresh strawberry purée, sieved

Whisk the cream until stiff and fold in the strawberry purée. Add a few drops of cochineal to the cream if you want a stronger pink.

STRAWBERRY ICE CREAM WITH PINK MERINGUES

3½ lb (1.5 kg) strawberries
1 pint (570 ml) double or whipping cream
6 oz (175 g) icing sugar

Keep back 8 oz (225 g) of the best strawberries for decoration. Liquidise the rest in a blender, or press through a sieve. Whip the cream with the sugar until it is thick, and stir into the strawberry purée. Pour into a mould and freeze in the coldest part of the freezer for several hours, preferably overnight. When you are ready to serve the pudding, turn out the mould by running it very quickly under the hot tap, invert on to the serving dish and give the mould a sharp tap. Decorate with the remaining strawberries and serve with a plate of pink meringues, sandwiched together with whipped cream (see above).

RHUBARB FOOL

¾ pint (425 ml) double cream, whipped
1 pint (570 ml) rhubarb purée, sweetened

Whip the double cream until stiff but not too stiff. Fold the purée into the cream, and refrigerate. (If you wanted to jazz up the flavour, grate some orange rind into the rhubarb purée.)

RASPBERRY OR STRAWBERRY SORBET

This can also be served with a lemon sorbet, which looks white. If you have a melon baller, and the time, make a heap of little balls for each person. Decorate with tiny mint leaves.

1 lb (450 g) caster sugar
1 pint (570 ml) water
juice of 2 lemons
1 pint (570 ml) fruit purée

Place the sugar and water in a small heavy-based pan. Dissolve over a low heat, bring to the boil and maintain for a minute. Remove from the heat, stir in the lemon juice and cool. Fold the fruit purée into the cold syrup. Freeze until slushy, beat until smooth, and freeze for a further 2 hours. Beat once more and freeze until firm. Remove from the freezer 20 minutes before serving.

If you want to serve the sorbets in individual wine glasses, frost the rims in pink coloured sugar first (as on page 21).

LEMON SORBET

12 oz (350 g) caster sugar
$\frac{3}{4}$ pint (425 ml) water
juice and finely grated rind of 4 lemons

Place the sugar and water in a small heavy-based pan. Dissolve over a low heat, bring to the boil and maintain for a minute. Remove from the heat, stir in the lemon juice and finely grated rind and allow to cool. Freeze until slushy, beat until smooth, freeze for a further 2 hours, and beat once more. Freeze the sorbet then until it is firm. Remove from the freezer 20 minutes before serving.

Green Party

STARTERS

SPINACH SOUP

This recipe allows for $1\frac{1}{2}$ small ladles of soup per child. You will need a food processor to make this soup.

2 lb (900 g) spinach
4 oz (110 g) butter
1 large onion, finely chopped
3 oz (75 g) flour
2 pints (1.1 litre) milk
salt and freshly ground pepper
$\frac{1}{4}$ pint (150 ml) cream (optional)
nutmeg (optional)

Wash the spinach thoroughly and take off the stalks. Process until finely chopped. You will need to do this in several goes. Melt the butter in a pan and fry the onion gently until it has softened. Add the spinach and cook for a few minutes. Stir in the flour, and cook, stirring constantly. Remove from the heat, and gradually add the milk. Return to the heat, stirring frequently, then bring the soup to the boil. Season to taste.

This soup can be made the day before the party and refrigerated. Reheat and, just before serving, decorate each portion with a swirl of cream and a grating of nutmeg if you wish. Some tiny croûtons (see page 99) add a touch of colour and dash.

WATERCRESS SOUP

Make this as in the above recipe, but substitute 3 bunches of watercress for the spinach. Decorate with tiny sprigs of watercress.

AVOCADO AND ORANGES WITH GREEN HERB DRESSING

4 oranges
3 ripe avocado pears
juice of 1 lemon
chopped parsley and chives
salad dressing

Cut the peel and pith off the oranges with a very sharp knife. Hold the orange over a bowl between your first finger and thumb, and cut each segment, leaving behind the membrane. Collect all the segments in the bowl with the juice. Peel the avocados and cut from top to bottom in thin slices. (Whether you do this with the pear left whole, or whether you remove the stone and cut the slices from the half pear, rather depends on the ripeness of the fruit.) Paint each slice of avocado with the lemon juice using a pastry brush (to stop it going black). Arrange each individual plate with alternative slices of avocado and orange. Mix the chopped herbs in with the salad dressing and pour a little over the fruit.

EGGS WITH GREEN MAYONNAISE OR SALAD CREAM

a bunch of watercress or lettuce leaves
8 hard-boiled eggs, peeled and halved
very finely chopped parsley and chives
½ pint (275 ml) mayonnaise or salad cream

Arrange a little bed of watercress or lettuce leaves on individual plates and place a halved hard-boiled egg on top of each. Mix the herbs in with your mayonnaise or salad cream and pour over. Place a small sprig of watercress on top of the eggs.

STARTER ACCOMPANIMENTS

BROWN BREAD AND GREEN BUTTER PINWHEELS

Thinly slice brown bread and cut off the crusts. Soften some butter and add enough finely chopped parsley to turn the butter green. Spread on the bread slices and roll the slice of bread up. Leave wrapped in damp greaseproof paper in the fridge. Just before serving slice these little rolls into pinwheels – they will look like mini slices of Swiss roll.

HEART-SHAPED BREAD WITH GREEN BUTTER

This can be a bit wasteful, but is a fun way of serving bread and butter. Spread your thinly sliced crustless bread with the green herb butter as above, and cut using a heart-shaped pastry cutter.

HOT FRENCH STICK WITH GREEN HERB BUTTER

Mix softened butter with either chopped fresh mixed green herbs or a little of the mixed herb purée which can be bought from any good supermarket. Carefully cut the French stick into slices (about 1 inch or 2.5 cm thick), but do not cut right through the bottom of the loaf. Spread between each slice with plenty of the butter mixture and, if you have any left over, then spread this over the top of the loaf. Wrap the bread in foil, and bake for about 10 minutes at 425°F, 220°C, Gas Mark 7, then open up the foil and brown and crisp the bread for a further 5 minutes, at 400°F, 200°C, Gas mark 6.

ROLLS OR FRENCH STICK WITH GREEN BUTTER

Just have rolls or French stick cut into slices on the table, and serve them with green butter. Make balls of butter and roll them in finely chopped parsley, or simply press finely chopped parsley all over a slab of butter.

MAIN COURSES

GREEN TAGLIATELLI WITH HAM AND CHICKEN CREAM SAUCE

2 oz (50 g) butter
1 large onion, finely chopped
8 oz (225 g) ham, cut into thin strips
8 oz (225 g) cooked chicken, cut into thin strips
½ pint (275 ml) single cream
salt and freshly ground black pepper
1¼–1½ lb (550–675 g) tagliatelli or any green pasta
4 oz (110 g) Cheddar cheese, finely grated
1 oz (25 g) Parmesan cheese, grated

Make the sauce first. Melt half the butter in a pan and cook the onion gently until soft. Add the ham and the chicken strips and heat through. Stir in the cream and some salt and pepper to taste.

Boil the pasta in a large pan of salted water for about 10 minutes: it should be tender, but not soft. Drain well and toss with the remaining butter. Mix the warm sauce with the pasta and the Cheddar cheese. Toss this mixture and, just before serving, sprinkle the Parmesan on top.

COLD CHICKEN WITH WATERCRESS SAUCE

You will need a processor for this recipe.

5½ lb (2.5 kg) roasting chicken
1 large onion, quartered
1 carrot, peeled and sliced
1 bay leaf
a blade of mace
8 peppercorns
a pinch of salt

Watercress sauce
2 bunches of watercress
½ pint (275 ml) cream
2 tablespoons mayonnaise
2 tablespoons lemon juice
salt

Cover the chicken with cold water in a large pan, and add the other ingredients. Bring to the boil and simmer gently for 1½ hours. Allow the chicken to go completely cold in the liquid before removing. Carve the flesh from the chicken and arrange on a serving dish. Clingfilm and refrigerate until the party.

To make the sauce, reserve a few sprigs of watercress for decoration and process the rest – a little at a time. Lightly whip the cream and add the mayonnaise, lemon juice and salt. Stir this in with the watercress, cover with clingfilm and refrigerate.

To serve, pour some of the sauce over the chicken in the centre of the serving dish. Offer the remaining sauce separately, and decorate the serving dish with the reserved watercress sprigs.

SPINACH AND HAM PANCAKES

Oven Temperature: 350°F, 180°C, Gas Mark 4

We suggest an average of $1\frac{1}{2}$ pancakes per child, thus the pancake batter is for 12 pancakes.

Pancakes

4 oz (110 g) plain flour
a good pinch of salt
1 egg
$\frac{1}{2}$ pint (275 ml) milk
a little lard for frying

Filling

1 lb (450 g) frozen spinach
$1\frac{1}{2}$ oz (40 g) butter
1 large onion, finely chopped
$1\frac{1}{2}$ oz (40 g) plain flour
juice of $\frac{1}{2}$ lemon
$\frac{1}{2}$ pint (275 ml) double cream
freshly grated nutmeg
salt and freshly ground black pepper
12 slices ham

Toppings

either
4 oz (110 g) Cheddar cheese, finely grated
or
$\frac{3}{4}$ pint (425 ml) Cheese Sauce (see page 100)

To make the pancakes, sieve the flour into a bowl with the salt, and make a well in the centre. Put in the egg and half the milk. Start to mix in gently, from the well outwards, with a wooden spoon. When all the flour has been mixed in, add the remaining milk gradually, beating continuously. Allow the batter to stand for at least half an hour before you make your pancakes.

Heat a little lard in a frying pan or on a griddle – it should be very hot before you pour any batter in. Coat the bottom of the pan with batter and swivel the pan. Cook until set and brown on the bottom, then turn over to brown the other side. Continue until all the batter is used up.

To make the filling, cook the spinach according to the packet directions. Melt the butter in another pan, and fry the onion gently until soft. Stir in the flour and cook for a little while. Take off the heat, add the lemon juice to the cream and pour this, together with the spinach, into the pan. Mix together and cook over a low heat. Season to taste with nutmeg, salt and pepper.

If you are making the pancakes well before the party, allow the mixture to go cold. Lay out your pancakes with a slice of ham on each, and divide the spinach mixture between them. Roll the pancakes up and put them in a buttered dish (freeze now if liked). Top with chosen topping and warm through in the oven for 15–20 minutes.

VEGETABLES

A green salad could include kiwi fruit, apple, sliced courgettes, watercress, green celery and pepper etc.

Hot green vegetables could include broccoli, peas, beans, spinach (not with the pancakes) and new potatoes with masses of chopped parsley.

ANNA'S GREEN DUCHESSE POTATOES

1 × 8 oz (225 g) packet chopped frozen spinach
2 lb (900 g) potatoes, peeled, cooked and mashed with butter and milk (page 81)
a pinch of nutmeg

Cook the spinach as instructed on the packet, and evaporate as much water as possible. Beat into the duchesse potato mix with the nutmeg. Pipe into a dish – allow one to two rosettes per child. Prepare these beforehand and heat them up gently.

PUDDINGS

MERINGUE WITH APPLE CREAM FILLING

You can have the meringue white or green, whichever you prefer.

Oven Temperature: 275°F, 140°C, Gas Mark 1

4 egg whites
8 oz (225 g) caster sugar
green food colouring
4 tablespoons sweetened apple purée
½ pint (275 ml) double cream, or ¾ pint (425 ml) if decorating the top with rosettes

You will need two baking sheets each covered with silicon paper. Draw a 10 inch (25 cm) circle on each piece of paper and turn the paper over.

Whisk the egg whites until they are stiff, but not dry, and add half the sugar. If you are colouring your meringue green add the few drops of food colouring now. Continue to whip until the mixture is thick and glossy and holds

a peak. Fold in the rest of the sugar. Divide the meringue equally between the two circles: either spread it with a palette knife or pipe it if you prefer. Bake at the bottom of the oven for 1–1½ hours, or until it is dry. Check occasionally that it is not browning. Carefully peel off the paper when the meringue is cold.

Make sure the fruit purée is quite solid, not runny. Whip the smaller quantity of cream, and fold in the apple purée. If you feel the colour is not strong enough add a few drops of green food colouring. Spread the cream on one of the meringue layers, and press the other half on lightly. If you have the extra amount of cream, whip this and decorate your meringue with rosettes just before the party.

KIWI FRUIT SORBET

12 oz (350 g) caster sugar
¾ pint (425 ml) water
6 kiwi fruit
¼ pint (150 ml) white wine
a few drops of green food colouring

You will need a food processor to make this sorbet. Make a syrup with the sugar and water as for Lemon Sorbet on page 89. Purée the kiwis with the wine: the little black seeds show up in the purée, and it looks rather pretty. Add a few drops of green food colouring. Mix the purée with the syrup and then continue as on page 89. Serve the sorbet in individual wine glasses, frosted with green sugar first (as on page 21).

APPLE SORBET

12 oz (350 g) caster sugar
¾ pint (425 ml) water
¾ pint (425 ml) thick apple purée
  (unsweetened)
a few drops of green food colouring

Using the apple purée, make as for the Lemon Sorbet on page 89. Serve the sorbet in individual wine glasses frosted with green sugar first (as on page 21)

GOOSEBERRY FOOL

2 lb (900 g) gooseberries
12 oz (350 g) sugar
6 fl. oz (175 ml) water
½ pint (275 ml) cold custard (use packet
  custard)
¼ pint (150 ml) double cream
a few drops of green food colouring, if
  necessary

Optional garnish
¼ pint (150 ml) double cream, whipped

Prepare the gooseberries and cook them with the sugar and water until they are very soft. Sieve them or process in a food mixer. Process or mix with the custard. Whip the cream to soft peak consistency and fold this into the fool. (If you feel the fool does not look green enough, add a few drops of green food colouring.) Pour the mixture into a glass bowl or divide between eight glasses. Cover with clingfilm and chill. Decorate with extra whipped cream rosettes, if you like.

GREEN AND WHITE FRUIT SALAD

It is most important to choose apples and pears with green skins and white flesh, and a melon with greenish coloured flesh.

4 oz (110 g) sugar
¼ pint (150 ml) water
juice of 2 lemons
2 green apples, cored and sliced
1 green melon, halved and scooped or sliced
8 oz (225 g) green seedless grapes
3 kiwi fruit, peeled and sliced
1 can lychees, drained
2 white pears, cored and sliced
2 bananas (optional)

Put the sugar and water in a small pan over a low heat, and when the sugar has quite dissolved, bring to the boil and simmer gently for 5 minutes. Add the lemon juice to the syrup, and cool. Combine all the fruit except the bananas in a bowl and pour the syrup over. Leave it for at least an hour before serving. Peel and slice the bananas and stir them into the rest of the fruit at the last minute.

CHEESE

If the children are older and if you think that they would appreciate a cheese board to precede or follow the dessert, then include on this Sage Derbyshire Cheese and Herb Roulé. Serve with as green a celery as you can find. (If you are doing a green and white party serve Bath Oliver Cheese Biscuits which are practically white.) Decorate the board with green watercress, parsley or green grapes.

Black and White Buffet Supper

STARTERS TO SERVE WITH DRINKS

CURRY DIP

6 oz (175 g) fresh cream cheese
2 tablespoons single cream
curry paste or powder to taste
salt and freshly ground pepper, to taste

Make sure the cream cheese is at room temperature and beat well with the cream and curry powder. Season to taste. Cover with clingfilm. Serve with cauliflower florets cut to manageable size, and sliced mushrooms (try to find some with a good dark inside).

HORSERADISH DIP

6 oz (175 g) fresh cream cheese
2 tablespoons single cream
1½ tablespoons horseradish sauce, or to taste
a few drops of Worcestershire sauce (optional)
salt and freshly ground pepper, to taste

Mix and serve as above.

PRUNES STUFFED WITH CREAM CHEESE

8 oz (225 g) cream cheese
salt and fresh ground pepper
1 packet of Sainsbury's ready prepared, ready to eat (really scrumptious) prunes

Have the cream cheese at room temperature and mix with the seasoning. Cut the prunes open and stuff them with the cream cheese.

CELERY STICKS WITH STILTON AND CREAM CHEESE FILLING

a few sticks of crisp celery, washed well
4 oz (110 g) cream cheese
4 oz (110 g) Stilton cheese
1 tablespoon single cream
freshly ground pepper

Have the cheeses at room temperature and blend them together until smooth with the single cream. Either pipe or spoon the mixture into the hollow of the celery sticks. Cut the sticks into 1 inch (2.5 cm) long pieces and season with pepper.

BLACK GRAPES STUFFED WITH CREAM CHEESE AND WALNUTS

8 oz (225 g) black grapes
4 oz (110 g) cream cheese
1 oz (25 g) finely chopped walnuts
salt and freshly ground pepper

Remove the pips from the grapes without cutting the grapes completely in half. Have the cream cheese at room temperature and thoroughly mix with the finely chopped walnuts and seasoning. Put a little of the stuffing into each grape.

BUFFET SELECTION

CHICKEN SALAD WITH BLACK GRAPES OR CHERRIES

4 lb (1.8 kg) cooked chicken
½ pint (275 ml) natural yoghurt
½ pint (275 ml) mayonnaise
2 tablespoons single cream
½ cucumber, peeled and chopped
2 apples, peeled, cored, chopped and
  sprinkled with lemon juice
3 sticks celery, chopped
8 oz (225 g) black grapes, pipped, or black
  cherries, stoned
salt and freshly ground pepper

Cut the flesh of the chicken into bite-sized pieces. Combine the yoghurt, mayonnaise and cream in a large bowl and add the fruit and vegetables and the chicken flesh. Season to taste, and chill in the fridge.

WHITE RICE SALAD WITH RAISINS AND ALMONDS

¼ pint (150 ml) French dressing
1 lb (450 g) cooked rice (use white long-grain
  not brown)
4 oz (110 g) raisins
4 oz (110 g) flaked almonds, toasted
2 sticks celery, chopped
freshly ground black pepper

Add the salad dressing to the rice while it is still hot, and mix thoroughly. Allow this to cool, then add the raisins, almonds, celery and freshly ground pepper.

EGG SALAD WITH MOCK CAVIAR

8 hard-boiled eggs, peeled and halved
  lengthways
lettuce
6 tablespoons mayonnaise
1 small jar lumpfish roe (mock caviar)

Arrange the eggs on a bed of lettuce on individual plates. Spoon a little mayonnaise on top of each, and decorate with some of the mock caviar.

CHINESE LEAF SALAD

1 head of Chinese leaves
1 head of chicory
4 oz (110 g) mushrooms, sliced (choose
  mushrooms which have a good contrasting
  white and dark brown inside)
1 bulb of fennel, sliced thinly
8 oz (225 g) black olives
salad dressing

Slice the Chinese leaves and put in the salad bowl. Place leaves of chicory upright around the edge of the bowl. Scatter the remaining ingredients on top.

PUDDINGS

PROFITEROLES AND DARK CHOCOLATE SAUCE

You could also make eclairs, large or small, with this choux pastry mixture. Simply pipe a line instead of a walnut, to whatever length or thickness you desire.

Makes 24

Oven Temperature: 400°F, 200°C, Gas Mark 6

$2\frac{1}{2}$ oz (65 g) plain flour
a pinch of salt
2 oz (50 g) butter
$\frac{1}{4}$ pint (150 ml) water
2 eggs (size 2)

Chocolate sauce
5 oz (150 g) sugar
3–4 tablespoons golden syrup
2 oz (50 g) cocoa powder
$\frac{1}{2}$ teaspoon vanilla essence
3 oz (75 g) butter
7 fl oz (200 ml) water

Filling
$\frac{3}{4}$ pint (425 ml) double cream

Sieve the flour and salt together. Put the butter and water in a heavy-based pan, and heat gently until the butter has melted. Bring to the boil, and tip in the flour and salt, beating until the mixture comes together and leaves the sides of the pan. Remove from the heat and allow to cool for 2–3 minutes. Beat in the eggs, one at a time, beating well until the mixture has taken up the egg before adding any more.

Place a large star nozzle in a piping bag and fill with the pastry mixture. Lightly dampen a baking tray. Pipe the mixture in small mounds about the size of a walnut. Bake for 20–25 minutes, and you must *not* open the oven door during cooking. Remove from the oven and make a small hole in the side of each profiterole. Return to the oven for 5 minutes. Remove again and cool on a wire rack.

To make the sauce, heat all the ingredients together over a gentle heat, stirring it. Bring the sauce to the boil and keep boiling for approximately 3–4 minutes. Leave to cool.

Whip the cream until stiff and put in a piping bag. Cut the cold profiteroles open on one side and pipe in the cream. Pile on to a dish and, just before serving, pour over the cold chocolate sauce.

LEMON SYLLABUB WITH BLACK CHERRIES

1 × 12 oz (350 g) can stoned black cherries (not *red*) or 12 oz (350 g) fresh black cherries, stoned
$\frac{3}{4}$ pint (425 ml) double cream
juice and finely grated rind of 3 lemons
3 oz (75 g) caster sugar
$\frac{1}{4}$ pint (150 ml) white wine

Strain the canned cherries of juice if you are using them and drain on kitchen paper. Divide the cherries between eight glasses. Whip the cream until soft and starting to thicken, then gradually add the juice and the rind of the lemons, together with the sugar and white wine. Continue whipping until the mixture is fairly thick. Pour the mixture over the cherries, and chill.

CHOCOLATE ROULADE

Oven Temperature: 350°F, 180°C, Gas Mark 4

6 eggs, separated
6 oz (175 g) caster sugar
2 oz (50 g) cocoa
icing sugar

Filling

8 oz (225 g) plain chocolate, broken up
2 tablespoons water
2 eggs, separated
$\frac{1}{4}$ pint (150 ml) double cream, whipped

To make the roulade, put the egg yolks and caster sugar into a bowl. Whisk until the mixture thickens. Add the cocoa and gently mix it in. Whisk the egg whites until stiff and then carefully fold into the chocolate mixture. Pour the mixture into a tin 12 × 7 inches (30 × 18 cm) which you have previously lined carefully with greaseproof paper. Cook for about 20 minutes until it has risen and is springy to the touch. Leave to cool (and incidentally to shrink somewhat).

To make the filling, put the chocolate pieces into a bowl with the water and melt over a pan of hot water. Beat it a bit to make sure it is smooth. Beat the yolks into the chocolate mixture. Whisk the egg whites and fold them in as well. Leave to cool.

To prepare the roulade, turn it on to a piece of greaseproof paper which you have sprinkled with icing sugar. Remove the paper from the bottom of the cake and spread it first with the cool chocolate filling, and then with the whipped cream. Roll up the cake into a log, and however gently you do this, you will probably get some cracks in the cake surface: this adds to its log-like look!

YOGHURT CREAM SURPRISE

$\frac{1}{2}$ pint (275 ml) double cream
$\frac{1}{2}$ pint (275 ml) natural yoghurt
dark soft brown sugar
fruit (optional)

Whip the cream until soft and thick, and stir in the yoghurt. If you want to add fruit – black grapes, for instance – put them at the bottom of a glass bowl. Pour the yoghurt and cream mixture on top and cover to a depth of about $\frac{1}{2}$ inch (1 cm) with the soft brown sugar. This must be done 24 hours before you intend to serve the pudding as then the topping becomes almost as crisp as if it had been grilled. The colour contrast is much better after 24 hours and although it is a dark brown, the contrast between the white bottom showing through the glass bowl and the dark top would be effective for this party.

BLACKCURRANT/BLACKBERRY SORBET AND LEMON SORBET

Make up the Lemon Sorbet as on page 89, and make a 'black' sorbet with a purée of either blackcurrants or blackberries and a sugar syrup. Follow the Lemon Sorbet recipe thereafter. Serve a scoop of black and of white per guest.

CHEESE

There are lots of black and white cheeses: Chèvre Blanc (white goat's cheese); Tomme aux Raisins (white cream cheese rolled in black grape seeds); Rambol au Poivre (cream cheese with black peppers); or Brie. Serve with Bath Oliver biscuits or black rye bread, and white celery.

A selection of food and drink.

The Pink Party (see page 22).

Mixed Dinner Parties

SUMMER MENU

CHILLED CUCUMBER SOUP

You will need a food processor or blender to make this soup. If it is a very cold night you could always heat this soup up and serve it with hot bread rolls or croûtons.

3 cucumbers
2 pints (1.1 litre) milk
3 oz (75 g) butter
1 large onion, finely chopped
3 oz (75 g) flour
1 pint (570 ml) good well flavoured chicken
  stock (or use a cube and add a bay leaf)
a couple of drops of food colouring (if required)
finely chopped mint, parsley or chives
¼ pint (150 ml) single cream

Cut off eight thin slices of cucumber, unpeeled. Peel the remaining cucumber and take out the seeds. Chop and process or blend with a little milk.

Melt the butter in a pan, add the onion and allow to cook gently until softened. Add the flour and cook for a few minutes, then add the cucumber purée. Mix thoroughly, and pour in the remaining milk and the stock. Bring to the boil and allow to cook for a few minutes. Pour the soup into a bowl and allow to cool. Cover and chill until you wish to serve it.

If you feel the colour is rather brown (this will depend on the stock you have used) add a couple of drops of green food colouring. Just before serving add chopped herbs, a swirl of cream and a slice of cucumber on the top.

CROÛTONS

6 slices white bread
½ pint (275 ml) cooking oil

Trim the crusts off the bread and cut into neat ½ inch (1 cm) squares. Heat the cooking oil in a frying pan and drop in one croûton to test the heat. It should sizzle, but not turn brown too quickly. Take it out and put all the others in, turning them after half a minute until they are golden brown all over. Watch them carefully because they can go too brown very quickly. Take them out and drain them on kitchen paper. Serve hot. You can make these in advance and reheat them when you need them.

CHERRY CHICKEN SALAD

5 lb (2.25 g) chicken, cooked with tarragon
1 lb (450 g) cherries
¼ pint (150 ml) double cream
½ pint (275 ml) mayonnaise
2 tablespoons tarragon vinegar
salt and freshly ground pepper
finely chopped parsley

Cut the chicken flesh into bite-sized pieces. Stone the cherries and leave them on kitchen paper to drain off juice while you prepare the sauce. (If you can get hold of a garlic press with a cherry stoner incorporated in the handle, these are excellent for the job.) Whip the cream lightly to a soft peak texture and mix with the mayonnaise and vinegar. If you feel you can't taste a sufficient tarragon flavour, add more vinegar here. Fold in the chicken and cherries and check the seasoning. Sprinkle with chopped parsley before serving. We suggest you make a rice and a green salad to serve with the chicken, but if it is a cold night you could bake some potatoes.

WINTER MENU

HADDOCK MOUSSE WITH HEART-SHAPED BREAD AND BUTTER

Cut the bread and butter into heart shapes as described on page 90 – or serve with rolls.

1 lb (450 g) smoked haddock fillet
4 peppercorns
a piece of onion
some parsley
bay leaf
1 pint (570 ml) cold water
½ oz (15 g) gelatine
½ lemon
½ pint (275 ml) double cream, lightly whipped
freshly ground pepper
chopped parsley

Place the haddock, peppercorns, onion, parsley, bay leaf and water in a pan and bring to the boil. Cover and allow to simmer for 5 minutes and then remove from the heat. Leave the haddock in the stock until it is cool. Drain and flake the flesh. Retain the stock.

Strain ½ pint (275 ml) fish stock into a small bowl, and sprinkle on the gelatine. Leave this to soak for 5 minutes. Place the bowl over a pan of hot water and allow the gelatine to dissolve. Cool the stock and when it begins to thicken, fold in the haddock, lemon juice and lightly whipped cream. Check the seasoning and divide the mixture between eight ramekin dishes. Cover with clingfilm, and chill. Before serving, sprinkle with chopped parsley.

LASAGNE

Oven Temperature: 350°F, 180°C, Gas Mark 4

12 oz (350 g) lasagne

Meat sauce
1 tablespoon oil
1 large onion, finely chopped
2 slices streaky bacon, chopped
1½ lb (675 g) lean beef, minced
8 oz (225 g) button mushrooms, thinly sliced
2 tablespoons flour
2 tablespoons tomato purée
1 tablespoon redcurrant jelly
1 × 15 oz (425 g) can tomatoes
1 carrot, thinly sliced
1 teaspoon mixed herbs (amount depends on children's taste)
salt and freshly ground black pepper
½ pint (275 ml) stock

Cheese sauce
2 oz (50 g) butter
2 oz (50 g) plain flour
1 pint (570 ml) milk
8 oz (225 g) Cheddar cheese, finely grated
2 oz (50 g) Parmesan cheese, grated, or extra grated Cheddar

Many people find it easiest to make the lasagne using the pasta which does not need any preliminary cooking. In this case, we suggest that you make an extra ½ pint (275 ml) of cheese sauce. However, if you prefer to boil the lasagne first – for about 15–20 minutes – the non-stick secret is not to drain the water off the lasagne, but, using two fish slices, take the pasta from the water just as you are assembling the dish. Just shake the excess water off, and you will find the pasta much easier to deal with.

To make the meat sauce, heat the oil in a large pan and fry the onion gently, until soft.

Add the bacon and fry a little before adding the mince. Turn the mince until it is brown, then add the mushrooms, and continue cooking for a couple of minutes. Then add the flour, tomato purée and redcurrant jelly, and stir well. Add the canned tomatoes, carrot, herbs, seasoning and stock, and bring to the boil. Allow to simmer for 45 minutes, and remember to stir occasionally.

To make the cheese sauce, melt the butter in a pan and stir in the flour. Cook gently for a couple of minutes. Take off the heat and gradually add the milk. Return to the heat, and bring to the boil until the sauce has thickened. (If your sauce is lumpy use a wire whisk to get rid of the lumps.) Add some salt and pepper and stir in the Cheddar cheese.

Grease a $5\frac{1}{4}$ pint (3 litre) dish. If you haven't got one large enough, simply divide the lasagne between two smaller greased dishes. Put a third of the meat sauce, topped by the cheese sauce and followed by half the lasagne into the dish or dishes. Repeat the layers and finish with the grated Parmesan on top. Bake in the oven for about 45 minutes until the top is nicely browned. This dish can either be made the day before, or it freezes extremely well. Allow the lasagne to defrost overnight and then reheat.

For an optional topping, you can sprinkle the lasagne with 2 oz (50 g) finely grated Cheddar cheese, topped by 1 oz (25 g) of breadcrumbs and 2 oz (50 g) of chopped almonds. This may sound strange, but the nuts give a lovely crunchy contrast to the rest of the dish. And for a sauce alternative, you could add a $\frac{1}{2}$ teaspoon of mustard to the cheese sauce, when you add the seasoning and cheese.

FRUIT FONDUE

Don't serve this after a meat fondue!

10 oz (275 g) plain chocolate
3 tablespoons orange juice
2 tablespoons cream (optional)
Selection of sliced or diced fresh fruit, eg nectarines, peaches, oranges or satsumas (in segments), kiwi fruit, grapes, half a small pineapple, bananas – don't slice these early – strawberries.

Melt the broken chocolate with the orange juice over a very gentle heat. Do not boil this mixture. Stir constantly until it is quite smooth. Pour it into the fondue pan and keep the mixture warm. Stir in the cream just before serving if you intend to include it.

Have a couple of bowls of mixed prepared fruits at either end of the table. The guests dip whichever fruit they wish on their fondue forks into the sauce.

ICED COFFEE

3 tablespoons instant coffee
sugar to taste (about 2 tablespoons)
$\frac{1}{4}$ pint (150 g) boiling water
2 pints (1.1 litre) cold milk
ice cubes

Put the coffee and sugar in a large jug. Add the boiling water and stir well. Add the cold milk and ice cubes. Keep in the fridge until needed.

Some people might prefer no sugar at all, in which case you might feel it would be safer to omit the sugar and serve caster sugar separately for anyone who wants it (although it won't dissolve so well in the cold coffee).

Match Party Food

The quantities given in this section are for either eight or twenty-four children, unless specified. If you are having more or fewer people adapt the quantities to fit your numbers.

LUNCHES

SAUSAGE MOUSSAKA

Oven Temperature: 375°F, 190°C, Gas Mark 5

For 24:
6 lb (2.7 kg) potatoes
3 onions, very finely chopped
2 oz (50 g) butter
6 lb (2.7 kg) sausages
1 lb (450 g) Cheddar cheese, grated
salt and pepper
½ pint (275 ml) milk

For 8:
2 lb (1.1 kg) potatoes
8 oz (225 g) onions, very finely chopped
1 oz (25 g) butter
2 lb (900 g) sausages
6 oz (175 g) Cheddar cheese, grated
salt and pepper
3 tablespoons milk

Peel the potatoes, and boil them until they are cooked, but still slightly firm. Drain, and when they are cool enough to handle, slice them. Fry the onion in the butter for at least 5 minutes until soft but not brown. Remove the onion, and cook the sausages in the pan for about 10 minutes. Layer the potatoes and sausages in an ovenproof dish (or dishes), adding the cheese and onion to each layer, together with a little seasoning. Pour on the milk and cook for about 20–25 minutes.

Meanwhile, prepare the cheese sauce. Make a roux with the butter and flour, stir in the milk to make a smooth sauce, then add three-quarters of the cheese and a little salt and pepper. When the meat is cooked, drain off any fat if necessary, and transfer to a larger ovenproof dish or dishes. Arrange the sliced potatoes on top of the meat, pour on the cheese sauce, sprinkle the remaining cheese over the top and cook for 30 minutes in the oven until the top is golden and bubbling.

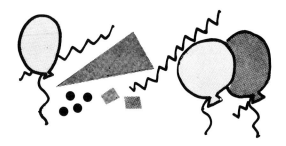

CHEESY MEAT AND POTATO PIE

Oven Temperature: 350°F, 180°C, Gas Mark 4

For 24:
6 lb (2.7 kg) minced meat
3 onions, very finely chopped
1½ pints (850 ml) stock
3 tablespoons tomato purée
salt and pepper
6 lb (2.7 kg) potatoes
6 oz (175 g) butter
6 oz (175 g) flour
2½ pints (1.4 litres) milk
1 lb (450 g) Cheddar cheese, grated

For 8:
2 lb (900 g) minced meat
1 onion, very finely chopped
½ pint (275 ml) stock
1 tablespoon tomato purée
salt and pepper
2 lb (1.1 kg) potatoes
2 oz (50 g) butter
2 oz (50 g) flour
¾ pint (425 ml) milk
6 oz (175 g) Cheddar cheese, grated

Combine the meat and onion in an ovenproof dish or dishes (use best quality minced meat, because there is so much less fat on it). Mix the stock, tomato purée, salt and pepper together and pour over the meat. Cook for 2 hours in the preheated oven, stirring occasionally.

Peel and cook the potatoes, taking them off the heat when they are still firm. Drain and slice them when they are cool enough to handle.

OSLO STEAK STEW

The tangy, slightly spicy flavour of this stew has a great appeal for children.

Oven Temperature: 325°F, 160°C, Gas Mark 3

For 24:
8 lb (3.6 kg) chuck steak, trimmed and cut into bite-sized pieces
cooking oil
8 onions, sliced
3 pints (1.75 litres) stock or water
3 Oxo cubes
3 level tablespoons mild curry powder
3 tablespoons Worcestershire sauce
3 oz (75 g) cornflour
¼ pint (150 ml) vinegar
6 oz (175 g) brown sugar
6 tablespoons tomato purée

For 8:
2½ lb (1.1 kg) chuck steak, trimmed and cut into bite-sized pieces
cooking oil
3 onions, sliced
1 pint (570 ml) stock or water
1 Oxo cube
3 teaspoons mild curry powder
3 teaspoons Worcestershire sauce
2 tablespoons cornflour
3 tablespoons vinegar
3 tablespoons brown sugar
2 tablespoons tomato purée

Fry the meat lightly on both sides in the cooking oil and remove to a casserole dish or dishes. Fry the onion and add to the meat. Mix all the other ingredients and pour into the dish or dishes. Put the lid on and cook in the preheated oven for 2–2½ hours, stirring occasionally.

ICE CREAM AND SAUCES

To serve twenty-four children you will need three large blocks (4 litres) of Neapolitan ice cream cut into portions. For eight children serve one block. We suggest using blocks because they are so much quicker and easier to serve for large numbers. All these sauces can be made in advance and left in a covered saucepan. All you have to do is reheat them just before serving. Add a little milk if the sauce has gone thick.

Mars Bar Sauce

For 24:
*2 packets mini or
12 large Mars Bars
a little milk*

For 8:
*4 large Mars bars
a little milk*

Chop up the Mars Bars and place in a heavy bottomed saucepan with a little milk. Melt over a low heat, stirring constantly. Add a little more milk if the sauce is a bit thick, or to eke it out!

Toblerone Sauce

If you prefer a nutty sauce, substitute Toblerone for the Mars Bars.

Marshmallow Sauce

For 24:
*12 oz (350 g) sugar
6 tablespoons water
2 packets (9 oz/250 g)
  marshmallows
a few drops vanilla
  essence
a few drops cochineal
3 egg whites*

For 8:
*4 oz (110 g) sugar
2 tablespoons water
8 pink marshmallows
a few drops vanilla
  essence
a few drops cochineal
1 egg white*

Dissolve the sugar in the water, bring to the boil and simmer for 5 minutes (8–9 minutes for the larger quantities). Cut up the marshmallows, add them to the sugar syrup and stir them until they have melted. Add the vanilla and cochineal. Whip the egg white stiffly and fold into the marshmallow mixture. Serve warm with the ice cream.

Chocolate Fudge Sauce

For 24:
*1½ pints (850 ml) milk
3 level tablespoons
  cocoa
1 lb 2 oz (500 g) sugar
9 oz (250 g) butter*

For 8:
*½ pint (275 ml) milk
1 level tablespoon cocoa
6 oz (175 g) sugar
3 oz (75 g) butter*

Heat the milk and pour a little over the cocoa in a bowl to make a smooth paste. Add the cocoa paste to the rest of the milk and add the sugar and butter. Stir over a gentle heat in a large heavy-bottomed pan until they are dissolved. Bring to the boil and boil briskly for about 5 minutes – up to 10 minutes for the larger quantity – until the mixture begins to thicken, stirring all the time. If you have a sugar thermometer, boil until it reads 217°F (100°C). Cool slightly before using.

Butterscotch Sauce

For 24:
*12 oz (350 g) light brown sugar
6 oz (175 g) butter
1¼ lb (600 g) golden syrup
¾ pint (425 ml) milk*

For 8:
*3 oz (75 g) light brown sugar
2 oz (50 g) butter
4 large tablespoons golden syrup
¼ pint (150 ml) milk*

Put the sugar, butter and syrup into a saucepan, and stir over a gentle heat until dissolved. Simmer for 3 minutes (5 minutes if you are making the larger quantity), stirring all the time. Take off the heat and slowly add enough milk to make a pouring consistency. Serve hot with the ice cream.

TEAS

BELLA'S CHEESE STRAWS

Makes 30

These puff up beautifully when they cook.

Oven Temperature: 425°F, 220°C, Gas Mark 7

3 oz (75 g) Cheddar cheese
2 oz (50 g) plain flour
1 level teaspoon baking powder
a pinch Cayenne pepper
2 oz (50 g) butter or margarine
2 egg yolks

Grate the cheese into a mixing bowl. Sift the flour, baking powder and Cayenne into the bowl. Cut the butter or margarine into small pieces and rub into the flour until the mixture resembles fine breadcrumbs. Add one of the egg yolks, and mix with a wooden spoon to a stiff dough. Shape the dough into a rectangle approximately 9 × 6 inches (23 × 15 cm) on a floured board. Cut into straws and place on ungreased baking sheet. Brush with the remaining egg yolk. Cook for 8–12 minutes towards the top of the oven until golden brown. Allow to cool on baking sheet.

SAUSAGE ROLLS

Makes 24
Oven Temperature: 350°F, 180°C, Gas Mark 4
After 15 minutes: 325°F, 160°C, Gas Mark 3

15 oz (425 g) packet Jusrol flaky pastry
8 oz (225 g) sausagemeat
a little milk

Make these the day before the party. Roll out the pastry into a rectangle on a floured board, and cut into two strips, lengthways. Divide the sausagemeat into two halves, and roll with your hands into two sausages the same length as the pastry. Brush the long edges of the pastry with milk, and lay the sausagemeat down the length of the pastry. Bring the edges up to the centre to cover the sausagemeat. Press the edges firmly together, making an indented edge with your fingertips and brush the pastry with milk. Place on a greased baking tray and cut into rolls $1\frac{1}{2}$ inches (4 cm) long, and cook for 15 minutes. Reduce the oven temperature, and cook for a further 10 minutes, but do not let them get too brown. They should rise well, and be deep gold to light brown in colour.

CHEESE SCONES

Makes 24

These can be made a day or two before the party, and kept in an airtight tin.

Oven Temperature: 350°F, 180°C, Gas Mark 4

12 oz (350 g) self-raising flour
1 level teaspoon salt
3 oz (75 g) butter
3 oz (75 g) Cheddar cheese, grated
a little milk

Stir the flour and salt together, and rub in the fat, until the mixture resembles fine breadcrumbs. Add the cheese and enough milk to make a stiff dough, but be careful not to make it too slack. Roll it out to a thickness of at least $\frac{1}{2}$ inch (1 cm), or pat it down with your hands, and cut it out into rounds with a 2 inch (5 cm) diameter pastry cutter. Place on a greased baking tray, brush the tops with milk and cook for about 10 minutes. You can cut them in half and spread the halves with butter before serving.

CHOCOLATE SHORTBREAD TREAT

These are at their best when freshly made, but will keep well if necessary.

Makes 24

Oven Temperature: 350°F, 180°C, Gas Mark 4

9 oz (250 g) flour
1½ oz (40 g) caster sugar
6 oz (175 g) butter

Filling
6 oz (175 g) butter
6 oz (175 g) soft brown sugar
3 level tablespoons golden syrup
1½ small cans condensed milk

Icing
12 oz (350 g) plain dessert chocolate
1½ oz (40 g) butter

Grease a baking tin. To make the shortbread base, sift the flour into a bowl, add the sugar and rub in the butter until the mixture resembles fine breadcrumbs. Knead it into a ball and press well into the tin. Cook for 15 minutes. Leave to cool in the tin.

To make the filling, put all the ingredients into a saucepan and stir over a gentle heat until the sugar has dissolved. Bring to the boil and, stirring continuously, boil gently for 7 minutes. Take off the heat and beat well, then pour on to the shortbread base. Allow to cool before adding the icing.

To make the icing, cut the chocolate up roughly and melt over a very gentle heat with the butter. Spread evenly over the filling. When the chocolate is quite cold cut into twenty-four fingers.

CHOCOLATE CRUNCH CAKES

Makes 24
Make two or three days in advance and keep in the fridge.

1 lb (450 g) plain chocolate
2 egg yolks
4 oz (110 g) unsalted peanuts, chopped
4 oz (110 g) Rice Krispies
24 paper cases

Melt the chocolate over a very gentle heat, and stir in the egg yolks. Then stir in the dry ingredients until they are well mixed. Put teaspoonsfuls of the mixture into paper cases and leave to set in the fridge.

NUTTY CHOCOLATE TREAT

Makes 24
These biscuits will freeze or you can make them several days in advance and keep them in the fridge.

8 oz (225 g) plain chocolate
8 oz (225 g) butter
2 level tablespoons golden syrup
8 oz (225 g) digestive biscuits, crushed
2 oz (50 g) raisins
4 oz (110 g) toasted flaked almonds

Line two 7 inch (18 cm) baking tins with clingfilm or grease a loose-bottomed tin, because otherwise the biscuits might stick.

Break the chocolate up into very small pieces – preferably in a food processor. Place the butter, syrup and chopped chocolate in a heavy-bottomed pan over a low heat. Once melted, take the pan off the heat and allow the mixture to cool. Add the biscuit crumbs, nuts and raisins. Place the mixture into your tin and smooth the top with a palette knife. Leave until cold, then cut into twelve slices per tin.

CORNFLAKE/RICICLE SPECIALS

These will keep fresh for several days in an airtight tin.

Makes 24

Oven Temperature: 200°F, 100°C, Gas Mark $\frac{1}{4}$

4 oz (110 g) cornflakes or Ricicles
12 oz (350 g) plain chocolate
2 oz (50 g) butter or margarine

Spread the cornflakes over a shallow baking tray and put in the bottom of the oven for 10 minutes. Remove from the oven and leave until cool, then crumble them up until fairly small. They should be very crisp. Melt the chocolate and butter over a gentle heat (do not add water as this will make the cornflakes go soggy). Stir in the cornflakes and shape the mixture into small conical heaps on a greased baking tray, then leave to set.

FABULOUS FLAPJACKS

These will freeze or you can make them several days in advance and keep in an airtight tin.

Makes 12 large or 24 small

Oven Temperature: 300°F, 150°C, Gas Mark 2

8 oz (225 g) butter
5 oz (150 g) caster sugar
2 tablespoons golden syrup
10 oz (300 g) porridge oats
2 oz (50 g) raisins

Melt the butter over a low heat with the sugar and the golden syrup. Stir in the porridge oats and add the raisins. Mix well. Pour into a greased Swiss roll tin, approximately 11 × 7 inches (28 × 18 cm), and cook in the centre of the oven for 30–35 minutes until golden brown. Remove from the oven and mark into fingers. Leave to cool in the tin.

PEANUT COOKIES

Makes 36

Oven Temperature: 350°F, 180°C, Gas Mark 4

2 oz (50 g) softened butter or margarine
4 oz (110 g) brown sugar
3 tablespoons crunchy peanut butter
1 tablespoon golden syrup
1 egg
6 oz (175 g) self-raising flour

Cream the butter and sugar. Add the peanut butter and syrup and mix well. Stir in the egg, and then gradually add the flour. Take small nut-sized pieces of the dough, lightly roll in a little extra flour, then flatten them gently on a greased baking tray. Cook for 10–15 minutes – don't let them get too brown. The uncooked dough freezes very well – just wrap in clingfilm.

CHOCOLATE PRALINE CAKE

Makes 32 fingers

1 tablespoon caster sugar
4 oz (110 g) margarine
2 oz (50 g) cocoa
1 tablespoon golden syrup
8 oz (225 g) digestive biscuits, crushed
2 oz (50 g) sultanas or raisins
2 oz (50 g) walnuts, chopped
4 oz (110 g) plain chocolate
a knob of butter

Cream the sugar and the margarine together. Melt the cocoa and golden syrup together in a saucepan and add to the margarine. Stir the biscuit crumbs, sultanas and walnuts into the mixture and press down into a greased 8 inch (20 cm) square tin. Melt the chocolate with a knob of butter, and pour over the top. Leave until cold, then cut into slices.

MATCH CAKE

If you are having a match party which is also a birthday party why not round off the tea with a match cake? You will need two 8 inch (20 cm) square cakes, placed together on a board to form an oblong 16 × 8 inches (40 × 20 cm). Make the following cake recipe up twice. To ice the cake you can either use green butter icing, or apricot glaze and green glacé icing. You will also need a small quantity of white glacé icing to mark out the pitch.

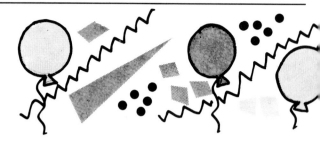

Oven Temperature: 350°F, 180°C, Gas Mark 4

6 oz (175 g) soft butter or margarine
6 oz (175 g) caster sugar
a pinch of salt
grated rind and juice of ½ orange
3 large eggs
6 oz (175 g) self-raising flour, sieved
1 tablespoon milk or water, if necessary

Grease the tin, and line the base with greased greaseproof paper, silicon paper or butter papers cut to fit.

It is very important to have your fat and eggs at room temperature and to warm your mixing bowl. Cream the fat, sugar and salt together until the ingredients are thoroughly combined and the mixture is like whipped cream. Add 1 teaspoon of the grated rind and the orange juice. Beat the eggs in a separate bowl and add them to the creamed mixture, a little at a time, beating well after each addition until the mixture returns to its fluffy state. Sift the flour into the bowl from a height, thereby allowing the flour to take in air. Carefully fold in the flour with a metal spoon. Add the milk or water if the mixture does not fall easily from the spoon. Turn the mixture into the prepared tin and bake for 45 minutes. To test if the cake is cooked, press it and if it springs back into

shape it is ready.

Take out of the oven, and after a minute run a palette knife along the edge of the container and turn the cake on to a wire tray. Peel off the greaseproof paper and allow to cool. See below for icings and assembly instructions.

Butter Icing

8 oz (225 g) butter, at room temperature
2 tablespoons liquid (orange juice from the other ½ orange)
a few drops green food colouring
1¼ lb (600 g) icing sugar, sieved

Cream the butter with a tablespoon of the liquid and the food colouring, and gradually beat in the icing sugar, and more liquid if required. Beat the mixture until the consistency is smooth and creamy.

Glacé Icing

1 lb (450 g) icing sugar, sieved
4–6 tablespoons hot water
1 tablespoon orange juice
a few drops green food colouring

Gradually mix the sieved icing sugar with the hot water, beating well until a smooth coating consistency is achieved. Add the hot water very cautiously as it is easy to make the icing too runny. When ready to use it should still seem a little stiff – this is the correct consistency. Reserve 2 tablespoons of the white glacé icing. Add the orange juice and green food colouring to the remainder.

Apricot Glaze

6 tablespoons apricot jam, sieved
2 tablespoons lemon juice

If you are using glacé icing you will need to cover the cake with a layer of apricot glaze first, to prevent the crumbs getting into the icing. Heat the jam with the lemon juice, and push through a plastic sieve into a basin with a wooden spoon. Use this mixture while still warm, but not too hot.

Match Cake Assembly

Drinking straws or construct-a-straws, cut into correct lengths, sellotaped together, or bent into shape (for the goalposts or whatever)
tiny plastic ball
a few players (from your local baker or use Subbuteo or similar, if you have them)
candles and holders

Place the cakes on the board. Coat the sides and top of the cakes either with the green butter icing or with the apricot glaze followed by the glacé icing, and smooth with a palette knife. When the cake covering has set, pipe white lines using a fine nozzle in the appropriate positions for a simple football pitch, and stick your straws in as goal posts. Place your players on the cake and your candles around the edge of it.

This football pitch could, of course, be adapted to make a cricket, rugby or rounders pitch or a tennis court.

ICED CUP CAKES

Makes 24
Oven Temperature: 350°F, 180°C, Gas Mark 4

8 oz (225 g) butter or soft margarine
8 oz (225 g) caster sugar
4 eggs
8 oz (225 g) self-raising flour
24 paper cake cases

Icing

8 oz (225 g) icing sugar
3 or 4 tablespoons boiling water
decorations (Smarties, hundreds and thousands, etc)

Beat the butter and sugar together until pale and smooth. Whisk the eggs in a separate bowl and add to the mixture a little at a time, beating all the time. Sieve the flour into the bowl and fold in. Fill the paper cases about two-thirds full, and cook for about 15 minutes, until they are well risen and golden brown.

When the cakes are quite cold, make up the icing – it should be quite stiff – and spoon it over the cakes. Smooth with a palette knife. Add the decorations, or pipe guests' names on in a contrasting colour.

Lunch and Activity Party Food

HOME-MADE BEEFBURGERS

Oven Temperature: 450°F, 230°C, Gas Mark 8

2 lb (900 g) lean beef mince
1 large onion, very finely chopped
1 tablespoon tomato sauce
1 tablespoon sweet pickle
1 heaped teaspoon tomato purée
1 teaspoon dried mixed herbs or some mixed
  herb purée
salt and freshly ground pepper

Place all the ingredients in a food processor for a couple of seconds or combine thoroughly. Form the mixture into eight thick burgers. Heat the frying pan and cook over a brisk heat turning once, or place in a hot oven and cook for 15 minutes. Serve with oven chips and peas, or in a soft roll.

PIGS IN A BLANKET

2 lb (900 g) big pork sausages
6 oz (175 g) Cheddar cheese
streaky bacon rashers

Grill the sausages for 15 minutes, then make a lengthways cut down each one and put a suitably sized slice of cheese into the cut. Grill the bacon rashers lightly (removing the rind if necessary). Wrap round the sausages and keep in place with cocktail sticks. Put under a hot grill for 5 minutes, until the bacon is crispy and the cheese has melted.

You can prepare these in advance, except for the final grilling, and leave them in the fridge. When you need them, put them under the grill for 10–15 minutes, until they are piping hot. They are also very good served cold, for a picnic or outdoor lunch.

DEVILLED CHICKEN DRUMSTICKS

A spicy recipe that older children will love.

Oven Temperature: 400°F, 200°C, Gas Mark 6

8 chicken drumsticks
$\frac{1}{4}$ pint (150 ml) vegetable oil
1 level teaspoon curry powder
1 level teaspoon paprika
$\frac{1}{2}$ level teaspoon allspice
$\frac{1}{2}$ level teaspoon ground ginger

Make a couple of shallow cuts in the flesh of each drumstick, then mix the oil and the spices. Pour the marinade over the chicken and leave for several hours, turning occasionally. Put the drumsticks in a roasting tin with the rest of the marinade and cook for 45 minutes, turning occasionally. Serve hot or cold. If you are taking them on a picnic, make sure they are completely cold before you pack them.

BACON JACKET POTATOES

Oven Temperature: 350°F, 180°C, Gas Mark 4

8 large potatoes
3 oz (75 g) butter
5 tablespoons milk
8 rashers streaky bacon
salt and freshly ground black pepper
3 oz (75 g) Cheddar cheese, grated

Clean the potatoes and bake for 1½–2 hours. Cut them in half lengthways and scoop out the middle. Mash well with the butter and milk. Grill the bacon (removing the rind if necessary) and chop it up. Add to the mashed potatoes with a little seasoning. Spoon back into the potato shells, sprinkle with grated cheese and grill until the cheese is golden and bubbly.

You can prepare these in advance except for the final grilling. When ready, give them a good 20 minutes under the grill, or 30 minutes in the oven.

LEMON PUDDING

6 oz (175 g) granulated sugar
2 heaped tablespoons plain flour
4 oz (110 g) butter
3 eggs, separated
rind and juice of 1½ large lemons
12¼ fl oz (350 ml) milk

Combine the sugar, flour, butter and egg yolks in a basin, and beat until well blended. Beat in the grated lemon rind and juice, then beat in the milk, a little at a time. Whip the egg whites until they are stiff and fold them into the mixture. Pour into an ovenproof dish, put the dish into a baking tin of hot water and cook for 30 minutes. The top should be well risen and golden, while the bottom is still runny.

CHOCOLATE MALLOWS

4 oz (110 g) plain chocolate
2 eggs, separated
1 oz (25 g) butter
20 marshmallows
1 tablespoon hot water

Melt the chocolate in a basin over hot water. Add the egg yolks, butter and marshmallows and continue to cook, stirring all the time until the mixture is smooth, then add the hot water and remove from the heat. Whisk the egg whites until they are stiff and fold into the mixture. Spoon into a serving bowl and decorate with whipped cream when it is set.

PLUM AND APPLE CRUMBLE

Oven Temperature: 350°F, 180°C, Gas Mark 4

1 lb (450 g) apples
1 lb (450 g) plums or 14 oz (400 g) can plums
sugar to taste
3 oz (75 g) butter
6 oz (175 g) flour
3 oz (75 g) demerara sugar
1 oz (25 g) walnuts or hazelnuts, chopped
 (optional)

Peel, core and slice the apples; halve the fresh plums and take out the stones. Simmer the fruit gently in a saucepan with the sugar and a very little water until they are soft. (If you are using tinned plums, you don't need to cook them first. Simply add them to the apples [once stewed].) Make the topping by rubbing the butter into the flour until the mixture resembles fine breadcrumbs. Add the sugar and the nuts. Spread the crumble over the fruit in a baking dish and cook for 20–30 minutes. Serve hot with vanilla ice cream.

Family Party Food

STARTERS

Remember, all these recipes are for fourteen people.

Instead of actually making a course where you all need to sit down, why not simply serve 'bits' with your pre-lunch or supper drinks? The children will love helping to hand these round, so you can leave them in charge!

MINI SAUSAGE ROLLS

Makes 30

Make these the day before the party, but do heat them up for serving.

Oven Temperature: 350°F, 180°C, Gas Mark 4

3 oz (75 g) butter (but do not cut it off the block)
4½ oz (125 g) self-raising flour
1½ dessertspoons water
or
12 oz (350 g) packet JusRol flaky pastry
6 oz (175 g) sausagemeat
a little milk

Use a block of very cold butter: better still, put it in the freezer for 2 hours. Unwrap one end of the block and mark off a 3 oz (75 g) section. Sift a little flour into a bowl and grate the butter coarsely on top of the flour. Add more flour and then butter, and continue until both are used up. Mix together very gently with a metal spoon until the mixture resembles fine breadcrumbs, then add water to mix. The finished mixture should feel light and require no kneading.

Roll out into a rectangle on a floured board, again very gently, and cut into two strips lengthways. Divide the sausagemeat into two halves, and roll with your hands into two sausages, the same length as the pastry. Brush the long edge of the pastry with milk, and lay the sausagemeat down the length of the pastry and bring up the edges to the centre to cover the sausagemeat. Press the edges firmly together, making an indented edge with your fingertips, and brush the pastry with milk. Place on a greased baking tray, cut into rolls 1 inch (2.5 cm) long, and cook for 15 minutes.

Reduce the oven temperature to 350°F, 180°C, Gas Mark 4, and cook for a further 10 minutes, but do not let them get too brown. They should rise well and be deep gold to light brown in colour.

DIPS AND BITS

Dips (see page 77).

Grapes stuffed with cream cheese: use white or black grapes (see page 95).

Celery stuffed with cream cheese (see page 95).

Radishes with cream cheese:
Choose large radishes and halve them horizontally. Cut off the tops and bottoms to allow them to stand firmly on a plate. Pipe a rosette of seasoned cream cheese on each half. For a Valentine Party, use a heart-shaped aspic cutter to cut tiny radish skin hearts and place one on each rosette.

CHEESE STRAWS

You can make these in the traditional cheese-straw shape or use cutters in the shape of animals, ducks, hearts, stars, etc., to make them look more interesting. Make them up to a week in advance, but store in an airtight tin and reheat if necessary to crisp them.

Makes 64
Oven Temperature: 350°F, 180°C, Gas Mark 4

4 oz (110 g) plain flour
1 teaspoon salt
2 oz (50 g) butter
2 oz (50 g) Cheddar cheese, grated
1 egg yolk
1 tablespoon cold water

Sift the flour and salt together and rub in the butter to give a texture like fine breadcrumbs. Stir in the cheese and egg yolk, and add enough cold water to give a stiff dough, but be careful not to add too much. Roll the pastry thinly and if you are making straws trim to 8 inch (20 cm) squares. Put on a greased baking tray and cut into straws, 2 inch (5 cm) long and $\frac{1}{2}$ inch (1 cm) wide, separating them gently with the knife. If you are using cutters, cut out shapes before putting them on the tray. Bake in the centre of the oven for 10–15 minutes, until golden.

POPCORN

Children enjoy helping to make popcorn, because the results are so spectacular, and a little corn makes a great deal of popcorn.

3 oz (75 g) popping corn
2 tablespoons cooking oil
2 tablespoons sugar or 1 tablespoon salt

Heat the oil until it is lightly smoking in a large heavy-bottomed saucepan with a tightly fitting lid. Add the popcorn, one kernel deep in the bottom of the pan, and shake it well while it is cooking. Keep the lid on! When it has finished popping, put it into bowls, sprinkle with the salt or sugar, and leave to cool slightly before handing it round.

MAIN COURSES

MEAT FONDUE

Allow $\frac{1}{2}$ lb (225 g) of meat per adult in total, and as far as the children are concerned, don't forget that a fourteen-year-old chap will eat as much as a father, if not more! So gauge the amount of meat you allow for the children according to their ages.

Have a selection of diced meats – chicken breast, sausages, steak, the best you can afford. Remember that although you are not actually cooking the meat, it does take a long time to dice. Make sure you have a good sharp knife. Try to avoid having frozen meat as it will spit more in the fondue because of the higher water content.

Chicken, sausage and pork should be cooked longer than the steak, and beware of spitting sausages too!

FONDUE SAUCES

Do not make enormous quantities of each sauce, say ½ pint (275 ml) of each. Have these on the serving table, and everyone can put a selection on their plates which will avoid stretching over and accidents happening.

Curry:
Mix mayonnaise with a little curry powder or curry paste to taste. Add a little lemon juice if you wish.

Tomato:
Mix mayonnaise with a tablespoon of tomato purée.

Mayonnaise:
With chopped chives, chopped parsley, lemon juice and whipped cream. Whip the cream. Add to the mayonnaise with the other ingredients and mix well.

Salad Cream:
Just plain for the children's sake – amazingly, some love it with anything and everything.

Barbecue Sauce:
See page 69.

Horseradish Sauce:
Don't try to make your own, buy a bottle and, if it is very hot, add some double cream.

Allow one fondue set per six people maximum. Your friends will not mind bringing theirs with them. Heat the containers of oil on the hob in the kitchen first, but be very careful of bringing them through to your dining area, and don't have children running around. Put them in the centre of the table out of harm's way – do remember to get enough fuel for the fondue before the party. Keep an eye on the sets used by the children to make sure they are not overheating. Test to make sure that the oil is hot enough by putting some diced bread in it. If it cooks fast and furiously you will know the temperature is correct. Serve some diced white bread together with some sliced mushrooms (allow one per person) for the children to pop in with their meat, as it will be delicious fried (French bread does not fry as well as ordinary bread).

No-one **should try to eat from their cooking fork – do remind the children – as it would burn them.**

COLD CHICKEN CONCOCTION
(with selection of cold meats)

3 × 3½ lb (1.5 kg) chickens, cooked

Sauce
½ pint (275 ml) mayonnaise
¾ pint (425 ml) cream
¼ pint (150 ml) yoghurt
2 tablespoons curry paste
1 tablespoon apricot jam, sieved
1–1½ tablespoons coconut cream
3–4 fresh peaches or nectarines
juice of 1 lemon
chopped parsley

Cook your chickens (we recommend simmering with onion, carrot, bay leaf, 6 peppercorns and water and/or wine for 1½ hours), then allow to cool in the liquid. Drain and strip off all the flesh (freeze the stock for use in a soup later). Keep some of the flesh separate, wrap in clingfilm and refrigerate (in case any children do not like curry sauce). For the sauce, mix the mayonnaise, cream, yoghurt, curry paste, apricot jam and coconut cream in the blender. Add the chicken and refrigerate.

Take the mixture out of the fridge an hour before serving to allow the flavour to develop.

Slice peeled peaches or nectarines and sprinkle and mix with lemon juice. Fold into the chicken and sprinkle with the chopped parsley.

BEEF CASSEROLE

Oven Temperature: 325°F, 160°C, Gas Mark 3

5 lb (2.25 kg) chuck steak, diced
4 tablespoons cooking oil
3 onions, diced
6 slices bacon, chopped
6 slices carrot
2 sticks celery, sliced
4 oz (110 g) mushrooms, sliced
5 heaped tablespoons flour
2½ pints (1.5 litres) good jellied stock (if
*   possible, otherwise use stock cubes)*
wine (optional, and cut down the stock if you
*   do use wine)*
oregano or mixed herbs to taste
salt and freshly ground pepper

Cut your meat into bite-sized cubes and fry fast in the oil in a flameproof casserole. Remove the meat when browned all over and fry onions over a gentler heat. When the onion is transparent, add the bacon and fry for a few minutes, then add all the other vegetables. Once these are softened check and see if you need a little more oil, and then sprinkle on the flour. Cook for a few minutes and gradually add the stock and/or wine, herbs and seasoning. Put the meat back into the casserole, and bring to the boil slowly. Taste the sauce and adjust the seasoning, and put in the oven for 2–2½ hours until the meat is tender. You may need to use two casserole dishes, as this recipe is for a large quantity.

SALAD

SALAD FOR 14

Try honey instead of sugar in your dressing – it's delicious and practically drunk separately by the children in our family.

2 large lettuces, or 2 different sorts of lettuce
*   (1 round and 1 Chinese leaf, etc.)*
3 large oranges, sliced
3 kiwi fruit, sliced
1 cucumber, sliced
1 bunch or packet watercress
1 green and 1 red pepper, sliced
1 head celery, chopped
chopped parsley
½ pint (275 ml) salad dressing

If you have a large bowl which will be suitable for salad, the easiest way to make sure that everybody gets a bit of everything is to make layers of the salad: start off with a bed of lettuce and cover it with one of the sliced oranges, one of the kiwi fruit, a few slices of cucumber and some of the watercress, peppers and chopped celery. Sprinkle on some parsley, then follow with the same layers again, so that in the end you will have about three layers altogether. Do not toss the salad in case some of the younger children would prefer not to have a dressing. Serve that separately, in a jug.

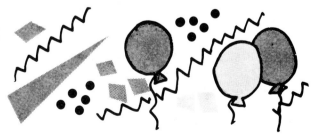

Drinks

Here we give drink recipes for every kind of party, from sophisticated sounding 'cocktails' for teenage discos and suppers, to sparkling thirst-quenchers for younger age groups and satisfying milk shakes for smaller parties.

The first big question with older children is the problem of alcohol. It is important to discuss this openly with your own children when you are planning the party. Remember that when you were young you wanted to experiment, and your children will too. But they must realise that as a parent you will have to keep a very close watch on what everyone is drinking. During the party you will be responsible not only for your own children but for all their guests as well. You must insist that people do not bring drink in with them, so don't be afraid to take it away if you see any evidence of extra alcohol. You can agree with your older children to serve a limited amount of alcohol at the party in exchange for nobody bringing their own. Then you can quietly reduce or cut out the alcohol after everyone has had their first glass.

By this stage children love to feel sophisticated so it is very important to give the drinks exciting and grown-up names, even if the content is totally innocuous. Dress up the concoctions with sliced fruit, ice and colouring, and the glasses (for a small party) with frosting, cocktail umbrellas or other decorations (see page 20).

The suggested recipes are all subject to your own taste, so mix and adjust them to suit yourself and your children. Always have a trial tasting well before the party. Perhaps the children could organise this, but be prepared for a messy kitchen.

With regard to quantities you will find that a 1 litre bottle will be sufficient for nine wine glasses. A bottle of wine (75 cl) will give seven wine glasses. Adapt these recipes to fit your numbers, but remember that children drink a lot at parties, particularly when being very active.

HARVEST PUNCH

A good 'cup' for larger parties.

1 carton apple juice
$\frac{1}{2} \times 2\frac{1}{2}$ pint (1.5 litre) bottle cider
$2 \times 2\frac{1}{2}$ pint (1.5 litre) bottles lemonade
sliced fruit
mint, if available

Mix all the liquid ingredients together, then add the chopped fruit and mint. Add ice direct to glasses. When refilling, use either less cider, or if preferred no more cider, but increase the proportion of apple juice. For a non-alcoholic cup omit the cider altogether and increase the apple juice (see page 17).

BUCKS FIZZLE

1 carton fresh orange juice
$1 \times 2\frac{1}{2}$ pint (1.5 litre) bottle lemonade
slices of orange

Mix the ingredients together, and serve immediately.

BUCKS FIZZ

2 cartons fresh orange juice
1 bottle sparkling white wine
1 bottle sparkling non-alcoholic wine or grape
  juice
slices of orange

Chill all the ingredients very thoroughly. Mix together and serve at once. When refilling, increase quantity of non-alcoholic wine, or see above for non-alcoholic recipe.

CHAMPAGNE COCKTAIL

1 bottle sparkling wine
1 bottle sparkling non-alcoholic wine or grape
  juice
sugar lumps
brandy essence

Chill the wine very thoroughly. Put a sugar lump in each glass and one or two drops of brandy essence. Either mix the non-alcoholic and alcoholic wines together to serve if you wish your guests only to have half a glass of wine, or fill each glass with the sparkling wine then refill with non-alcoholic.

KIR

(for pink parties)

1 bottle dry white wine
1 bottle non-alcoholic wine or grape juice
Ribena

Chill the wine thoroughly. Pour a little Ribena into the bottom of each glass and fill up as above, either with a mixture of the non-alcoholic and alcoholic wines, or start with the wine and refill with the non-alcoholic wine. Serve at once.

ROYAL KIR

(for pink parties)

1 bottle sparkling white wine or grape juice
1 bottle non-alcoholic white wine
strawberry syrup as used in milk shakes

Chill the wine thoroughly. Put a little strawberry syrup in the bottom of each glass and fill up as above.

PINK POTION

(for pink parties)

$1 \times 3\frac{1}{2}$ pint (2 litre) bottle of lemonade
strawberry syrup or cochineal food colouring

Chill the lemonade thoroughly. Pour a little strawberry syrup or food colouring in each glass and fill up with lemonade. Serve at once.

GREEN GIGGLES

(for green parties)

$1 \times 3\frac{1}{2}$ pint (2 litre) bottle of lemonade
green food colouring

Chill lemonade thoroughly. Pour a couple of drops of food colouring in each glass and fill up with lemonade. Serve on a tray immediately, or pour quite a few drops of green food colouring into a jug and fill up with lemonade. Watch out for green mouths! Serve at once.

LIME COCKTAIL

(for green parties)

*1 × 3½ pint (2 litre) bottle of lemonade
lime concentrate*

Chill lemonade thoroughly. Pour some concentrate in the glasses and fill with lemonade, or make up a jug. Serve at once.

GREEN LIGHT GO-GO

(for green parties)

*1 bottle sparkling white wine
1 bottle non-alcoholic white wine or grape juice
green food colouring*

Chill the wine thoroughly. Put a couple of drops of food colouring in each glass and fill up with white wine and refill with the non-alcoholic wine, or just half a glass of wine and half of grape juice. Serve at once.

TROPICAL PUNCH

*1 carton tropical fruit juice
1 bottle sparkling wine
1 bottle sparkling non-alcoholic wine or grape juice
slices of kiwi fruit, mango or other tropical fruit*

Chill all ingredients and mix together. Serve at once.

TROPICAL TREAT

*1 carton tropical fruit juice
1 bottle Perrier
slices of fruit as above*

Chill all the ingredients and mix together. Serve at once.

SANGRIA

*1 bottle dry white or medium dry wine, or 1
  box of grape juice
1 bottle Perrier
sliced fruit*

Chill all ingredients and mix together. Serve at once.

RED SANGRIA

*6 lemons
2 oz (50 g) sugar
1 bottle red wine
1 × 3½ pint (2 litre) bottle lemonade*

Slice the lemons and put in a bowl with the sugar. Leave for 24 hours then squeeze and strain. Mix the wine and lemonade and add the strained lemon juice.

SPRITZER

*1 bottle dry or medium dry white wine
soda water*

Chill the ingredients and mix together. (Put in more soda than wine for younger children.) Serve immediately.

PIMMS

*Pimms
lemonade
sliced fruit
mint*

We have not specified quantities for this recipe as it depends on the age of your guests. Serve this with a drop of Pimms to the younger and a stronger mix, if you want, for the older children, and weaken as necessary for refills.

MULLED MYSTERY

8 fl oz (225 ml) Ribena
3½ pints (2 litres) orange juice
3 oranges, each stuck with 6 cloves
1 teaspoon ground cinnamon
red wine (optional)

Place all the ingredients in a heavy-based saucepan and allow to simmer gently for 30 minutes. It does *not* taste of pure Ribena! Serve hot after a cold outing, like a fireworks party. Have prepared beforehand and heat up when you get in.

WINE CUP

This wine cup is alcoholic. It is included in case you need a drink for much older teenagers. As the evening progresses increase the lemonade in the mix.

1 × 2½ pint (1.5 litre) bottle lemonade
1 × 2½ pint (1.5 litre) bottle cider
1 bottle white wine
a scant pint (500 ml) grape juice
⅛ bottle orange Curaçao

Mix all the ingredients together.

HOME-MADE LEMONADE

4 lemons
4 tablespoons sugar
3 pints (1.7 litres) boiling water
10 ice cubes

Cut the lemons into quarters. Put them with the sugar into a heat-resistant jug. Pour on the boiling water and leave to stand for thirty minutes. Strain, cool, add the ice cubes and serve.

HOME-MADE ORANGEADE

Follow the recipe for lemonade as above. When it is cool, squeeze the juice of 4 oranges into the lemonade, add the ice cubes and serve.

SPARKLING APPLE PUNCH

2 red-skinned eating apples
juice of 1 lemon
2 large oranges
1 large bottle concentrated apple juice
2 pints (1.1 litre) soda or tonic water
2 pints (1.1 litre) dry ginger ale

Wash and dry the apples, then quarter, core and slice them. Pour lemon juice over them to stop them going brown. Slice the oranges into small pieces, discarding the pips. Place the apple juice and prepared fruits into a large bowl. Cover and chill for about 2 hours. Chill the soda or tonic water and ginger ale. Just before serving measure out soda or tonic water and ginger ale and combine with the apple juice. Ladle into glasses for serving.

SPARKLING FRUIT BOWL PUNCH

2 red-skinned eating apples
lemon juice
2 large oranges
½ lb (225 g) grapes
fresh strawberries or raspberries, if in season
2 pints (1.1 litre) soda water
2 pints (1.1 litre) ginger ale
1 large cup concentrated fruit syrup (as used in milk shakes)

Follow the recipe as above.

HOME-MADE BLENDER LEMONADE

4 thin-skinned lemons
4 tablespoons sugar
10 ice cubes
3 pints (1.7 litres) cold water

Cut the lemons into quarters. Put all the ingredients, reserving 2 pints (1.1 litre) of water and 5 ice cubes, into the blender and blend for 10 seconds. Strain, add remaining water and ice cubes and serve.

FIZZY APPLE PUNCH

½ pint (300 ml) concentrated apple juice
2 pints (1.1 litre) soda water
2 pints (1.1 litre) ginger ale
2 eating apples (red if possible)

Chill all the ingredients (except the apples) for 2 hours. Quarter and core the apples, but do not peel them, and cut the quarters into small chunks. Put into a large jug. Pour over the other ingredients and serve.

FIZZY APRICOT PUNCH

2 lemons
1 × 10 oz (275 g) can apricots (stoned)
3 pints (1.7 litres) fizzy lemonade

Chill all the ingredients for at least 2 hours. Cut the lemons into quarters, and put into a blender with the apricots. Blend for 20 seconds. Strain into a serving jug, and mix well with ½ pint (300 ml) lemonade. Add the rest of the lemonade, and serve.

FIZZY ORANGE PUNCH

1 pint (570 ml) orange juice
2 pints (1.1 litre) tonic water
10 ice cubes
a few orange slices

Chill the ingredients in the fridge for at least 2 hours. Pour the orange juice into a jug. Mix well with ½ pint (300 ml) of the tonic water. Add the rest of the tonic water, the ice cubes, the slices of orange, and serve.

COLA SURPRISE

3 pints (1.7 litres) Coca-Cola or Pepsi-Cola
small carton of ice cream

Spoon or scoop the ice cream into each serving glass. Pour the Cola over and serve.

PINEAPPLE DREAM

1 × 10 oz (275 g) can pineapple chunks
2 pints (1.1 litre) cold milk
vanilla ice cream

Put the pineapple, its juice and 1 pint (570 ml) milk into the liquidizer, and blend for 20 seconds. Add remaining milk. Pour into serving glasses and top with a scoopful of vanilla ice cream. Serve with straws.

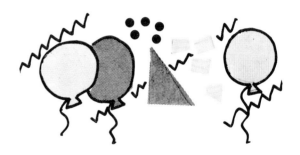

BANANA WHIZ

2 bananas
1 egg
2 pints (1.1 litre) cold milk
1 tablespoon sugar
chocolate vermicelli

Peel the bananas, chop, and put in the blender. Break the egg into the blender and add the other ingredients, reserving 1 pint (570 ml) of milk. Blend for 20 seconds until foaming. Add the remaining milk. Pour into tall glasses and serve with straws. Just before serving sprinkle with vermicelli.

CHOCOLATE BANANA SHAKE

2 bananas
2 pints (1.1 litre) cold milk
2 heaped tablespoons drinking chocolate or 1
  tablespoon each cocoa and sugar

Peel the bananas, chop, and put into the blender. Add the other ingredients, reserving 1 pint (570 ml) of milk, and blend for 20 seconds until foamy. Add remaining milk. Pour into tall glasses and serve with straws.

BLACKCURRANT DELIGHT

5 tablespoons Ribena
2 pints (1.1 litre) cold milk
vanilla ice cream
hundreds and thousands

Mix the Ribena and milk together. Pour into tall glasses. Top with a scoop of vanilla ice cream and just before serving sprinkle with hundreds and thousands. Serve with straws.

PEPPERMINT DELIGHT

a few drops peppermint essence
a few drops green colouring
1 tablespoon sugar
2 pints (1.1 litre) cold milk
soft ice cream

Add the peppermint essence, green colouring and sugar to the cold milk, and stir well. Pour into tall glasses and top with a scoop of ice cream.

APRICOT DELIGHT

1 × 10 oz (275 g) can apricots (stoned)
1 tablespoon sugar
2 pints (1.1 litre) milk
6 ice cubes

Put all the ingredients into a blender, reserving 1 pint (570 ml) milk, and blend for 20 seconds. Add remaining milk. Pour into tall glasses and serve with straws.

RASPBERRY SODA

8 oz (225 g) fresh or frozen raspberries
2 pints (1.1 litre) milk
1 small bottle tonic water
1 small block of Raspberry Ripple ice cream

Partially defrost the frozen raspberries. Put the raspberries and 1 pint (570 ml) milk into a blender and blend for 20 seconds. Strain. Add remaining milk and tonic water. Pour into serving glasses. Top with a scoop of ice cream.

Home-Made Sweets for Presents

Sweets are really quite easy to make and are popular presents. Wrap four or five sweets together in a 6 inch (15 cm) square of clingfilm or cellophane and tie with freezer ties and colourful narrow ribbons. Remember that you could also use these to serve with coffee after a party for older children: put the green peppermint creams on the table following the green party; serve dark chocolate truffles following the black and white party; and pink coconut ice for pink parties . . .

FUDGE

1 lb (450 g) sugar
5 oz (150 g) butter
$\frac{1}{4}$ pint (150 ml) milk

Grease a tin about 8 inches (20 cm) square. Put all the ingredients into a saucepan over a gentle heat and stir until the sugar is dissolved. Bring to the boil, stirring all the time, and boil until a small spoonful of the mixture dropped into a cup of cold water forms a ball. Take off the heat and beat for a couple of moments until the mixture has cooled slightly. Pour into the tin and cut into squares when cold.

CHOCOLATE FUDGE

Make as above, adding 2 tablespoons cocoa, and make sure the cocoa is completely dissolved before the mixture comes to the boil.

VERY EASY CHOCOLATE FUDGE

A very quick and easy recipe. It doesn't need cooking, so children can make it themselves, but it tastes just like the real thing.

10 oz (275 g) icing sugar
3 oz (75 g) cream cheese
3 oz (75 g) plain chocolate, broken up
3 level tablespoons cocoa
2 oz (50 g) raisins or chopped walnuts
  (optional)

Sieve the icing sugar and mix well with the cream cheese. Melt the chocolate with the cocoa in a basin over hot water. Mix into the cheese and add the raisins or nuts. Line a 7 inch (18 cm) square tin and spread the fudge, smoothing it with a palette knife dipped into boiling water. Put it in the fridge and cut it into squares when it is set. The fudge will keep for at least a month if you store it in the fridge.

TOFFEE APPLES

6–8 unblemished eating apples
1 lb (450 g) demerara sugar
2 oz (50 g) butter
$\frac{1}{4}$ pint (150 ml) water
2 tablespoons golden syrup
1 wooden stick per apple (or lolly stick)

First of all prepare your apples; wipe them clean, dry them and insert the sticks. In a large heavy-bottomed pan melt the remaining ingredients over a gentle heat (do not stir too much as this may cause the toffee to crystallise). When the sugar has dissolved, boil rapidly for about 5 minutes. If you have a sugar thermometer, boil until the temperature is 290°F (143°C), otherwise test the toffee by popping a little into cold water – it should set quite hard. Remove the pan from the heat. Tipping it slightly, dip in your apples and coat each one completely. Stand the apples either on a buttered tray or on wax paper. When quite cold, wrap each one in a piece of cellophane, clingfilm or waxed paper, and fasten with ribbon or freezer twists ties. You can prepare these toffee apples a couple of days before the party but keep them somewhere dry.

PEANUT AND CHOCOLATE BALLS

$3\frac{1}{2}$ oz (100 g) plain chocolate, broken up
1 oz (25 g) butter
2 oz (50 g) peanuts
1 teaspoon vanilla essence

Put the chocolate in a bowl and stand over heated hot water. Add the butter and leave until both are melted. Chop the peanuts coarsely and add to the chocolate with the vanilla essence. Form into balls, and leave to firm before wrapping.

COCONUT ICE

1 lb (450 g) sugar
$\frac{1}{4}$ pint (150 ml) milk
5 oz (150 g) desiccated coconut
pink food colouring

Grease a tin, 8 inches (20 cm) square. Put the sugar and milk into a saucepan and heat gently until the sugar has dissolved. Bring to the boil, stirring continuously, and cook until a spoonful dropped into cold water forms a soft ball. Remove from the heat and stir in the coconut. Pour half the mixture into the tin, add pink colouring to the remaining half, and then pour over the first portion. Divide into 1 inch (2.5 cm) squares, while the coconut ice is cooling. Don't take out of the tin until completely cold.

PEPPERMINT CREAMS

If you like leave half the mixture plain and make a mixture of green and white peppermint creams, or pink and white if you use pink food colouring.

10 oz (275 g) icing sugar, sieved
1 egg white, stiffly beaten
a few drops of peppermint essence
green or pink food colouring

Add the sieved icing sugar to the whisked egg white, and mix with a wooden spoon (if not stiff enough add a little extra icing sugar). Stir in the peppermint essence and green food colouring. Roll out peppermint mixture on to a board sprinkled with icing sugar and cut out shapes (diamonds, stars, etc) with a knife, the smallest size pastry cutter, or a suitably sized lid. Leave the peppermints in a cool place until they are set hard (this may take several hours).

ROSIE'S CHOCOLATE TRUFFLES

*8 oz (225 g) good quality plain chocolate,
  broken up*
4 oz (110 g) unsalted butter
8 oz (225 g) sieved icing sugar
4 fl oz (100 ml) double cream
4 tablespoons ground almonds
2 tablespoons brandy, rum or orange juice
Cocoa

Melt the chocolate in a double boiler. Mix in all the other ingredients, excepting the cocoa. Pour into a bowl and leave to cool in the fridge. Wash your hands in very cold water, and form the mixture into balls. Put some cocoa on a plate and roll the balls in it. Leave overnight in the fridge before you wrap them, if you are giving them as presents. If serving with coffee then put into little petits-fours cases. Store them in an airtight tin in the fridge. You can make these a couple of days before you need them.

BISCUITS TO HANG ON A CHRISTMAS TREE

1 recipe Shortbread (see page 106)
star or suitable Christmas shaped cutters
*$\frac{1}{4}$–$\frac{1}{2}$ inch (5–10 mm) diameter circular cutter
  (even a pencil would do)*
very narrow ribbon or parcel ribbon

Roll out the shortbread mixture and cut into shapes. Before cooking, make a hole in the top of each biscuit, through which you can put the hanging ribbon. You do not want the hole to be too near an edge or the shortbread will break, and you want it centrally positioned so that the shape will hang properly and not be overweighted on one side. Decorate your shape with icing and silver balls if you wish.

General Index

Recipe Index

Picture credits
Tony Stone (opp. p. 33)
Vision International (centre spread, Anthea Sieveking left).